HOUSING, FINANCIAL MARKETS AND THE WIDER ECONOMY

WILEY

SERIES IN
FINANCIAL ECONOMICS
AND QUANTITATIVE ANALYSIS

Series Editor: Stephen Hall, *London Business School, UK*

Editorial Board: Robert F. Engle, *University of California, USA*
John Flemming, *European Bank, UK*
Lawrence R. Klein, *University of Pennsylvania, USA*
Helmut Lütkepohl, *Humboldt University, Germany*

Further titles in preparation
Proposals will be welcomed by the Series Editor

HOUSING, FINANCIAL MARKETS AND THE WIDER ECONOMY

David Miles
Merrill Lynch Limited

JOHN WILEY & SONS

Chichester • New York • Brisbane • Toronto • Singapore

Other Wiley Editorial Offices

John Wiley & Sons, Inc., 605 Third Avenue,
New York, NY 10158-0012, USA

Jacaranda Wiley Ltd, 33 Park Road, Milton,
Queensland 4064, Australia

John Wiley & Sons (Canada) Ltd, 22 Worcester Road,
Rexdale, Ontario M9W 1L1, Canada

John Wiley & Sons (SEA) Pte Ltd, 37 Jalan Pemimpin #05-04,
Block B, Union Industrial Building, Singapore 2057

Library of Congress Cataloging-in-Publication Data

Miles, David (David K.)
    Housing, financial markets and the wider economy / David Miles.
        p.   cm. — (Series in financial economics and quantitative analysis)
    Includes bibliographical references and index.
    ISBN 0-471-95210-9 (cloth)
    1. Housing — United States.   2. Housing — United States — Finance.
    I. Title   II. Series.
    HD7293.M467   1994
    338.4′33635 — dc20   94 – 17863
                                                                    CIP

British Library Cataloguing in Publication Data

A catalogue record for this book is available from the British Library

ISBN 0-471-95210-9

Typeset in 10/12pt Times from author's disks by Laser Words, Madras
Printed and bound in Great Britain by Biddles Ltd, Guildford, Surrey

To my parents

Contents

Series preface

This series aims to publish books which give authoritative accounts of major new topics in financial economics and general quantitative analysis. The coverage of the series includes both macro- and microeconomics, and its aim is to be of interest to practitioners and policy makers as well as the wider academic community.

The development of new techniques and ideas in econometrics has been rapid in recent years and these developments are now being applied to a wide range of areas and markets. Our hope is that this series will provide a rapid and effective means of communicating these ideas to a wide international audience and that in turn this will contribute to the growth of knowledge, the exchange of scientific information and techniques and the development of cooperation in the field of economics.

Stephen Hall
London Business School, UK

Preface

This book is about the economics of housing — how their values are determined, how their purchase is financed, how the amount of new building is affected by the structure of financial markets and by the tax system, and how changes in house values affect the wider economy.

The conceptual framework for the analysis of housing issues is developed in detail in the first part of the book. Dynamic models of forward-looking agents are used to derive the impact of changes in current, and expected future, credit conditions and house prices upon the demand for property and household saving. The impact of financial liberalization is analysed and the implications of greater integration in European financial markets for the availability of loans to finance house purchase is considered. Of particular importance is assessment of the time-frame over which adjustments to new equilibria in the housing and financial markets occur.

The book will use empirical evidence from the UK, the USA, continental Europe and Japan to assess the impact of changes in housing markets and in financial markets. Both aggregate, time-series evidence and also results from the analysis of disaggregated, household data will be used. The empirical work will test specific hypotheses about the links between house values, consumer spending and the lending policies of financial institutions. The extent to which conditions in housing markets within Europe, and the ways in which finance for house purchase is provided, may converge is assessed.

The issues addressed in this book have implications for the formulation of macroeconomic policy and for the design of policies specifically aimed at housing — policy towards rental markets; policy for the tax treatment of housing; policy towards the regulation of financial intermediaries involved in the provision of housing finance; and policy on the availability of land for residential development.

Acknowledgements

In writing this book I have benefited from written comments, conversations and arguments with numerous people. I should especially like to thank Orazio Attanasio, Martin Brookes, David Begg, Hugh Davies, John Flemming, Charles Goodhart, Vittorio Grilli, Yannis Ioannides, Georges de Menil, Ben Lockwood, Costas Meghir, Andrew Oswald, Hashem Pesaran, Danny Quah, Steve Satchell, Andrew Scott, Miguel Sebastian, Dennis Snower, Alan Timmermann, Martin Weale, Guilelmo Weber, Stephen Zeldes and members of the Clare Group and the Financial Markets Group at the LSE.

Some of the chapters in this book draw upon papers which have appeared in various journals. In particular, Chapter 3 draws on material which appeared in my article in the February 1992 edition of the National Institute Economic Review. Chapter 4 is an extensively rewritten and extended version of a paper that originally appeared in the Manchester School in 1993 ('House prices, consumption and personal sector wealth: some conceptual and empirical issues'). Chapter 5 is based upon a model developed in my paper in the European Economic Review in 1992 (vol. 36, no. 5). Chapter 8 draws upon my entry 'European Financial Deregulation', in the New Palgrave Dictionary of Money and Finance (1992), edited by Eatwell, Millgate and Newman. That chapter also includes material which appeared in my article in the February 1994 Bank of England Quarterly Bulletin ('Fixed and floating-rate finance in the United Kingdom and Abroad'). I should like to thank editors of those journals and, particularly, anonymous referees who made numerous helpful comments.

Much of this book was written at Birkbeck College, University of London where my colleagues, on the faculty and on administration, helped in ways too numerous to list. Sharon Agard and Jim Lewin provided excellent research help.

I owe special thanks to Ron Smith for *always* sparing time to discuss problems.

The research reported here benefited from a grant from the Leverhulme Trust.

CHAPTER 1

Introduction: the economics of residential property

1.1 INTRODUCTION

Few people are nomads by choice. Most of us live in the same place for years, often decades, on end. There are few places more evocative of our past than the spaces in which we have lived. As with other commodities, the houses in which we live reflect our tastes and our resources; but they also mould our lives. Here is John Burnett, chronicler of the social history of housing in England, describing the importance to the new London middle classes in the inter-war years of their newly built, semi-detached, suburban homes:

> They opened up possibilities of a new and decent life away from the noise and dirt of Victorian cities, of healthier children and of parents who, through the ownership of property, could elevate themselves in the estimation of the world. Physically, the minimal five-roomed semi made civilized life, in middle class terms, possible for a small family. It allowed for a proper separation of eating and living, for a proper separation of ages and sexes for sleeping, for cleanliness, order, ventilation and recreation. Emotionally, it satisfied the deeply felt needs of ownership, of security and of control of one's environment.
>
> (Burnett 1986)

Most houses and flats are more durable than the people who live in them; they remain after we have used them. Many people can remember the lives of that first generation of new, suburban home-owners of the 1920s and 1930s, but we can only imagine the lifestyles of the urban Victorians who came before them; we can, however, still live in the homes that were once theirs. These features of houses — their durability; their being the space in which so much of our lives are lived; their appropriability; their malleability (so that they often come to reflect us more the longer we live in them); their uniqueness, if only in location but so often in hundreds of other ways — account for their economic importance. Were they not durable we should not be willing to trade the value of several years of labour for ownership rights to them; if they were not appropriable we could not. And were they not so central to our comfort and our health, were access to them not for many of us a prerequisite for enjoyment of so many other things of value, then durability and appropriability would not be sufficient to give them value.

The factors which determine the quantity, the value, and the pattern of ownership of housing within a country reflect fundamental characteristics of its economy: the way people work and how they form attachments will affect where they want to live and what sorts of houses they wish to live in; the legal and political environment will affect the type of contracts for home ownership and for financing house purchase which are permissible and enforceable; the technology available to construct buildings will determine the type and cost of houses; the geography of the country and its level and rate of change of population will influence the density of housing and the value of land; the technology of financial intermediation will affect the spread of home ownership and the age at which owner-occupation becomes feasible. These things are not independent and each of them changes through time. One of the aims of this book is to analyse systematically how changes in these factors impact on the housing market and how changes in that market, in turn, affect households, companies and governments.

This book is about the economics of housing — how their values are determined, how their purchase is financed, how the amount of new building is affected by the structure of financial markets and by the tax system, and how changes in house values affect the wider economy. Our subject is the housing markets of developed economies over the post-war period; a period during which the patterns of ownership of homes, their values and the ways in which they are bought and sold have changed significantly.

There are three reasons for writing a book on this subject.

First, houses are important commodities — what happens in housing markets is of macroeconomic significance. In the most developed economies the value of residential property is several times that of aggregate annual output. In the UK and USA investment in residential property since the Second World War has typically accounted for between 3% and 4% of GDP; in countries where war damage was more serious investment has been even higher. Changes in the prices of housing relative to other goods have a major impact on the value, the composition and the distribution of wealth. None of these things are unique to houses; so while the scale of the macroeconomic impact of changes in housing markets may be greater than comparable changes in the markets for most other durable goods — computers, aeroplanes, arms, cars — that would not in itself warrant their being treated separately. But houses have features which would make it misleading to treat them in the same way as most other durable assets. To a large extent this is because houses are both an important (and often *the* most important) component of the net worth of their owners but they also directly yield services to those that live in them. This makes the analysis of changes in the price of houses very different from investigation of the impact of, for example, stock price movements or changes in commodities' prices or changes in the prices of machines. A major theme of this book is that much research on the effects of changes in housing markets ignores special features of the market; the second aim of the book is therefore to develop a framework which pays attention to the unique characteristics of these assets.

The third reason for writing this book is that in the last twenty years there have been significant changes in supply and, especially, demand conditions in housing. In the US and UK perhaps the most important change has been the greater availability of housing finance. In the course of the 1980s it became easier in the UK than ever before to borrow against the collateral of owner-occupied housing; in the US this had happened some years before; in Continental Europe and in Japan it may happen over the next ten years. Within the UK changes in the tax treatment of housing; the spread of owner-occupation; and, for the first time in the 1980s, the phenomenon of widespread inheritance by existing home owners of (largely) unmortgaged property from their parents are interrelated phenomena which — along with financial deregulation — all have macroeconomic impacts. The dramatic rise in the importance of housing in the wealth of the personal sector is not only an effect of these changes but also enhances the impact of events which cause prices and quantities of houses to change. There have been few attempts to analyse the impact of all these relatively recent, and interrelated, changes within a coherent framework.

Sorting out the mechanisms which are at work in the housing market — distinguishing between cause and effect; between exogenous and endogenous factors — is crucial if we are to understand the economics of housing. The strategy followed in this book is to use economic theory to guide the empirical analysis of household behaviour and of housing markets; our aim is to assess the role of housing in the macroeconomy and to better understand the impact that future changes in financial markets and in government policy towards housing might have.

Our concerns are macroeconomic; this is a book about economic aggregates, though one which I hope is based upon good microeconomic principles. Housing economics is no longer the sole preserve of micro-economists focusing upon the welfare effects of the system of housing provision or on analysis of the implications of the tax treatment of housing (for an excellent and recent analysis of this sort see Hills (1991), for a survey of earlier work see Mclellan (1982)); macro-economists now see developments in the housing markets as of prime importance to the wider economy. There have recently appeared several important studies analysing the macroeconomic impact of various changes in the housing market and in the market for home loans (some of the more controversial being Mankiw and Weil (1989), Manchester and Poterba (1989), Muellbauer and Murphy (1990) and Bover, Muellbauer and Murphy (1988)). But there have been few attempts to study the interactions between, and the overall effects of, the changes in housing finance; in home ownership; and in house values that have occurred over the past twenty years. The aim of this book is to provide a comprehensive analysis of these issues.

The conceptual framework for the analysis of housing issues will be developed in detail in the first part of the book. Dynamic models of forward-looking agents will be built so as to derive the impact of changes in current, and expected future, credit conditions and house prices upon the demand for property and household saving. Aggregating from the household to the whole economy will allow one to derive the general equilibrium impact of exogenous shocks. The impact of financial liberalization will be analysed and the implications of greater integration in European financial markets for the availability of loans to finance house purchase will be considered. Throughout we will stress the general equilibrium effects of changes—the impact on house values, on consumer spending, on trade flows and on bequests of wealth. Of particular importance will be assessment of the time-frame over which adjustments to new equilibria in the housing and financial markets occur.

The book will use empirical evidence from the UK (but also from the US, continental Europe and Japan) to assess the impact of changes in housing markets and in financial markets. Both aggregate, time-series evidence and also results from the analysis of disaggregated, household data will be used. The empirical work will test specific hypotheses about the links between house values, consumer spending and the lending policies of financial institutions.

The issues addressed in this book have implications for the formulation of macroeconomic policy and for the design of policies specifically aimed at housing—policy towards rental markets; policy for the tax treatment of housing; policy towards the regulation of financial intermediaries involved in the provision of housing finance; and policy on the availability of land for residential development. We shall consider the implications of our analysis for policy in all these areas.

1.2   THE IMPORTANCE OF UNDERSTANDING THE HOUSING MARKET: AN EXAMPLE FROM RECENT HISTORY

The importance of understanding the impact of changes in housing conditions for macroeconomic policy is nicely illustrated by considering the role of falling house prices in the rise in consumer saving in the UK between 1989 and 1992—a period during which real house prices fell by around 25%, the savings rate almost doubled (from just over 6% to around 12%), GDP stagnated and business confidence slumped. It was common in that period to hear the view that until house prices stopped falling consumer expenditure would remain depressed and economic recovery would, at best, be sluggish. There are two reasons why this argument appears, on the surface, to be plausible. First, housing wealth held by the personal sector—that is the value of the owner-occupied housing stock net of the value of outstanding mortgages—is the largest single component of their total net worth; at the end of 1992 almost 40% of total household net wealth was in the form of net equity in owner-occupied, residential property. (This compares with a figure of around 20% in the early 1960s.) The life-cycle theory of consumption implies that consumers' expenditure should depend on human capital (the present value of expected incomes from the supply of labour) and the value of tangible and financial assets (Deaton, 1992). Unanticipated changes in wealth should affect expenditure so unexpected house price rises should stimulate consumption and, because of the higher proportion of household wealth in the form of housing, to a greater extent now than in the past.

Second, the dramatic rise in consumer expenditure in the UK in the mid- and late 1980s coincided with a boom in house prices. The boom in consumption was financed to a significant extent by equity withdrawal — that is households borrowed against rising housing wealth and used the proceeds to finance consumption (a phenomenon to which we will return in Chapter 3). So it seems that changes in house prices — both in theory and in practice — have a direct and powerful impact on consumption.

But once one thinks through the economics of decisions made by households about where they live and how they pay for housing these arguments look less convincing in proving a *causal* link between rising house prices and consumption. Most fundamentally, it is far from clear why changes in house prices at the aggregate level should be expected to affect consumption. The reason is that increases in house prices benefit those who aim to trade down — i.e. move to a smaller house — but harm those who aim to trade up. At a point in time the supply of housing is fixed so the extra demand from those trading up must be matched by the extra supply from those trading down; gainers and losers tend to balance out in *aggregate*, so it is unclear why there should be an *aggregate* impact on confidence and expenditure. At the individual level, of course, things are clearer — those who own homes and are prepared to trade down to less valuable dwellings, either in the rented sector or within the owner-occupied sector, are better off when the relative price of property increases. If you move from one house to another whose value is 75% of the original you are able to buy goods worth 25% of the value of a house; the more valuable are houses the greater the quantity of such goods can be bought from trading down. But at any point in time for society as a whole there is only one means of trading down — selling off the housing stock to foreigners; all house moves between domestic residents simply cancel out with the gain of those trading down after real house prices rise exactly offsetting the loss of those trading up. But notice that domestic residents would not necessarily gain from increases in real house prices by selling their homes to overseas property developers and renting them back since rental costs will generally be proportional to house values, at least in the longer run; so the only way for UK residents as a whole to gain is to simply trade down *en masse*. The scope for this is clearly somewhat limited and the demand from overseas for UK residential property might be relatively small. Clearly if the real value of houses were to become astronomical *and* overseas buyers could be found then only a rather limited degree of trading down would be needed to realize large welfare gains. But such a scenario seems rather far-fetched and is reminiscent of the story that the land in the Imperial Palace in Tokyo, when valued at the same price per square metre as adjacent land in the business district, was (at least before the slump in prices in the 1990s) more valuable than the whole of California. The relevance of that story is not that the calculation was inaccurate but that no American who might be lucky enough to own even a smallish fraction of California would ever trade it to use, rather than rent out, a small piece of land on the other side of the Pacific.

The general point being made here is quite simple, but has been overlooked by most economists who continue to treat housing wealth in the same way as other components of household net worth. Assuming that the overall economy-wide scope to substitute out of housing is insignificant, *aggregate* wealth effects from real house price rises are zero. This argument casts doubt on the belief that house price rises fuel consumption due to a wealth effect. Those who believe that house price rises fuel consumption via wealth effects are either relying on the propensity to consume of those who are able to trade down (e.g. those who have been owner-occupiers for many years) exceeding the propensity to consume of those who aim to trade up (e.g. first time buyers) *or* that rises in house prices have an impact on consumption which works through an alternative mechanism to a simple wealth effect. One such mechanism is if rises in house values increase the scope of home-owners to borrow and thereby relax binding credit restrictions — a collateral enhancement effect rather than a wealth effect. Estimating the scale of such effects is one of our aims in Chapter 7.

There remains the argument that the 1980s house boom coincided with the consumption boom. The point here is that coincidence is not causation. A plausible (but no more than that) explanation of the simultaneous rise in house prices and rapid growth in consumer expenditure is that financial deregulation and rising expectations of future income caused both. If, in the mid-1980s, UK households *revised* up their expectations of *future* incomes it would be natural that they felt inclined to consume more *now* and finance that extra expenditure by borrowing against future incomes. Since the cheapest and easiest way to borrow was on mortgage the result was massive equity withdrawal. The greater availability of mortgage finance allied with more optimistic expectations of future incomes would also have increased the demand for housing; given that supply is more or less fixed in the short term, rising house prices were inevitable. The key point with this interpretation of events in the mid- and late 1980s is that rising house prices may not have been the *cause* of rapidly rising consumption expenditure; rather they may have been the effect of changing credit conditions and of upwards revisions to income expectations, the same factors which account for high consumption. Whether this interpretation is consistent with the evidence is the subject of Chapter 6.

Let us take this argument one step further. *If* changes in house prices do not, in themselves, drive consumption, then those proposals made in the depths of the UK recession in the early 1990s to stimulate the housing market so as to boost aggregate demand were wrong-headed. Amongst these were proposals to boost house prices by (further) increasing the favourable tax treatment of owner-occupied housing. The implications of proposals to increase the £30 000 limit on mortgage tax relief, or to target benefits at first-time buyers, were rarely thought through by their advocates. There are at least three arguments as to why such moves would have been ill-considered and we shall consider each of them in some detail in later chapters. First, because they are likely to increase house prices, such tax changes would have harmed those who were yet to enter the market and those who were in small houses and needed to trade up — since these are likely to be the least well off the redistributive aspects of such a tax change were likely to be harmful (Chapter 9). Second, as noted above, theory suggests that increasing house prices is an indirect and perhaps unreliable means of boosting aggregate demand (Chapter 4). Third, changing the relative costs of renting and owner-occupation by increasing the favourable tax treatment of the latter distorts the market; extending tax breaks to home-owners would have been a setback to the advances made since the mid-1980s in resurrecting the rental market.

In practice, the government resisted the pressure to give the housing market a boost by extending tax relief; tax breaks on owner-occupied housing were actually reduced in the two budgets of 1993, though only after interest rates had fallen enough to more than cushion the impact on the cash flow of households with mortgages.

The reason for reflecting on this episode is that I hope it illustrates how thinking about the economics of housing markets is both helpful in evaluating the merits of a policy of engineering economic recovery by boosting house values and useful in assessing whether tax changes which might reduce house prices may depress consumption.

1.3 THE SPECIAL FEATURES OF HOUSING

I think that this example from the somewhat parochial debate about the way out of the UK recession of the early 1990s helps makes a general point about the economics of housing; this is that it is essential to think clearly about some of the special features of houses which make the determinants of housing demand and the conditions of supply specific to this market. These are features which once properly specified in a dynamic model of rational, optimizing agents can, for example, help make clear the ways in which houses are comparable to equities and ways in which they are quite different (the subject of Chapter 4).

It is helpful at the outset to list some of these special features of houses and of housing markets.

(1) *Durability*: It is hard to think of many durable assets which have a longer useful life than houses; a substantial proportion of houses in most European cities were built before the First World War. In the UK in 1991 over 20% of houses were built before 1919 *(Housing Finance Review*, 1993).

(2) *Uniqueness*: Unlike other consumer durables (computers, cars, fridges or tools) no two houses are the same.

(3) Uniqueness implies a complete *inelasticity of supply*—there can never be more than one building at the North West intersection of Oxford Street and Regent Street. There are of, course, close substitutes; but the inelasticity of the supply of land with certain characteristics—land with planning permission and within a given distance of particular places—means that houses cannot be treated like most reproducible, tangible assets.

(4) The ability of households to raise loans against housing *collateral* is greater than for most other assets; in many developed countries people can borrow more money, and at lower cost, to finance house purchase than for other purposes. In the UK an overwhelming proportion of the debt of the personal sector is in the form of mortgages (over 80% at the end of 1992).

(5) Part of the reason why housing is good collateral is that there is a *well-developed secondary market* in houses. Yet transactions costs associated with house purchase are substantial. Smith, Rosen and Fallis (1988) estimate that transactions costs typically amount to between 8% and 10% of the purchase price of a home in the US; costs in France are probably twice as high and the degree of turnover substantially lower *(Journal of Housing Research,* **3** (1), 1992).

(6) *Price volatility* in housing markets may be no greater than for many other assets—indeed exchange rates, bond prices and equity values may be substantially more volatile (Chapter 3)—but the implications of changing house prices on the distribution of wealth may have been of greater importance. The combination of sharply rising real house prices and the spread of owner-occupation has been one of the main factors behind the trend to more equal ownership of wealth in the UK over the twentieth century (Atkinson, 1983; Hamnett 1991; Hamnett, Harmer and Williams, 1991).

(7) A further implication of the rise in home ownership and of the relative price of houses is that housing wealth has come to be the most important component of the value of *estates bequeathed* in the UK. Hamnett (1991) reports that by the mid-1980s around 55% of estates bequeathed contained housing wealth; in most of those estates housing wealth was the largest component. This phenomenon is not confined to the UK. In the last thirty years the value of residential property in Japan has risen astronomically; land prices have risen even faster. Yoshikawa and Ohtake (1989) report that in 1983 70% of the value of bequests in Japan was accounted for by land.

(8) *Tax treatment*: In many countries the tax regime favours home ownership. This has been, and remains, the case in the UK; capital gains on (first) houses used for owner-occupation are untaxed as is the imputed rent from them. Interest on the first £30000 of mortgage debt is tax deductible (though now at a lower rate than the tax rate on income); interest on no other household loans receives tax relief.

(9) *Financial intermediaries* — primarily banks, savings and loans, building societies and other specialist housing finance companies — are more closely involved in the housing market than in the markets for other consumer durables. Given the cost of houses and, at least in the UK, the early age at which people buy them (in 1990 35% of adults below the age of 25 were home-owners), the lending practices of financial firms have a great impact upon the demand for housing.

In analysing housing markets it is essential to keep these special features in mind, and in the models developed in later chapters we aim to capture — often in a stylized way — these distinctive characteristics of the market. The reliance on formal models itself warrants some justification. Mine is simple; without a clear framework within which to analyse the determinants of the prices and quantities of houses it is hard to see how the implications of the distinctive features of houses, and of changes in them, can be assessed; we should be left only with the choice over how we should describe recent events — as political history, as sociology or simply as tables of statistics. We rely upon theoretical models to provide our framework for analysing the housing market. But in constructing these models we shall be forced to abstract from many features of real housing markets. We shall, for example, repeatedly make three assumptions, none of which is innocuous and any of which might result in misleading conclusions and create a straitjacket — rather than a guide — for empirical work. It is worth describing these assumptions at the outset.

First, we shall assume that individual houses can be compared and aggregated. We shall talk about units of housing in the same way as we talk about gallons of oil. This does not imply that a twelve-bedroom mansion in London's Belgravia or on the edge of Central Park in Manhattan is assumed to be the same commodity as a one-bedroom flat in Toxteth or a tenement in the Bronx; merely that there is embodied in each a certain quantum of constant quality units of housing. How many units of housing are embodied in a particular house or flat will depend upon its size, location, design, state of repair and a host of other factors. For our purposes the nature of the mapping from a vector of house-specific characteristics to an'output' of housing units is of secondary importance and will not be specified. But the assumption that such a mapping exists, that houses can be compared in some objective way independent of preferences, is a strong one (Mclellan, 1982, Chapter 2). We are assuming that homes created in cellars can be compared with the town houses of the upper middle classes. Before one is too quick to reply that it is innocuous to assume that there is always some way of measuring the quantity of housing services provided by these different spaces, consider the following descriptions, both written about housing conditions in the UK in the 1830s:

> From some recent enquiries on the subject, it would appear that upwards of 20,000 individuals live in cellars in Manchester alone.... These cells are the very picture of loathsomeness — placed upon the soil, though partly flagged, without drains, subjected

> to being occasionally overflowed, seldom cleaned—every return of their inmates
> bringing with it a further succession of filth—they speedily become disgusting recep-
> tacles of every species of vermin that can infest the human body...
>
> (P. Gaskell, 1833, quoted in Burnett, 1986)

Burnett goes on to describe the kind of home available at around the same time
for a rent of £75—about 10% of the peak earnings of a middle class man:

> It is a house of 'character' in the fashionable 'Gothic' style, with ten rooms—not
> counting the spacious hall—a large dining room and an elegant drawing room opening
> to a conservatory, a study, a kitchen and adjoining domestic offices sufficient for the
> manservant, cook and two maids who are now kept, six bedrooms, the principal one
> having its own small dressing room, and, for the first time, a bathroom with a fixed
> bath and piped water supply.

Quite how many units of housing are embodied in a Manchester cellar relative to
the number in a 'Gothic style' house is a matter for speculation.

Our second assumption is that we can treat preferences over houses and over
other commodities as being, in some sense, fundamental; that is as being unchanged
by the particular history of bundles of commodities (including past housing services)
consumed. To most economists this is natural enough, and only usually thought
unacceptable in the analysis of habit-forming drugs or alcohol. Although I will
always make this assumption I am not convinced that in the analysis of housing it
is entirely harmless. Consider the following accounts from the 1850s:

> Home has no attraction for the young labourer. When he goes there, tired and chilly,
> he is in the way amidst domestic discomforts; the cottage is small, the children are
> troublesome, the fire is diminished, the solitary candle is lighted late and extinguished
> early.... He naturally, then, goes to the public house, where a cheerful fire and jovial
> society are found, and becomes a loose character...
>
> (Sir A. H. Elton in the 'Agricultural Gazette' (1853))

The effect of housing conditions on Victorian preferences was not believed to be
confined to men:

> When young girls are brought into contact with men by overcrowding in that sort
> of way, and by going to offices (privies) which are exposed to public view, the fine
> edge of modesty must, of course, be very much blunted; and there is no doubt that
> that does lead...in the end to immorality, to communication with each other before
> marriage, and such like.
>
> (Canon Girdlestone, quoted in Burnett, 1986)

One does not need to share the Victorian high-mindedness to see the point.

A third, and related, assumption which we shall make is that household labour
incomes are independent of housing. This implies that wage rates and the supply of
labour from households are not affected by changes in house values or in the type of
housing they have. In turn this implies that labour productivity and access to work
are unaffected by housing conditions, assumptions which the recent research on the

interaction between regional disparity in house prices and labour mobility suggests are not innocuous (Bover, Muellbauer and Murphy, 1988). Indeed the fact that there is now a substantial literature on efficiency wages that stresses the relation between labour productivity and remuneration (e.g. Shapiro and Stiglitz, 1984) suggests the importance of the links between the effectiveness of labour and its material conditions. The perception of the links between housing standards and labour productivity was a major factor in the development of employer housing estates at the end of the nineteenth century (as, for example, with W. H. Lever's Port Sunlight, George Cadbury's Bourneville and Joseph Rowntree's New Earswick; the development of housing estates by Robert Owen at New Lanark is an example from an earlier era). Burnett (1986) suggests that for the late nineteenth century urban poor, the links between housing markets and household income were complex and many:

> No matter what the cost and quality of accommodation, they [the poor] were inevitably tied to locations where a day's work might be picked up if a man were on the spot at 5 or 6 am, and where his wife and daughters could work as charwomen, seamstresses and at sweated domestic industries not available in the suburbs. Cheap markets meant that food prices were lower than further out, while debts to local shopkeepers also tended to tie the poor to areas where they were known and could obtain credit.

We ignore these factors — the difficulty of comparing different houses and the effects of housing conditions upon consumer preferences and upon labour incomes — not just because they are hard to quantify, but more because their inclusion is likely to prove unhelpful in analysing, say, the impact of changes in the tax treatment of housing or of financial liberalization. To allow, for example, for the impact of housing quality upon labour productivity would add a spurious generality to results while in reality merely peppering extra partial derivatives around the pages of the text the magnitude, often even the sign, of which is unclear.

1.4   A PLAN OF THE BOOK

In Chapter 2 we develop a model of the housing market which can be used to analyse the short-run and long-run impact of changes in financial markets, in tax rates, in demographics and in supply conditions on the prices of houses and on the stock of dwellings. We derive a more general measure of the cost of housing services for a forward-looking consumer than has been used in the literature. This way of measuring the user cost of housing will be used throughout this book. Chapter 3 puts recent developments in the UK housing market into a long-term context. We focus there on the process whereby housing wealth has been accumulated. The impact of price changes and of new building in accounting for the rise in the real value of the housing stock is analysed. We study how the tax and financial system have influenced the real cost of housing services. The impact of changes in demographics and the importance of housing wealth in the transfer of wealth across generations is analysed.

In Chapter 4 we use the model of household consumption decisions developed in Chapter 2 to derive the optimal response of consumer spending and household saving to various types of house price shock. We show how the response of saving to house price shocks is sensitive to the time horizon of the household, the degree of substitutability between housing and other consumption goods, the nature of the shock and the composition of household assets before the shock occurs. We use data on the consumption decisions of households and on real house prices to assess whether the model of rational, forward-looking agents is consistent with the time-series evidence on price shocks and consumption growth.

Chapter 5 considers the impact of financial deregulation. We use the framework developed in Chapter 2 to analyse the ways in which greater access to credit affects housing demand, consumption, bequests of wealth and house prices. The nature of the adjustment path in the wake of unanticipated relaxations of the lending criteria used by financial firms is derived. Simulations with a calibrated model are undertaken to assess the different ways in which financial liberalization might affect the economies of the major developed countries.

Chapters 6 and 7 use first aggregate, and then micro, data to assess whether the impact of house price shocks, of financial deregulation and of shocks to income are in line with the predictions of the theoretical models developed in Chapters 4 and 5. It is far from clear what the relative importance of easier credit and changing expectations of future disposable incomes is in accounting for the sharp fall in the savings rate in many countries in the 1980s. The aim of Chapter 6 is to address that issue. Using a model of household intertemporal optimization the differences in the time-series properties of income and consumption when the driving force behind lower saving is shocks to income rather than easier credit conditions are analysed. The properties of the simple model of household behaviour are used in designing tests to discriminate between those accounts which make financial deregulation central to recent changes in UK savings (e.g. Muellbauer and Murphy, 1990) and those which place more emphasis on changes in expectations of future incomes (King, 1990; Pagano, 1990; Attanasio and Weber, 1992). We find evidence that credit-easing has been more important than changing expectations of future incomes.

Chapter 7 uses micro-data to estimate the determinants of household permanent income and to measure how human capital and earnings uncertainty affect consumption. We also estimate how home-owners react to capital gains on housing and assess whether these gains are treated in the same way as other sources of income. Since house price rises simultaneously increase the market value of the assets of home-owners *and* the opportunity cost of consuming current and future housing services, it is in theory unclear whether we should expect a wealth effect on consumption. Using UK micro-data we find that capital gains on housing do not show up as a major determinant of household consumption, a result consistent with the theoretical work of Chapter 4. Estimates of permanent income and of earnings uncertainty do, however, have powerful effects on spending. We find that precautionary motives may account for a substantial proportion of household saving.

In Chapter 8 we turn to the design of contracts to finance house purchase. We consider the differences between the markets for housing finance within Europe and, more specifically, in the types of loan contract available in them. The risk characteristics of alternative types of mortgage contract are analysed and the implications of greater mobility of capital on the ways in which house purchases are financed, and on the demand for and price of housing, is considered.

The final chapter considers the policy implications of the study. Four issues are addressed: the tax treatment of owner-occupied housing; the ways in which financial intermediaries are regulated; policy towards the rental sector; and the macroeconomic policy implications of financial liberalization in the market for home loans.

1.5   WHO IS THIS BOOK FOR?

It would be misleading to claim that having an interest in the economics of housing is either a necessary or sufficient condition for reading this book. It is not sufficient because I take for granted a familiarity with undergraduate principles of microeconomics and, to a lesser extent, macroeconomics. The more technical sections — which could be skimmed on a first reading — require at least a familiarity with dynamic and constrained optimization; the empirical chapters (particularly 6 and 7) assume at least undergraduate econometrics. Having a specialist interest in housing is not a necessary condition for this book to be helpful. This is because this book is as much about the economics of consumer behaviour, of financial markets and of macroeconomic policy as it is about the construction and exchange of houses; and because houses are such important commodities what happens in housing markets is of macroeconomic significance and cannot fail to have implications for public policy.

REFERENCES

Atkinson, A. (1983) *The Economics of Inequality*, 2nd edition, Clarendon Press, Oxford.

Attanasio, O. and Weber, G. (1992) The UK Consumption Boom of the Late 1980s: Aggregate Implications of Microeconomic Evidence, Mimeo, University College London.

Bover, O., Muellbauer, J. and Murphy, A (1988) Housing markets and UK labour markets, *Oxford Bulletin of Economics and Statistics*, **51**, 97–136.

Burnett, J. (1986) *A Social History of Housing*, 2nd edition Methuen, London.

Deaton, A. (1992) *Understanding Consumption*, Clarendon Press, Oxford.

Gaskell, P. (1833) *The Manufacturing Population of England*, reprint, 1972, p. 133.

Hamnett, C. (1991) Home Ownership, Housing Wealth and Wealth Distribution in Britain. Paper presented to a conference on *Housing Policy as a Strategy for Change*, Oslo, June.

Hamnett, C., Harmer, M. and Williams, P. (1991) *Safe as Houses*, Paul Chapman Publishing, London.

Hills, J. (1991) *Unravelling Housing Finance*, Oxford University Press, Oxford.

Housing Finance Review (1993), prepared by Steve Wilcox and published by the Joseph Rowntree Foundation, York.

Mclellan, D. (1982) *Housing Economics*, Longmans, London.

Manchester, J. and Poterba, J. (1989) Second Mortgages and Household Saving. NBER Discussion Paper No. 2853.

Mankiw, G. and Weil, D. (1989) The baby boom, the baby bust and the housing market, *Regional Science Urban Economy*, **19**, 235–58.

Muellbauer, J. and Murphy, A. (1990) Is the UK balance of payments sustainable?, *Economic Policy*, **11**, 345–83.

King, M. (1990) Discussion of 'Is the UK balance of payments sustainable?', *Economic Policy*, **11**, 383–87.

Pagano, M. (1990) Discussion of 'Is the UK balance of payments sustainable?', *Economic Policy*, **11**, 387–90.

Poterba, J. (1984) Tax subsidies to owner occupied housing, *Quarterly Journal of Economics*, November, 729–52.

Shapiro, C. and Stiglitz, J. (1984) Equilibrium unemployment as a worker discipline device, *American Economic Review*, **74**, 433–44.

Smith, L., Rosen, K. and Fallis, G. (1988) Recent developments in economic models of housing markets, *Journal of Economic Literature*, **XXVI**, 29–64.

Yoshikawa, H. and Ohtake, F. (1989) An analysis of female labour supply, housing demand and the saving rate in Japan, *European Economic Review*, **33**, 997–1030.

CHAPTER 2

Theoretical building blocks for the analysis of housing markets

2.1 INTRODUCTION

Our aim here is to develop a theoretical framework which will be used in subsequent chapters to analyse housing markets. Some of the features which make houses different from other commodities — distinct even from other expensive, durable goods — were described in the previous chapter. In developing models, there is inevitably a tension between providing a structure rich enough to allow for these distinctive features of housing and providing tractability. We can only face the resulting trade-off once we fix our goal. Our own is to see how the demands of individuals for the services of housing — demands which are conditional upon household resources, perceptions of the current and future values of houses and of other goods, the availability of finance and the tax treatment of loans — interact with the supply conditions in the construction industry to determine the price and quantity of housing. In later chapters we investigate more closely how the determination of prices and quantities in the housing market fits in with other household decisions over consumption and the allocation of savings; we will also investigate the implications of these decisions for aggregate trade flows. As the range of issues which we analyse changes the appropriate degree of abstraction in the description of housing markets alters; the number of simplifying assumptions made about housing structures, tax rates and financial markets varies. But in all cases without some formal model of how the determinants of the demand and supply of housing interact it is hard to know where to begin in tracing through the impact of changes in the lending policies of financial firms or of alterations in the tax treatment of capital gains on housing or of shifts in demographics or in the supply of land for house building.

The key element in the analysis of housing markets will turn out to be the derivation of an expression for the user cost of housing. In this chapter we derive a more general formula for the user cost than has been used in the literature, special cases of which will be used often in subsequent chapters. Having derived the user cost we look at the supply side of the market for residential property and analyse equilibria in the markets for existing homes and in the construction industry. The long-run impact of exogenous changes that affect either the demand for, or the supply of, housing services is then determined. The nature of dynamic adjustment paths to new equilibria in the market are analysed. We go beyond some earlier models of the housing market (e.g. Poterba, 1984) in explicitly modelling the impact of restrictions on the availability of funds to households; in particular we will pay attention to differences in the availability of credit to finance various sorts of consumption. Houses are durable assets which are hard to conceal or smuggle and for which a well-developed second-hand market exists. Therefore the risks faced by lenders who take residential property as collateral are (or at least in many countries have been perceived to be) lower than the risks for most other types of credit. As a consequence the cost of mortgage debt has been lower and its availability greater than with other types of loan. In comparison, loans backed by human capital are very hard to obtain, for well-known reasons stemming from asymmetries in information which create moral hazard and adverse selection problems, (Stiglitz and Weiss, 1981). We analyse how greater availability of credit to finance house purchases affects the housing market; we also investigate the impact of changes in credit conditions in the mortgage market.

2.2   THE USER COST OF HOUSING

We begin by modelling the demand for housing at the household level. We will assume that agents aim to maximize the expected value of a time-separable, lifetime utility function which depends upon consumption of housing services and of a composite consumption good. We assume that housing services are proportional to the quantity, or number of units, of housing owned (H). The flow of utility derived in period t will be written $U(H_t, c_t)$, where c_t is consumption at t of the consumption good.

Agents are assumed to earn income from their fixed supply of labour at employment terms which are exogenous; they receive (or pay) interest on net financial assets. We will assume that agents are only able to borrow against housing wealth. This is an extreme assumption. While there are good reasons why it is easier to borrow against housing wealth than against almost any other household asset it is clearly unrealistic to assume zero supply of other credit. It would be less restrictive to assume that credit to finance other consumption were available but at a higher interest rate. Formally, however, there is no difference between our assumption and a weaker one that the cost of other credit is so high that no households use it.

We assume that there is a *maximum* ratio of mortgage debt to house value of β. This limit is set by lenders and may change over time. The existence of a limit might reflect an optimal response of financial firms to problems of asymmetric information. Despite the fact that houses are good collateral there is still a risk that lenders will lose money if they attract borrowers who know they face above average risks of not repaying loans; furthermore the incentive households have to preserve the value of the lender's collateral may decline if the loan is so high that the owner's expected, residual claim on the home is low and if lenders cannot monitor how they care for their home. For either of these reasons asymmetric information between borrowers and lenders may prompt financial firms to put a limit on the loan-to-value ratio. A quite different reason for limits on the size of loans is that financial intermediaries may themselves face binding restrictions; government regulations, or political pressure (so-called moral suasion), may prevent banks, building societies and savings and loans from lending as much as they would like. Restrictions on their ability to raise deposits may have the same effect. Both types of restriction have existed in the UK.

From the household's point of view the source of a borrowing limit is not very important; only the size of β matters. Credit restrictions will be relaxed by increasing β. Households at the limit of their mortgage are unable to borrow more to smooth consumption optimally; borrowing against future expected labour income is impossible once the mortgage limit has been reached. For a household at the limit of its mortgage, credit can only be extended if the value of its house (the only acceptable collateral) increases, either through price rises or by a move to a more expensive home. House price rises allow the credit-restricted home owner to borrow more and to increase non-housing consumption. Moving to a more costly home, however, will only allow a credit-restricted agent to increase non-housing consumption if $\beta > 1$. If $\beta < 1$, then for a household at the limit of its mortgage there is a down-payment constraint that any additions to investment in housing must be financed, in part, from own resources.

Until the credit limit is reached households are assumed to be able to cost-lessly vary the size of their mortgage. This implies that a household with spare borrowing capacity can top up its existing mortgage without being constrained to use the funds for home improvements or other uses which enhance the value of the lender's collateral. In practice, in both the US and UK it has not been easy until quite recently for households to borrow on mortgage without at least claiming that the funds were being used for some sort of investment in housing. Of course any household which borrows to finance housing expenditure while also holding financial assets is in some way using the loan for non-housing purposes, since it becomes a liability against which a portfolio of both housing and financial assets are held. Furthermore, there is anecdotal evidence from the UK that even when households have claimed that mortgage loans are being used to finance housing expenditure that is not where the money has ended up. Certainly estimates of aggregate equity withdrawal described in the next chapter suggest that leakage of funds from the UK housing market had been substantial well before building societies' range of permitted types of lending was extended in 1986. (Hence the following joke from the early 1980s: Building Society manager, on seeing a client who recently extended his mortgage, 'How is the loft conversion?'. Client: 'Pretty good, but it's a bit sluggish in third gear.')

For simplicity we initially assume that real interest rates are constant. Future labour incomes and real house prices are, however, variable and uncertain.

The household optimization problem at time $t = 0$ is

$$\max E_0(U_0) = \sum_{t=0}^{T} E_0[U(H_t, c_t)/(1 + \rho)^t] \tag{2.1}$$

The period to period budget constraint is

$$c_t = y_t + (1 + r)S_{t-1} - S_t - (1 + r_m)M_{t-1} + M_t - p_t(H_t$$
$$- (1 - \delta)H_{t-1}) - p_t H_t(\tau_p + \mu) \tag{2.2}$$

the constraints are

$$S_t \geq 0 \qquad\qquad \text{for all } t \tag{2.3}$$

$$M_t \leq \beta(p_t H_t) \qquad\qquad \text{for all } t \quad (\beta \geq 0) \tag{2.4}$$

$$S_T + p_T H_T - M_T \geq 0 \tag{2.5}$$

where
$E_t(.)$ is the expectations operator conditional on information at time t
c_t = consumption in period t
y_t = labour income (in terms of consumer goods) in period t
S_t = net financial assets (*excluding* mortgage debt) at beginning of time t
M_t = the outstanding mortgage at beginning of time t ($M_t \geq 0$)
p_t = price, in terms of consumer goods, of a unit of housing at start t
H_t = number of units of housing owned at the beginning of t
r = real interest rate earned on financial assets
r_m = real interest rate (in terms of *consumer goods*) paid on mortgages. (In measuring the user cost of housing for the UK in the next chapter we will see that it can be helpful to decompose the real rate into the nominal rate and an inflation term.)
ρ = discount rate
δ = depreciation rate on housing
τ_p = property tax rate (households who own a home are assumed to pay a proportion of its current market value each period in tax)
$\mu(p_t H_t)$ = insurance costs, repairs and maintenance costs; such costs are assumed to be a constant fraction, μ, of the value of the home and are assumed to be non-discretionary. (This is a simplification; while financial firms generally insist that building insurance is in place on houses they lend against, and that essential repairs are undertaken, there clearly remains some choice for households over the scale of insurance and the degree of maintenance.)

Net worth at t, denoted W_t, is

$$W_t = S_t + p_t H_t - M_t \tag{2.6}$$

i.e. the sum of financial and physical assets net of mortgage debt.

$U(H_t, c_t)$ is the time-separable and time-invariant utility function describing preferences over consumption of housing services (which are proportional to H) and of consumption goods. U is assumed to be increasing, twice differentiable and concave in its arguments.

We assume that all purchases of goods, receipts of income and payments of interest are made at the beginning of each period. Equation (2.5) states that at the end of a household's life at time T, net worth must be positive. If, in addition, $\beta < 1$, constraints (2.3) and (2.4) imply that household net worth (excluding the value of human capital), the sum of gross housing wealth and financial assets net of mortgage debt, must *always* be positive ($W_t > 0$, for all t). The implication of this is that if house prices were to fall suddenly households that were highly geared might need to pay off some of their mortgage. In practice, although lenders generally do have an upper limit on the ratio of house value to mortgage size for a household wishing to buy a new house, or extend a mortgage on an existing property, they could not insist that a household reduce its outstanding mortgage balance when house prices fall. This is an important point; if lenders cannot force households to repay early if the value of collateral *falls* — and so long as regular mortgage payments are met lenders would not be able to do this — but will lend more if the value of collateral *rises*, then there will be asymmetries between the effect of price rises and falls. Price rises increase the borrowing potential for home owners and for the credit restricted may cause increased consumption of both housing services and of other goods; reductions in prices may make it hard for households to trade up (or even trade down!), but may cause no change in current consumption. Modelling how these asymmetries work is important. We return to this in Chapter 5; Stein (1993) presents an interesting model where these asymmetries are modelled and can have a significant effect on house prices and the volume of transactions.

The budget constraint (2.2) says that consumption must equal labour income (y), *plus* the income from financial wealth ($r S_{t-1}$), *minus* additions to financial wealth ($S_t - S_{t-1}$), *plus* the excess of new mortgage loans over net additions to housing ($M_t - M_{t-1} - p_t(H_t - (1-\delta)H_{t-1})$), *minus* the cost of paying interest on existing debt ($r_m M_{t-1}$), and net of the direct costs of home ownership, i.e. *minus* taxes and maintenance ($p_t H_t(\tau_p + \mu)$).

The first-order conditions from the optimization problem are

$$U_c'(c_t, H_t) = E_t[((1+r)/(1+\rho))U_c'(c_{t+1}, H_{t+1})] + \lambda_{1t} \tag{2.7}$$

$$
\begin{aligned}
U_H'(c_t, H_t) = U_c'(c_t, H_t) \cdot p_t \cdot \Big\{ & (1-b) + \tau_p + \mu + b(1+r_m)/(1+r) \\
& - E_t(1+\dot{p}_t)(1-\delta)/(1+r) - ((1-\delta)/(1+\rho))\sigma_{u\dot{p}} \\
& - [\lambda_{1t}/U_c'(c_t, H_t)][b(1+r_m)/(1+r) \\
& - E_t(1+\dot{p}_t)(1-\delta)/(1+r)]\Big\}
\end{aligned}
\tag{2.8}
$$

where
$U'_c(c_t, H_t)$ is the marginal utility of (non-housing) consumption at t; $U'_c(c_t, H_t) = \partial U(c_t, H_t)/\partial c_t$
$U'_H(c_t, H_t)$ is the increment to utility in period t from a marginal increase in housing;
λ_{1t} is the Lagrange multiplier associated with the restriction $S_t \geq 0$;
b is the proportion of the value of an *increment* in house size financed on mortgage;
$\sigma_{u\dot{p}}$ is the conditional covariance between the increase in the marginal utility of consumption $(U'_c(c_{t+1}, H_{t+1})/U'_c(c_{t+1}, H_{t+1}))$ and the proportionate rate of change of house prices between t and $t+1$, denoted $(\dot{p}_t)$.

The derivation of (2.8) is explained briefly in an appendix to this chapter. The complementary slackness conditions are:

$$\lambda_{1t} S_t = 0 \tag{2.9}$$

$$\lambda_{2t}(\beta p_t H_t - M_t) = 0 \tag{2.10}$$

λ_{2t} is the Lagrange multiplier associated with the restriction $\beta \dot{p}_t H_t \leq M_t$; An implication of (2.10) is $\lambda_{2t}(\beta - b) = 0$ so that a household which is credit-restricted in the mortgage market (for whom $\lambda_{2t} > 0$) will choose to finance as high a proportion of incremental housing expenditure as possible on mortgage ($\beta = b$). (On our assumptions a household that was not credit constrained could finance more than $100\beta\%$ of marginal housing expenditure by mortgage debt, though it might, of course, choose a lower proportion of debt finance.)

It is important to note that (2.7) and (2.8) are valid whether $r = r_m$ (in which case the opportunity cost to a household of consumption today in terms of consumption tomorrow is the same whichever way expenditure is financed) or whether $r_m \neq r$, in which case the household will be at a corner solution and *at least* one of the constraints will bite. Consider, first, the case where the mortgage rate exceeds the return on financial assets. In this case the household will not simultaneously hold mortgage debt ($M_t > 0$) and financial assets ($S_t > 0$). If $r_m > r$ it is cheaper for the household to finance house purchase by running down financial assets rather than using mortgage debt. Mortgage debt would only be used if a household could reduce its stock of financial assets no further ($S_t = 0$). So when $r_m > r$, $M_t > 0$ only if the restriction $S_t \geq 0$ binds and $\lambda_{1t} > 0$. It may be that even though the mortgage rate exceeds the return on financial assets the borrowing limit is still binding, so $M_t = \beta p_t H_t$ and $\lambda_{2t} > 0$; such may be the desire to consume today that, given current income, the household would prefer to borrow more than the criteria used by financial firms allow, even though the cost of borrowing is relatively high.

If $r_m < r$ the household faces an arbitrage opportunity so long as $M_t < \beta p_t H_t$ since it could then borrow more against the value of its house and re-invest the proceeds in assets earning a higher return than the cost of debt. Since arbitrage cannot exist in equilibrium we infer that if $r_m < r$ households must face binding restrictions in the mortgage market, so $M_t = \beta(p_t H_t)$ and $\lambda_{2t} > 0$. Once again, it may be that both constraints bind, so $S_t = 0$ and $\lambda_{1t} > 0$ also. In this case the desire to consume more today outweighs the incentive to save — even at the relatively high rate r — so that all available funds are spent.

In the simplest case when $r = r_m$ there is only one constraint because mortgage debt and financial assets are perfect substitutes; the two constraints (2.9) and (2.10) reduce to a single condition with $\lambda_{1t} = \lambda_{2t} = \lambda_t$.

Whether, in practice, the net cost of mortgage debt (r_m) exceeds or falls short of the net rate of return on financial wealth (r) is unclear; in the UK at least part of the interest payments on mortgage debt are tax deductible, while for many households the income on financial assets is subject to a different (and sometimes zero) marginal rate of tax. So even if the gross interest rate on mortgages and the pre-tax returns on financial assets were equal the net rates would, in general, not be; and it is not clear which is lower.

Equation (2.7) is the standard Euler equation which, for a non-credit-restricted household, relates the marginal utility of consumption at t to the expectation of marginal utility at $t + 1$. If credit restrictions bind, so that a household holds no financial assets, $\lambda_{1t} > 0$ and the marginal utility of current consumption is higher than the adjusted (for interest and discount rates) expectation of future marginal utility. Condition (2.8) equates the marginal utility of housing to the product of the marginal utility of consumption and the effective user cost of housing. (2.8) implicitly defines the user cost of housing, which is the marginal rate of transformation between housing services and consumption goods. At an optimum this must equal the marginal rate of substitution, which is ($U'_H(c_t, H_t) / U'_c(c_t, H_t)$). Equation (2.8) is rather unwieldy and we shall consider special cases that are easier to interpret shortly. But the general version reveals the components of the user cost of housing — i.e. the determinants of the correct measure of the real cost of enjoying housing services within a particular period. From (2.8) it is apparent that the user costs depends upon the purchase price of housing units (p_t); the durability of the house (as reflected in the depreciation rate δ and the maintenance rate μ); the tax treatment of housing (reflected in τ_p and also, perhaps, in the differential between r and r_m); the expected rate of change of house prices; the means of financing house purchase (i.e. b); the risk characteristics of housing (measured by the conditional covariance between house values and the marginal utility of income ($\sigma_{u\dot{p}}$)); and the extent of credit restrictions (as reflected by λ_{1t}/U'_c).

In some special cases (2.8) simplifies to a more familiar form. Consider first the case where $\lambda_{1t} = 0$; $r_m = r$; and $\sigma_{u\dot{p}} = 0$. In this case credit restrictions do not bind; there is no difference between the net of tax cost of mortgage debt and the returns on financial assets; and there is no risk premium on houses because unanticipated fluctuations in the value of homes are independent of fluctuations in the marginal utility of wealth. In this case (2.8) simplifies to

$$U'_H(c_t, H_t)/U'_c(c_t, H_t) = p_t\{1 + \tau_p + \mu - E_t(1 + \dot{p}_t)(1 - \delta)/(1 + r)\} \quad (2.11)$$

For small values of $E_t(\dot{p}_t)$, δ, and r, $E_t(1 + \dot{p}_t)(1 - \delta)/(1 + r) \cong 1 + E_t(\dot{p}_t) - \delta - r$ in which case (2.11) implies that the user cost can be well approximated by

$$p_t\{\tau_p + \mu + \delta + r - E_t(\dot{p}_t)\}$$

which is a formula familiar in the literature (see, for example, Poterba (1984), or Smith, Rosen and Fallis (1988)).

If either $r_m \neq r$ *or* if $\lambda_{1t} > 0$ the user cost depends upon b; the way in which marginal house purchases are financed then influences the user cost. Denoting the user cost by uc_t, noting that in equilibrium $uc_t = U'_H(c_t, H_t)/U'_c(c_t, H_t)$, and using (2.8) we can derive the sensitivity of the user cost to variations in the (marginal) gearing ratio:

$$\partial(uc_t)/\partial(b) = p_t\{(1 + r_m)/(1 + r) - 1 - (\lambda_{1t}/U'_c(c_t, H_t))(1 + r_m)/(1 + r)\} \quad (2.12)$$

Since $\lambda_{1t} \geq 0$, if $r_m < r$ then $\partial(uc_t)/\partial(b) < 0$ and it pays households to finance as high a proportion of the cost of house purchase as is possible on debt — gearing reduces the effective cost of housing. While $r_m < r$ is a sufficient condition for high gearing to be desirable, (2.12) reveals that it is not necessary. Clearly

$$\partial(uc_t)/\partial(b) < 0 \quad \text{as} \quad (1 + r_m)/(1 + r) < 1/(1 - (\lambda_{1t}/U'_c(c_t, H_t))) \quad (2.13)$$

The non-negative quantity $\lambda_{1t}/U'_c(c_t, H_t)$ is an index of the degree to which current consumption is constrained by binding credit restrictions. (2.13) shows that if restrictions are severe enough they can make debt financing of house purchase attractive even if the mortgage rate is higher than the return on financial assets. The intuition is obvious: for the liquidity constrained $\lambda_{1t} > 0$ and from (2.9) $S_t = 0$, so the option of financing house purchase out of financial assets is not available; there is a value of credit to such a household which can more than compensate for the higher mortgage interest rate, so that the user cost declines as the proportion financed on credit increases.

An important point to note is that the degree to which constraints bite can be affected by the level of house prices; so it is not generally legitimate to take b (the marginal gearing ratio on housing) as independent of p_t. For example, a household that is currently constrained by the lending rule (2.4) has its marginal gearing rate constrained to equal β. A sudden rise in house prices may ease the restriction so much that the unconstrained marginal gearing rate then differs from β; the endogeneity (at least for some households) of b makes analysis of general equilibria in the housing market difficult.

2.3   THE SUPPLY AND DEMAND FOR HOUSING

The first-order condition (2.8) can be used to work out the effect upon the demand for housing services of changes in the determinants of the user cost. To analyse the aggregate effects of changes in the user cost upon house values and upon the total stock of housing we need to model how such changes affect the total demand for housing and we also need to specify how the supply of residential property is determined.

The simplest strategy is to assume the existence of a representative household and to assume that interest rates, depreciation and tax rates are independent of aggregate house prices, aggregate lending or the total stock of housing. We could, for example, assume that domestic financial firms can raise funds in a world capital market so that the cost of lending to domestic households is exogenous. We now interpret (2.8) as the first-order condition for this representative household. We write the marginal rate of substitution:

$$U'_H(c_t, H_t)/U'_c(c_t, H_t) \equiv f(H_t, c_t) \tag{2.14}$$

and we shall assume that $f'_H(H_t, c_t) < 0$.

Using (2.8), and from the definition $\dot{p}_t \equiv (p_{t+1} - p_t)/p_t$, we now write

$$f(H_t, c_t) = p_t(\gamma) - E_t(p_{t+1} - p_t)(\varphi) \tag{2.15}$$

where:

$$\gamma = 1 - b + \{1 - \lambda_{1t}/U'_c(c_t, H_t)\}[b(1 + r_m)/(1 + r) - (1 - \delta)/(1 + r)]$$
$$+ \tau_p + \mu - \sigma_{u\dot{p}}(1 - \delta)/(1 + \rho) \tag{2.16}$$

$$\varphi = (1 - \delta)/(1 + r)\{1 - (\lambda_{1t}/U'_c(c_t, H_t))\} \tag{2.17}$$

Notice in (2.16) that we have implicitly assumed that b is independent of p for the representative household. This is a simplification. Equally important is the implicit assumption that $\lambda_{1t}/U'_c(c_t, H_t)$ is independent of p_t. The importance of making these assumptions, and the effects of relaxing them, is discussed in more detail below.

The signs of γ and φ in (2.15) are crucial. Provided

$$E_t\{((1 + r)/(1 + \rho))[U'_c(c_{t+1}, H_{t+1})]\} > 0$$

and so long as the interest rate exceeds -100% this condition must hold, then from (2.7) $\{1 - (\lambda_{1t}/U'_c(c_t, H_t))\} > 0$ and $\varphi > 0$. If $\sigma_{u\dot{p}}$ is not significantly positive, $\gamma > 0$. If unexpected increases in house prices coincide with unanticipated declines in marginal utility $\sigma_{u\dot{p}}$ is actually negative and $\gamma > 0$. Indeed a negative value for $\sigma_{u\dot{p}}$ seems more plausible than a positive one. A negative value for $\sigma_{u\dot{p}}$ would follow, for example, if the main source of shocks to house prices stemmed from surprises in household incomes — positive surprises in household incomes increase the demand for housing and hence its price, but they also allow households to consume more generating a negative covariance between the impact on house prices and on marginal utility. In contrast a positive value for $\sigma_{u\dot{p}}$ implies that houses are a hedge against other risks to households. We cannot rule this out on theoretical grounds, but the likelihood that regional house prices are strongly positively correlated with regional employment prospects and that for many households mobility is limited makes it unlikely that empirical measures of $\sigma_{u\dot{p}}$ would be negative. For these reasons it seems reasonable to make the mild assumption that relative to the values of interest rates, taxes, depreciation rates and maintenance charges, σ_{u_p} is not so positive as to make γ negative.

We now move on to consider the supply side of the market. Following Poterba (1984) we shall assume that the quantity of housing units constructed in a period (gross of depreciation of existing houses) is a positive function of the real house price, p_t. Denote this quantity I (for gross investment in housing). Thus

$$I_t = \Psi(p_t) \quad \Psi'_p(p_t) \geq 0 \qquad (2.18)$$

(2.18) can be derived from the optimization problem of a representative house builder that aims to maximize at each point in time the sale value of houses built $(p_t I_t)$ net of costs of construction. Costs of construction include the costs of labour, materials and land. If there are diminishing returns to scale in the production technology then even if factors are instantaneously variable there will be a unique and finite level of output at any price. Gross investment is simply the sum of these optimal outputs across producers.

Constant returns to scale in the construction industry would mean that at the average cost of housing, denoted (say) by ac^*, the long-run elasticity of supply should be infinite ($\Psi'_p(ac^*) = \infty$). This would imply that the equilibrium price of housing should equal ac^* regardless of the level of demand, which would only determine the equilibrium stock of housing. But the existence of factors of production used in construction that are in inelastic supply — most obviously land — means that even if there were constant returns to scale at the firm level there would still be a finite aggregate response of investment to increases in the sale price of completed houses ($0 < \Psi'_p(p) < \infty$); land prices would be driven up by a surge in housing production so that the cost of producing a new house would rise.

The net addition to the aggregate housing stock in a period is gross investment net of depreciation. Denoting the aggregate stock of housing $\bar{H}$, and noting that all houses are assumed to depreciate at the same rate δ, we can use (2.18) to write the net supply of new housing:

$$\bar{H}_{t+1} - \bar{H}_t = \Psi(p_t) - \delta\bar{H}_t \qquad (2.19)$$

The representative agent assumption means that the demand condition relating the quantity of housing to its price and to the expected rate of change of price (equation (2.15)) can be interpreted in terms of aggregates. Thus we rewrite (2.15):

$$E_t(p_{t+1} - p_t) = p_t(\gamma/\varphi) - f(\bar{H}_t, \bar{c}_t)/\varphi \qquad (2.20)$$

where $\bar{c}$ is aggregate consumption and $f'_H(\bar{H}_t\bar{c}_t) < 0$.

(2.19) and (2.20) form a pair of difference equations in the expected change in house prices and the change in the housing stock. If time periods becomes smaller and smaller we converge to the continuous time analogues to (2.19) and (2.20), which are

$$\dot{\bar{H}}_t = \Psi(p_t) - \delta\bar{H}_t \qquad (2.21)$$

$$\dot{p}_t^e = p_t(\gamma/\varphi) - f(\bar{H}_t, \bar{c}_t)/\varphi \qquad (2.22)$$

Where $\dot{\bar{H}}_t$ is the rate of change of the aggregate housing stock at instant t and $\dot{p}_t^e$ the expected rate of change of house prices at t; δ should now be thought of as the instantaneous depreciation rate on housing. We can analyse the properties of (2.21) and (2.22) with a phase diagram. (See Blanchard and Fisher (1989) for a discussion of phase diagrams; Leonard and Van Long (1992) provide a detailed treatment, while Begg (1982) offers a less technical introduction.) To construct the diagram we need to relate actual price changes to expected price changes; the simplest assumption to make is that expectations are fulfilled, and we make it.

The two solid lines in the diagram (Figure 2.1) are derived from (2.21) and (2.22) and are the loci of points along which house prices are unchanging (aa) and on which the housing stock is constant (bb). There is a unique stationary equilibrium at $\bar{H}^\varepsilon$, p^ε where the two loci intersect. The arrows show the direction of motion of the system out of equilibrium, which can be inferred from (2.21) and (2.22). The assumption that γ is positive is crucial; conditional on it there is a unique level of prices for any given stock of houses which is consistent with equilibrium in the market for existing homes. We should point out here that assuming γ is positive is *not* innocuous. Were it not for the possible effects of credit restrictions, the assumptions required to ensure that the net effect upon housing demand of a price rise is negative (which effectively means that $\gamma > 0$) are not exceptionable; essentially they boil down to plausible restrictions on the risk premium on housing. But the existence of credit restrictions makes things much less straightforward. A rise in house prices may so enhance the borrowing capacity of a credit-restricted household that its response is to increase both non-housing

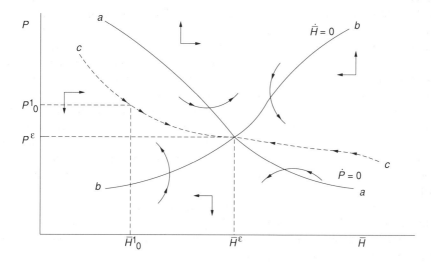

Figure 2.1 Equilibrium in the housing market

consumption *and* to consume more housing. A simple example helps make the point. Suppose a household cannot borrow more than 90% of the value of a house ($\beta = b = 0.9$). Let the household find it optimal, at given house prices and given expectations of future incomes, to have a £100 000 house with a £90 000 mortgage. Now assume house prices rise by 10%. The household could sell its current house and release £20 000 equity. This would allow it to buy a house in value up to £200 000. The household may find it optimal to use some of the equity for consumption *and* move to a more valuable house — e.g. it could sell the current home, spend £6000 on current consumption and buy a new house for £140 000 (with a £126 000 mortgage and using the proceeds of the first house as a deposit). This example shows that the marginal utility of non-housing consumption, the extent to which credit restrictions bind *and* the marginal gearing ratio on housing may all respond to changes in the level of house prices.

If this sort of effect is relevant for a large number of households, perverse effects of house price rises upon the demand for housing services are likely and a negative value for γ could arise. The loci of points of zero house price change (*aa*) would then slope up, creating the possibility of multiple intersections with the *bb* line. Multiple equilibria, unstable equilibria and perverse effects of changes in housing tax or in interest rates could all follow if γ were negative. (For an interesting model of multiple equilibria in the housing market based on credit restrictions see Stein (1993)).

We shall make the assumption for the rest of this chapter that although credit restrictions may be significant, they are not such as to generate a negative value of γ; we should still recognize that credit restrictions are likely to generate a smaller value of γ than if they were absent. This is significant. The smaller is γ the steeper is the *aa* schedule. This means that the impact of shocks to the housing market will be different when credit restrictions matter. For example, the steeper is *aa* the greater is the price effect, and the lower is the quantity effect, of changes in the supply function for housing; prices are more volatile the steeper is *aa*. The insight that credit restrictions might make house prices *more* variable is valuable and has not been noted in the literature; indeed it is more common to hear the opposite view that credit limits dampen swings in house prices.

Figure 2.1 reveals that, given our assumptions about parameter values, the conditions for saddlepoint stability hold and the housing market will converge on an equilibrium where the real price and the quantity of housing units is unchanging and where anticipations are fulfilled. The loci of points showing equilibrium prices for (predetermined) stocks of housing is the dashed line *cc*; this is the saddlepoint path implied by the schedules *aa* and *bb*. If, starting from equilibrium, 40% of houses were unexpectedly destroyed — reducing the stock to $\bar{H}_0^1$ — the price would jump to p_0^1. The housing market would asymptotically approach the old equilibrium along the path *cc* with prices falling, and net new houses being built, along the way. Any price other than p_0^1 at the instant after the reduction in the housing stock would put the housing market on an explosive path; forward-looking agents would recognize that prices could not move along such a path indefinitely and that an equilibrium condition would eventually have to be broken. Only along the path cc can all the equilibrium conditions continue to hold.

Phase diagrams can be used to study how changes in the current (or anticipated) tax treatment of housing, shifts in interest rates, or changes in the availability of finance affect both the long-run price and quantity of housing and how that equilibrium is reached.

Consider, first, the impact of a change in the tax system which makes housing more attractive. This could be a reduction in the rate of property tax (τ_p)—for example the abolition of a rating system, where the amount payable is a function of an estimate of the value of imputed income from owner-occupation, and its replacement with a poll tax amounts to a reduction in τ_p to zero. The introduction of more favourable tax breaks on mortgage loans, which reduces r_m, is an alternative way in which the tax system can become more favourable to owner-occupation. From (2.16) we see that *either* of these changes reduces γ. This has the effect of moving the loci of points of price stability (aa) to the right. Figure 2.2 traces through the implications of such a change on the assumption that it had not been anticipated and that the market had been in long-run equilibrium at $\bar{H}_0$, p_0 before the shock. The loci of combinations of prices and housing stocks which are stable moves from cc to c^1c^1. Because the housing stock is fixed at $\bar{H}_0$ in the short run (i.e. the housing stock is predetermined, or is a state variable) then in order for the market to move on to the new unique path of convergence, c^1c^1, the price must jump to p_0^1. The price of housing, unlike the housing stock, can move discontinuously, as indeed it must to preserve equilibrium in the market.

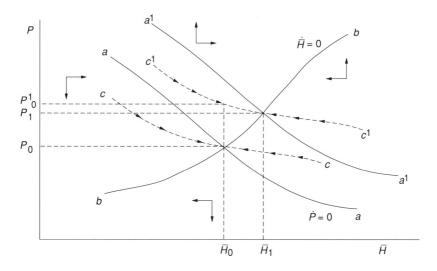

Figure 2.2   A favourable change in the taxation of housing

The diagram shows that provided the supply of houses is not perfectly inelastic (and if it were bb would be vertical), the unique convergent path to the new long-run equilibrium (c^1c^1) will involve falling prices. But provided that the supply is not perfectly elastic (and if it were bb would be horizontal), the new long-run equilibrium price (p_1) will be higher. The diagram shows that at the time of the tax change prices overshoot the new long-run equilibrium so that, in the short-run, demand is choked off to match the unchanged supply. As higher prices bring forth net investment, and the housing stock rises, the price of housing falls. Clearly, this type of overshooting of house prices is not a sign of inefficiency nor is it an indication of speculative bubbles or frenzy — despite the fact that these are interpretations routinely trotted out as 'explanations' of periods when house prices rise sharply and then fall. An important implication of this is that tests of 'efficiency' in the housing market, which assess whether, conditional on past prices, house price changes are unpredictable, are *not* informative about the efficiency of the market; Figure 2.2 shows that price changes *should* be serially correlated. Numerous papers test for efficiency by checking if price changes are unforecastable (recent examples being Case and Shiller (1989, 1990) and Ito and Hirono (1993)). Analysis of the interaction of the demand and supply sides of the market shows why this is not a valid test of asset market efficiency. Recall that Figure 2.2, which shows that price changes will be serially correlated after a shock, is constructed on the assumption of perfect foresight and market clearing. We shall see shortly that exactly how price changes are correlated depends crucially on the nature of the shock to the market.

It is important to stress that this analysis applies to changes in the housing market which are unanticipated. Had the change analysed in Figure 2.2 been forecast, the expectation of favourable tax breaks would have increased the demand for housing before the introduction of the measure, as individuals rationally aimed to build up their stake in housing in anticipation of an upwards price shock; of course the attempt by all agents to do this would drive the current price up so that on the implementation of the tax change there would be no price jump. Unless this were to happen unexploited arbitrage opportunities would exist. The path of adjustment can only follow the discontinuous route shown in Figure 2.2 if the tax change is *not* anticipated. So the implementation of a widely expected change in the tax treatment of housing or in the level of interest rates will not have an impact on prices at that date. (There would, however, have been an impact on price at the (earlier) time when it *first* became clear that a change was to be introduced.)

Consider next the impact of financial liberalization — an increase in the availability of funds to finance house purchase. We assume now that agents had been credit rationed before the increase in β. This implies, from (2.10), that prior to financial liberalization $b = \beta$, and so a rise in the maximum loan-to-value ratio will certainly have some impact.

Using (2.16), and imposing $\beta = b$, it follows that

$$\frac{\partial \gamma}{\partial \beta} = -1 + \{1 - \lambda_{1t}/U_c'(c_t, H_t)\}[(1 + r_m)/(1 + r)]$$

The derivative shows that the effect of increasing β upon γ will depend upon several factors. Higher gearing is more valuable the lower is r_m relative to r, so the impact of financial liberalization is dependent upon $(1 + r_m)/(1 + r)$. Increases in gearing are also more valuable the greater is the extent to which constraints bite, a natural measure of which is $\lambda_{1t}/U'_c(c_t, H_t)$. From (2.13) we know that $\partial\gamma/\partial\beta$ is negative provided the constraint was binding before credit liberalization. This follows because if credit restrictions are binding, so that households would prefer to finance a higher proportion of the purchase cost of housing on credit, any increase in the maximum loan-to-value ratio must reduce the effective cost of housing. This implies that $\partial(uc)/\partial(\beta) < 0$ which, by (2.13), means

$$(1 + r_m)/(1 + r) < 1/(1 - (\lambda_{1t}/U'_c(c_t, H_t)))$$

so that $\partial\gamma/\partial\beta < 0$. Since the impact of greater availability of mortgage debt is to reduce γ, the qualitative effect on the housing market is the same as the impact of lower taxes and can be traced through in Figure 2.2. The long-run price and quantity of housing will be higher as a result of credit liberalization; the short-run effect upon price will be greater than the long-run effect and real house prices, having jumped up, will gradually fall after the easing of restrictions.

The long-run and short-run effects of a rise in the mortgage interest rate can be analysed in the same way. From (2.16) a rise in r_m increases γ provided $b > 0$. The effect is to move the aa schedule down (Figure 2.3). There is an initial drop in prices from p_0 to p^1_0. At that lower price net housing investment is negative — depreciation exceeds gross investment, which may indeed have fallen

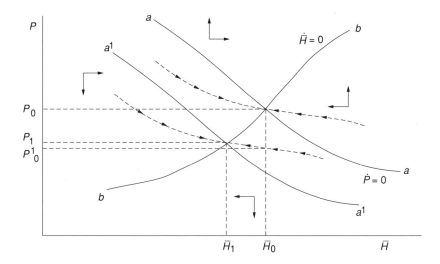

Figure 2.3 A rise in the cost of mortgages

to zero. The contraction in the stock of housing along the path to the new equilibrium causes a gradual increase in the market clearing price until we reach the new
steady-state. Activity in the construction industry is at its lowest immediately after
the increase in interest rates when house prices are also at their lowest.

Shifts in the demand for houses — stemming, for example, from increases in
current, or anticipated, incomes or from demographic factors which increase the
marginal utility of the existing housing stock — can be analysed with the same tools.
A demographic shift at time t which increases the number or size of households,
for example, will increase $U'_H(c_t, \bar{H}_t)$ and therefore raise $f(\bar{H}_t, \bar{c}_t)$. From (2.22)
we see that a rise in $f(\bar{H}_t, \bar{c}_t)$ moves the locus of points of zero expected house
price change to the right so that the impact on the housing market is the same as
in Figure 2.2.

Changes in the supply conditions in the construction sector shift the $\dot{H} = 0$
locus. Unexpected restrictions on the availability of land for residential development, or sudden rises in the cost of labour and materials used in the construction
industry, will reduce the flow of housing investment at any given price. Reductions
in construction costs or in the price of land will increase the flow of new houses
that are built at a given house price. Both the height and the slope of the $\dot{H} = 0$
locus may be altered. Figure 2.4 shows the impact of a decrease in housing cost.
The effect is to shift the locus of points of zero net investment (bb) to the right
(to b^1b^1). An important point to note here is that prices *undershoot* the new equilibrium. In the short run prices decrease from p_0 to p_0^1 and housing investment
rises. Net investment remains positive on the path to the new equilibrium and house
prices continue falling to the new steady-state level (p_1). An unexpected increase in
material costs or in land prices would also result in undershooting of the real house

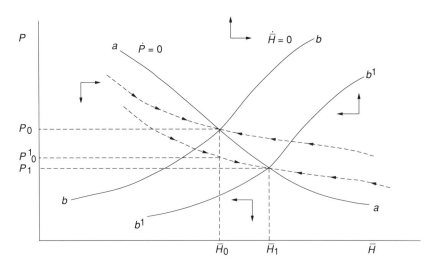

Figure 2.4   An adverse supply shock in the housing market

price; the initial rise in prices would be less than the eventual increase and along the transition path net housing investment would be negative as we converged to an equilibrium with a lower housing stock.

The implication of these results is that demand side shocks lead to *overshooting* of prices and to periods of rapid rises (or falls) in house values being followed by more gradual declines (or recoveries) in prices. Supply side shocks do not generate overshooting; they have a smaller immediate impact on price, which is followed by gradual changes of the same sign, i.e. *undershooting*. These differences in the time-series properties of prices can be useful in identifying the sources of shocks in the housing market. (Simulations reported in the *Bank of England Quarterly Bulletin* (1992, p. 177) using an estimated model of the housing market show that overshooting of house prices to various demand side shocks does appear to be significant).

2.4 THE PRICE OF HOUSES
AND THE SERVICES OF HOUSING

The first-order condition (2.8) equates the marginal rate of substitution between the services of housing and consumption with the user cost of housing. We could express this condition as a relation between the price of housing, the expected future house price and the marginal utility derived from housing relative to the utility of consumption goods. Using (2.15) we can write

$$p_t = (U'_H(c_t, H_t)/U'_c(c_t, H_t))/(\gamma + \varphi) + E_t(p_{t+1})(\varphi/(\gamma + \varphi)) \qquad (2.23)$$

where γ and φ are given by (2.16) and (2.17). By repeated forward substitution we can solve (2.23), subject to a transversality condition that the utility derived from a unit of housing increases less rapidly than the rate used to discount the future. Doing this allows us to express the house price in terms of the present value of the current and future housing services that a unit of housing yields. The forward solution of (2.23) is

$$p_t = \sum_{j=0}^{\infty} \{(U'_H(c_{t+j}, H_{t+j})/U'_c(c_{t+j}, H_{t+j}))\}[\varphi^j/(\varphi + \gamma)^{j+1}] \qquad (2.24)$$

Using the definitions of γ and φ , and making the approximation that $(1 - \delta)/(1 + r) \cong 1 - \delta - r$, we can write (2.24) for the simplest case where $\lambda_1 = \sigma_{\dot{p}u} = 0$ and $r_m = r$ as

$$p_t = \sum_{j=0}^{\infty} \{(U'_H(c_{t+j}, H_{t+j})/U'_c(c_{t+j}, H_{t+j}))\}$$

$$[(1 - \delta - r)/(1 + \tau_p + \mu)]^j (1/(1 + \tau_p + \mu)) \qquad (2.25)$$

The intuition behind (2.23) is fairly straightforward: $U_H'(c_{t+j}, H_{t+j})/U_c'(c_{t+j}, H_{t+j})$ is the relative value of the benefits from enjoying the services of a unit of housing at time $t+j$ to the benefits derived from consuming the non-durable good. Assuming that there is a rental market for housing units, this ratio should equal the cost in terms of consumer goods of renting a unit of housing for period $t+j$. (2.25) then says that the price of a house is the present discounted value of the future rental values of the property. The discount rate is $(1 - \delta - r)/(1 + \tau_p + \mu)$ which takes into account the physical depreciation of housing, the costs of maintenance, the rate of property taxes and the rate of time preference (as reflected by r). The value of a house is a decreasing function of each of these factors.

The two fundamental conditions derived in this chapter allow us to express the price of housing in two different ways. (2.25) relates the price of a unit of housing to the present value of the flow of future services that it yields. Equation (2.15), which is derived from the first-order condition (2.8), relates the price of housing to the expected rate of change of house prices and to the current flow of housing services. There is a close analogy between these two relations and two ways in which in an efficient market stock prices can be expressed. In simple models of an efficient capital market the price of a stock can be expressed as the present discounted value of the (expected) future dividends; this is sometimes referred to as the 'fundamentals' solution. Equation (2.25) is the 'fundamentals' solution to the equilibrium house price. But a condition that expected (risk-adjusted) returns should not be excessive also allows the stock price to be expressed as the discounted value of the expectation of its price 'tomorrow' plus the current dividend. With a slight abuse of language we might call this the 'arbitrage price' (the abuse stems from the use of the arbitrage concept in a context where expectations of future prices are not held with certainty). Equation (2.15) is the 'arbitrage' solution to the price of housing. Just as it is sometimes more useful in the analysis of stock markets to use one relation over the other, we will find it helpful in the rest of this book to sometimes focus on one or other of the two expressions for house prices. It is essential to note that there is no conflict between these two conditions; they are both derived from the same model of rational, forward-looking agents.

2.5   CONCLUSIONS

In this chapter we have derived a very general measure of the user cost of housing which goes beyond earlier work by explicitly accounting for the impact of credit restrictions. Combining the user cost measure — which is forward-looking — with a specification of the supply of new property allowed us to show how various shocks (for example unanticipated policy changes) affect the price and quantity of housing in the short and long run. We described conditions under which overshooting and undershooting of house prices arise and showed how standard tests of market efficiency are flawed.

REFERENCES

Bank of England (1992) House prices, arrears and possessions, *Bank of England Quarterly Bulletin*, May, 173–9.

Blanchard, O. and Fisher, S. (1989) *Lectures on Macroeconomics*, MIT Press, Cambridge, Mass.

Begg, D. (1982) *The Rational Expectations Revolution in Macroeconomics*, Phillip-Allen, Oxford.

Case, K. and Shiller, R. (1989) The efficiency of the market for single-family homes, *American Economic Review*, **79**, 125–37.

Case, K. and Shiller, R. (1990) Forecasting Prices and Excess Returns in the Housing Market. NBER Working Paper No. 3368, May.

Ito, T. and Hirono, K. (1993) Efficiency of the Tokyo Housing Market. NBER Working Paper No. 4382, June.

Leonard, D. and Van Long, N. (1992) *Optimal Control Theory and Static Optimization in Economics*, Cambridge University Press, Cambridge.

Poterba, J. (1984) Tax subsidies to owner-occupied housing, *Quarterly Journal of Economics*, November, 729–52.

Smith, L., Rosen, K. and Fallis, G. (1988) Recent developments in economic models of housing markets, *Journal of Economic Literature*, **XXVI**, 29–64.

Stein, J. (1993) Prices and Trading Volume: A Model with Down-payment Effects. NBER Discussion Paper, No. 4373, March.

Stiglitz, J. and Weiss, A. (1981) Credit rationing in markets with imperfect information, *American Economic Review*, **71**, 393–440.

APPENDIX: THE DERIVATION OF EQUATION (2.8)

Along an optimal path for the levels of consumption and for house size it must be the case that any deviation which satisfies the constraints should not increase expected utility. A *marginal*, sustainable deviation from the optimum path should leave the value of the maximand (equation (2.1) in the main text) unchanged. Equation (2.8) expresses an implication of that condition, which is that at an optimum the change in expected utility from a marginal increase in investment in housing at time t, which is unwound in the next period, should be zero.

A marginal increase in investment in housing at t in itself increases utility by $U'_H(c_t, H_t)$; but in order to satisfy the budget constraint (2.2) consumption of the other good both at t and in the next period must change. The right-hand side of (2.8) is simply the amount of consumption foregone at t in order to finance extra expenditure on housing, multiplied by the period t marginal utility of consumption, plus the expected value of the required change in consumption at $t+1$ multiplied by that period's marginal utility of consumption. So the right-hand side is the expected change in utility resulting from the rearrangement in the path of consumption necessitated by the extra expenditure on housing in period t; in equilibrium this must equal $U'_H(c_t, H_t)$. We shall show how the right-hand side of (2.8) is built up by considering first the change in consumption at t, and then focus on the expected change in consumption at $t + 1$ and how that change affects expected utility.

That part of the cost of a unit more of housing not financed on debt — that is $(1 - b)p_t$ — must, other things equal, reduce current consumption. Current consumption also has to be sacrificed to pay for the extra taxes and maintenance charges from home ownership. Hence the first part of the cost — in terms of utility foregone as a result of lower consumption — of extra housing is

$$U'_c(c_t, H_t)p_t\{(1 - b) + \tau_p + \mu\} \tag{A2.1}$$

The rest of the cost of house purchase, bp_t, is financed by increasing debt today; the implication of this change in debt is that consumption must be lower next period by an amount $bp_t(1 + r_m)$. Against this obligation to repay is the value of the extra housing; each unit of housing acquired at t is worth $p_{t+1}(1 - \delta)$ in the next period. The net resources which need to be diverted from consumption at $t + 1$ are therefore

$$p_t\{b(1 + r_m) - (p_{t+1}/p_t)(1 - \delta)\}$$

or

$$p_t\{b(1 + r_m) - (1 + \dot{p}_t)(1 - \delta)\} \tag{A2.2}$$

The effect on utility of reducing consumption by this amount is given by its product with marginal utility tomorrow — $U'_c(c_{t+1}, H_{t+1})$. The expectation of this product can be written

$$E_t\{(U'_c(c_{t+1}, H_{t+1}))p_t[b(1 + r_m) - (1 + \dot{p}_t)(1 - \delta)]\}$$
$$= [E_t(U'_c(c_{t+1}, H_{t+1}))]p_t\{b(1 + r_m) - (1 + \dot{p}^e_t)(1 - \delta)\}$$
$$- (U'_c(c_t, H_t))p_t(1 - \delta)\sigma_{u\dot{p}} \tag{A2.3}$$

where

$$\sigma_{u\dot{p}} = \{E_t([\dot{p}_t - \dot{p}^e_t][U'_c(c_{t+1}, H_{t+1}) - E_t(U'_c(c_{t+1}, H_{t+1}))])\}/U'_c(c_t, H_t)$$

$\sigma_{u\dot{p}}$ is the conditional covariance between the rate of increase in the marginal utility of consumption between t and $t + 1$, $U'_c(c_{t+1}, H_{t+1})/U'_c(c_t, H_t)$, and the percentage change in house prices ($\dot{p}_t$).

(A2.3) shows by how much utility is expected to decline at $t + 1$ as a result of the decision to enjoy more housing services at t.

Using (2.7) from the main text we can express the expectation of marginal utility at $t + 1$ in terms of marginal utility at t; λ_{1t}; ρ; and r:

$$E_t(U'_c(c_{t+1}, H_{t+1})) = [U'_c(c_t, H_t) - \lambda_{1t}](1 + \rho)/(1 + r) \tag{A2.4}$$

Using (A2.4) in (A2.3), and dividing by $(1 + \rho)$ to account for the discounting at t of utility which accrues at $t + 1$, we have

$$E_t\{(U'_c(c_{t+1}, H_{t+1}))p_t[b(1 + r_m) - (1 + \dot{p}_t)(1 - \delta)]\}/(1 + \rho)$$
$$= -p_t(U'_c(c_t, H_t))\sigma_{u\dot{p}}(1 - \delta)/(1 + \rho) + [U'_c(c_t, H_t)]$$
$$\times [1 - \lambda_{1t}/U'_c(c_t, H_t)]\{p_t\{b(1 + r_m)/(1 + r)$$
$$- (1 + \dot{p}^e_t)(1 - \delta)/(1 + r)\}\} \tag{A2.5}$$

The sum of (A2.5) and (A2.1) is the cost, in terms of foregone expected utility, of paying for the services of a marginal unit of housing in period t; at an optimum this utility cost must equal $U'_H(c_t, H_t)$. Thus

$$U'_H(c_t, H_t) = U'_c(c_t, H_t)p_t\{(1 - b) + \tau_p + \mu\} - p_t(U'_c(c_t, H_t))\sigma_{u\dot{p}}(1 - \delta)/(1 + \rho)$$
$$+ [U'_c(c_t, H_t)][1 - \lambda_{1t}/U'_c(c_t, H_t)]\{p_t\{b(1 + r_m)/(1 + r)$$
$$- (1 + \dot{p}^e_t)(1 - \delta)/(1 + r)\}\} \tag{A2.6}$$

Rearranging (A2.6) yields equation (2.8) in the main text.

CHAPTER 3

Housing and the wider economy in the short and long run

3.1 INTRODUCTION

This chapter describes the links between developments in the housing market and in the wider economy. Our aim is to look at the facts — concentrating on the experience of the UK, where financial liberalization has gone further than in most European countries and where the scope for the effects of changes in the housing market to spread to the rest of the economy is, consequently, greater. The experience of the UK and the US, and also of the Scandinavian economies, is contrasted with those of other countries where financial deregulation has been slower and where the scope to borrow against housing wealth is more restricted.

Five questions are addressed. First, what have been the forces behind the dramatic increase over the century in the proportion of wealth that is held by the personal sector in the form of owner-occupied housing? Second, what does the interaction of past investment decisions in the housing stock and future demographic trends suggest about the resources which will be channelled into housing over the next fifty years? Third, how has the personal sector responded to easier access to credit available against the collateral of housing? Fourth, what might be the short-run and long-run causes of changes in the price of houses relative to other goods? Fifth, how have changes in house prices, in interest rates and in the tax treatment of housing influenced the returns to home ownership and the incentives to owner-occupation? These questions are analysed by focusing on long-term trends — in the stock of houses, in house prices, in the demand for houses, in bequests of property and in financing patterns. It is important to take a long-term view of the housing market because the process whereby housing wealth has been accumulated, and the ways in which any discrepancy between actual and desired holding of housing wealth is removed, are slow-moving. More fundamentally, it is worth thinking about the links between housing and other markets because they are likely to be quantitatively significant, reflecting the economic importance of houses which are expensive[1], last a long time[2], yield a substantial flow of real services each year[3] and constitute a significant part of national net wealth[4]. These facts are, of course, not unconnected.

Within the context of the long-term trends in housing wealth and home ownership there are two important recent developments which will be described here and analysed in more detail in later chapters. First, in the 1980s housing wealth in the UK became relatively fungible; it can now be transformed into other commodities more easily than other forms of wealth which are important to the personal sector. For example, at the beginning of 1993 the value of personal sector wealth in the forms of pensions and life assurance policies was only slightly less than their total net financial worth and was approximately the same size as the value of net (of mortgage debt) owner-occupied housing. But it is still difficult for households to liquidate that part of their wealth which is in pensions or life policies while it has become relatively easy for households to take out second mortgages or top-up mortgages against the collateral of accumulated equity.

Second, the fact that prior to the 1980s it was relatively hard for older households to extract housing wealth without moving to the rented sector, or else to a smaller house, means that the stock of net housing wealth held may have been (and more than a decade later might still be) significantly different from its equilibrium value. Had the existence of rent controls and the presence of tax breaks on owner-occupied housing (Hills, 1991) not made the rented option relatively unattractive to both households and landlords, the difficulty of extracting accumulated net housing equity might not have had much effect on saving and consumption; people could have sold their homes to liquidate the equity and rented comparable property. But it is now widely agreed that rent controls have made private sector renting uneconomic (see, for example, Ashton, Minford and Peel (1987) and Black and Stafford (1988)). For these reasons the financial liberalization of the 1980s in the housing finance market may have had, and might continue to have, a significant effect on spending plans. Thus, it is both the fungibility of housing wealth *relative* to that of other important components in total wealth and the quite recent *change* in the degree of fungibility of housing equity that makes housing wealth special. In the light of this it is not surprising that the combined effects of rapidly rising real house prices in the 1980s and the greater ability of households to borrow against housing wealth — phenomena which I will argue are not unconnected — have been widely seen (though not convincingly proved) to have caused the sharp fall in the personal sector saving rate in the second part of that decade (Muellbauer and Murphy, 1989, 1990; Congdon and Turnbull, 1982; Lee and Robinson, 1990).

These factors which make housing wealth special — the degree of, and changes in, fungibility and the dual aspect of houses as durable assets and consumption goods — prompt many of the questions which I will address in later chapters. Here we focus on the historical record.

The plan of this chapter is as follows. Section 3.2 describes long-run trends in the UK housing market and makes some international comparisons. Section 3.3 analyses the scale of housing inheritances. Section 3.4 focuses on financial liberalization and the size of equity withdrawal. In Section 3.5 demographic factors are considered. The effects of taxes, interest rates and expected house price changes on the real cost of housing are analysed in Section 3.6.

3.2   UK HOUSING IN THE TWENTIETH CENTURY

Tables 3.1 and 3.2 reveal some of the main trends in UK housing over the century. Table 3.1 shows that the stock of dwellings has risen dramatically, though far from smoothly, over the past ninety years. The proportionate increase in the number of dwellings over the century has been almost twice as great as the rise in the population. Although the increase in the real stock of housing per capita is very imperfectly measured by the ratio of dwellings to persons (for example houses vary through time both in average quality and size) it is clear that there has been substantial accumulation over the century; the ratio of rooms to persons, a no more precise (but different) measure of real housing per person, has also doubled. Table 3.2 shows that owner-occupation has also risen enormously over the past eighty years. Almost 70% of households are now owner occupiers. A comparison with the UK on the eve of the First World War reveals just how dramatic the change in housing tenure has been; only 10% of households were owner-occupiers in 1914. Much of the rise in owner-occupation over the century has been concentrated in the post-war period; mass home ownership in the UK is a relatively recent phenomenon.

Table 3.1   The stock of housing

	Stock of dwellings (million)	UK population/ stock of dwellings
1901	8.01	4.78
1911	8.94	4.71
1921	7.98	5.52
1931	9.40	4.90
1939	11.50	4.20
1945	11.10	4.32
1951	12.39	4.05
1961	16.42	3.21
1971	18.20	3.05
1981	20.96	2.64
1991	23.14	2.48
1992	23.30	2.46

Source: *Annual Abstract of Statistics*
Note: Mean number of persons per room in 1911 was 1.10
      Mean number of persons per room in 1971 was 0.60
(Source: Burnett, J. *A Social History of Housing*, Methuen (2nd edn), 1986).

Table 3.2   Trends in owner-occupation

	Rate of owner-occupation (%)	Index of real house prices	
1914	10.0	1934/39	51
		1945	61
1939	33.0	1950	87
		1955	69
1953	34.5	1960	71
		1965	92
1961	42.3	1970	100
		1975	128
1971	50.6	1980	140
		1985	142
1981	56.6	1988	210
		1989	209
1991	67.7	1990	184
		1991	177
1992	68.0	1992	161

Sources: (1) Owner-occupation data from Holmans (1987), Table V.1; Housing Finance (1993).
(2) Real house-price data from Department of Environment index of house prices relative to retail prices, RPI. From 1965 the series is the mix-adjusted index which standardizes for changes in the number of habitable rooms per dwelling and allows for regional variation in house prices. No adjustments are made for other quality changes (Holmans, 1990, pp. 12–14)

The rise in the rate of home ownership may not be over. Surveys undertaken by the Building Societies Association (BSA) consistently reveal a strong preference for owner-occupation. Hamnett, Harmer and Williams (1991) report that a 1989 BSA survey revealed that 85% of the sample interviewed expressed a desire to be home owners; an even higher proportion of the young aimed to own homes. Despite the falls in nominal house prices in the early 1990s, and the sharp increase in repossessions of property from those unable to keep up mortgage payments (Bank of England, 1992), the proportion of young people aiming to become home owners remains high. Coles and Taylor (1993) report that a survey undertaken on behalf of the Council for Mortgage Lenders in early 1993 showed that 90% of under-25's expected to be owner-occupiers within ten years. By 2014 it is possible that more than three quarters of households will be owner-occupiers; a century before 90% of households lived in rented accommodation.

Table 3.2 also shows that real house prices have been on an upward trend through the century. Comparisons of real prices across such a long period are, however, problematic because adjustments for quality changes become increasingly difficult, so Figure 3.1 focuses on the quarter-century from 1966 to 1993. Over that period *real* prices (using either the Department of Environment mix adjusted price index

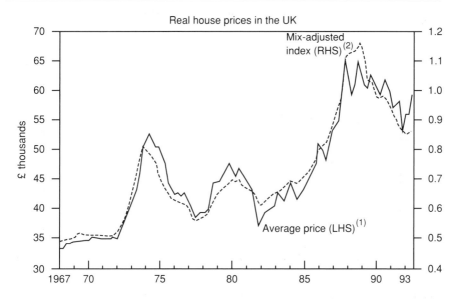

Figure 3.1   Real house-price measures: (1) average current price of all houses at mortgage completion stage deflated by the RPI (1990 = 100); (2) house price index deflated by the RPI (1990 = 100) (Source: *Housing Finance* (various issues))

or the average price of homes purchased with mortgages, both relative to retail prices) have almost doubled, even after allowing for the decline in nominal house values between 1990 and 1992. The mix-adjusted series makes some allowance for changes in the quality of homes by standardizing for the number of habitable rooms; but other quality changes, for example double glazing and central heating, are not accounted for. At least part of the apparent rise in the real price of houses is therefore due to home improvements. As regards the real value of the housing stock — the product of the number of dwellings and the average real price of homes — it is, of course, appropriate that quality changes should be reflected and it is right that that part of the rise in real house prices that reflects tangible improvements be included. But an important issue, to which we will return in the next chapter, is whether the effect of pure relative price changes should be counted as contributing to national, net worth.

The combination of an increasing stock of dwellings (both absolutely and relative to the population), rising rates of owner-occupation, mortgages which (at least in the past) have had to be fully repaid over periods rarely exceeding 25 years and rising real house prices has meant that real, net owner-occupied housing wealth held directly by the personal sector has increased sharply. Figure 3.2 shows net wealth in residential housing (the value of the owner-occupied housing stock net of outstanding mortgage debt) relative to total personal sector net worth (the total value of *all* tangible *and* financial assets net of all liabilities). That ratio had risen

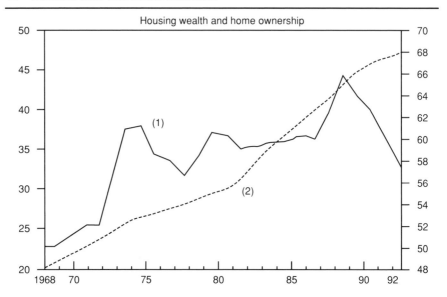

Figure 3.2 Housing wealth as a percentage of total net wealth and owner-occupation rates: (1) personal sector holding of net housing wealth as a proportion of total net worth. Housing wealth is the value of the owner-occupied housing stock less any mortgages outstanding (LHS) (Source: from *Financial Statistics* (Table S2) various issues); (2) owner-occupation rate — owner-occupied dwellings as a proportion of total dwellings (RHS). (Source: *Housing Finance* (various issues))

from around 20% in the early 1960s to around 45% by 1989, before falling back to around 35% by the end of 1992. Over a longer time horizon the increase in this ratio would be far more dramatic — Tables 3.1 and 3.2 reveal that since 1939 real house prices have more than trebled; over that period the stock of dwellings per person has risen by 70% and the rate of owner-occupation doubled. The combination of these three factors will have increased the value of directly held, per capita, real housing wealth (in terms of consumer goods) by over tenfold. Clearly that part of this rise simply due to the switch in ownership of existing houses from landlords to owner-occupiers does not represent a real increase in overall, national, housing wealth. But as the tables reveal, the rise in total dwellings (owner-occupied *and* rented) and in real house prices over the century has generated enormous increases in per capita housing regardless of the change in tenure. These increases have been substantially greater than the rise in real GDP — in the period since 1939 the total number of dwellings has doubled and the real price of houses more than trebled, generating a six-fold increase in the value of the real stock of housing; over the same period real GDP has risen roughly threefold.

To see more clearly the influences of real investment, price rises and shifts in ownership on the value and composition of personal wealth it is helpful to develop a simple accounting framework. Denote the market value, in current prices, of the

ith house at time t by P_{it}. Let the *number* of owner-occupied dwellings at time t be denoted H_t, so that i runs from 1 to H_t at time t. Let an index of consumer goods' prices at t be denoted PC_t. The population at t is N_t. A natural index of the gross (of mortgage debt) value of the per capita, real, owner-occupied housing stock at time t, which we denote WH_t, is

$$WH_t = \sum_{i=1}^{H_t} P_{it}/(PC_t N_t) \tag{3.1}$$

we can write (3.1) as

$$WH_t = (H_t P_t)/(PC_t N_t) \tag{3.2}$$

where $P_t = \sum_{i=1}^{H_t} P_{it}/H_t$ and is the average nominal price of dwellings at time t. Note that variation in P through time reflects two factors: (1) changes in the average quality of dwellings (e.g. changes in the number and average size of rooms; variation in the proportion of houses with central heating, double glazing and garages) and (2) changes in the market price of constant-quality units of housing.

We can write the number of owner-occupied dwellings as the product of the total number of all dwellings (HA_t) and the owner-occupation rate (ooc_t): $H_t \equiv (ooc_t)HA_t$. Thus

$$WH_t = (ooc_t)(HA_t/N_t)(P_t/PC_t) \tag{3.3}$$

and the value of per capita real housing wealth at t is written as the product of three factors: the owner-occupation rate; the total number of dwellings (rented and owner-occupied) per capita; the relative price of a typical dwelling to the price of all goods.

Table 3.3 presents some of the information from Tables 3.1 and 3.2 in a way which allows us to use equation (3.3) to construct an index of real, per capita, owner-occupied housing wealth. The table shows the rate of owner-occupation, an index of real house prices and the number of dwellings (both absolutely and relative to total population) at ten-yearly intervals since 1939. The final column in the table is the implied value of WH_t, i.e. the product of columns one, two and four. The price index for houses, which is deflated by the Retail Price Index (RPI) to generate column 2, does not adjust for quality changes; but from 1968 the series is the Department of Environment mix-adjusted series which adjusts for changes in the number of rooms.

Table 3.3 shows that since 1939 the constructed index of the value of the real, per capita, owner-occupied housing stock has increased by more than twelvefold. Over the same period real per capita GDP rose by a factor of just over two and a half. But a substantial proportion of the increase in housing wealth is simply due to changes in the rate of owner-occupation which, while reflecting an important change in the pattern of ownership of national wealth, do not change aggregate net worth. Ignoring the impact of these changes in owner-occupation, real per capita housing wealth between 1939 and 1991 rose just over sixfold. Of that sixfold increase by

Table 3.3   Per capita real housing wealth in the UK

	(1) ooc_t	(2) P_t/PC_t	(3) HA_t stock dwellings (million)	(4) HA/N_t Stock dwellings /population	(5) $(1) \times (2) \times (4)$ WH_t
1939	0.33	51	11.50	0.24	4.04
1945	0.33*	61	11.10	0.23	4.63
1951	0.34	86	12.39	0.25	7.31
1961	0.44	75	16.42	0.31	10.23
1971	0.52	103	18.20	0.33	17.63
1981	0.59	131	21.18	0.38	29.37
1991	0.68	177	23.14	0.40	48.14

*Estimate

Sources: HA_t and HA/N_t: figures for the stock of all dwellings and for total population are from *Annual Abstract of Statistics* (various issues) and Holmans (1987).

P_t/PC_t: Figures are from Holmans (1990), Table A.1. To construct the real house price measure we use the Department of Environment index of house prices relative to retail prices (RPI = 1.0 in 1991). Other sources are given in Table 3.2.

far the greater part has been due to changes in the relative value of houses. If *all* of these relative price changes were assumed to generate only nominal, and not real, wealth, then per capita housing wealth would have risen only 70% over the past fifty years; the housing wealth to GDP ratio would have fallen significantly.

Key to the measurement of the real wealth in housing is therefore the question of the treatment of price changes. Clearly any changes in the market price of dwellings which reflect quality changes should be included in a measure of real wealth; so to exclude all the dramatic relative price increase in houses (column 2 of Table 3.3) certainly leads to an underestimate of housing wealth. Estimates of the increase in the quality of dwellings using the value of home improvements, DIY expenditure and other small building work suggest that the average annual increase in quality over the post-war period is unlikely to exceed 1% (Holmans, 1990). Using the 1% a year figure generates a quality effect of around 60% over the period 1939–1991 (assuming no home improvements in the war years). Including only that part of the rise in the relative price of houses to other goods attributable to this quality adjustment (i.e. 1% a year) in the measure of real per capita housing wealth generates an increase over 1939–91 of 170%; this is only just over one third the increase if *all* the rise in the real price of dwellings, relative to the RPI, is counted as adding to real wealth. Furthermore, excluding the pure relative price effect of the change in the real value of houses over the period since 1960 would remove *all* of the, apparently substantial, increase in the proportion of the wealth of the personal sector in the form of housing noted at the beginning of this chapter.

Clearly then the question as to whether pure relative price changes should contribute to wealth is of great quantitative importance. In the next chapter we will examine the case for including such price increases in a measure of real wealth.

Table 3.4 Housing markets in the developed world

	Owner-occupation (%)		Stock of mortgage debt/household disposable income (%)	
US	65	(1990)	60	(1987)
Japan	61	(1988)	38	(1986)
Spain	77	(1980)	10*	(1986)
Italy	70	(1988)	7	(1987)
France	54	(1989)	48	(1987)
UK	67	(1990)	67	(1987)
Switzerland	30	(1980)	64*	(1982)
Canada	63	(1990)	50	(1986)
Netherlands	48	(1990)	—	
Germany	40	(1990)	2†	(1987)
Denmark	55	(1990)	66	(1990)

* Mortgage debt as proportion GDP rather than household income
† The OECD figure reported for Germany is implausibly low and counts only debt explicitly reported as mortgage lending; a calculation using a wider definition of household lending gives a debt/GDP ratio of 23% for 1990, in line with that of France.
Sources: Owner-occupation rates are taken from Bank of England (1991), International Housing Finance Factbook (1987), *Urban Housing Finance* (1989), *United Nations Compendium of Housing Statistics*, *Housing and Construction Statistics* (1990), and *Journal of Housing Research* (**13**(1), 1992). Ratios of mortgage debt to disposable income are from *OECD Economic Outlook*, 1989. For France and Italy ratios of long-term liabilities to income are shown.

Tables 3.4 and 3.5 compare the UK housing market with those of other major economies. Although there are enormous difficulties in comparing ownership patterns, house prices and mortgage debt across countries (Holmans, 1990) certain conclusions are robust to even significant measurement errors. First, the owner-occupation rate in the UK is amongst the highest in the developed world. Second, the stock of mortgage debt relative to household income is also one of the highest in the world and is far higher than in most other countries with comparable levels of owner-occupation. Indeed what is surprising about Table 3.4 is that there is little relation between owner-occupation and the mortgage debt to income ratio; both Spain and Italy have high rates of owner-occupation but little mortgage debt. Variation across countries in the use of credit to buy homes is far greater than variation in the value of homes or in rates of owner-occupation. An interesting feature which we consider in later chapters is the link between *changes* in the availability of housing finance and house price volatility. In the UK, Denmark, Sweden, Norway and Finland, credit — and finance for house purchase in particular — became more readily available in the 1980s. In the Scandinavian countries financial liberalization and the surge in borrowing came later than in the UK; but the sharpness of the boom in house prices — and the severity of the subsequent fall — was even greater than in the UK. In Finland, for example, house prices more than doubled between 1987 and 1989 and then fell 30% by mid-1992.

Table 3.5   Personal sector net equity in housing relative to GDP

UK	1.37	(1991)
US	0.73	(1989)
Germany	1.22	(1989)
Japan	3.64	(1989)
France	0.91	(1984)

Sources: For the UK and US estimates of the value of residential housing and mortgage debt are made directly by the Central Statistical Office (Table S2, *Financial Statistics*, CSO, 1990); and by the Board of Governors of the Federal Reserve (*Balance Sheets for the US Economy*, 1990). For the US the gross value of residential housing is used. For Germany and France average house prices were calculated from the survey of house prices in major cities and towns reported in Holmans (1990). Estimates of the number of owner-occupied houses were taken from Holmans (1990) and Boleat (1987); net equity is the product of average house values and the number of owner-occupied units, relative to GDP, less the ratio of mortgage debt to GDP. For Japan data from the survey of personal sector wealth were reported by the Economic Planning Agency.

The third feature to emerge from a comparison of developed countries is that the net housing equity of the personal sector in the UK is relatively high; amongst the countries for which estimates can be made only in Japan is the ratio of equity to GDP higher (Table 3.5).

What emerges from these international comparisons is that the UK is a country where the personal sector holds a comparatively large part of its wealth in the form of residential property and where mortgage debt has been more widely used to finance house purchase than in most other countries. In Chapter 2 we analysed the links between the availability of credit and the demand for, and price of, housing; in the light of the model developed there it seems likely that there is a relation between the relatively high value of housing in the UK and the extensive use of debt financing. We shall consider the nature of that link more closely in Chapter 5.

3.3   HOUSING BEQUESTS AND THE INTER-GENERATIONAL TRANSFER OF WEALTH

One implication of the trends in UK home ownership and real house prices outlined in the previous section is clear — while most children born in the early part of this century would have lived in rented accommodation for much of their lives and could not have expected to receive a bequest of a house from their parents, children born in the post-war period in the UK have a high probability that their parents will die as owners of very valuable properties. The importance of housing wealth in total bequests is *already* great. The study by Hamnett, Harmer and Williams (1991) reports the results of a 1988 survey into inheritance. 60% of a random sample of households who had ever received an inheritance of over £1000 had inherited housing or money derived from the sale of housing. But although a high proportion of households who had received a substantial inheritance had been bequeathed housing wealth, the number of such households was still quite small — only 15% of the random sample of households had ever inherited significant wealth.

The number of properties which are bequeathed to succeeding generations, rather than to a surviving spouse, and are released onto the market is estimated to be currently of the order of 160 000 a year (Hamnett, Harmer and William, 1991, p. 73). But the dramatic rise in owner-occupation over the post-war period and the increases in life expectancy suggest that the surge in bequests is yet to come and that property inheritance will increase sharply over the next fifty years. The rise in the real price of housing in the post-war period further boosts the total value of homes which will be bequeathed and implies that the proportion of the total value of estates accounted for by property is likely to be higher in the future. While it is the total value of bequests, rather than just that part which is in the form of housing wealth, which really matters for the spending decisions of inheritors, the rises in home ownership, in the stock of dwellings and in the real value of dwellings means that property inheritance will be a key factor behind trends in bequests. Again, the Hamnett study provides fascinating evidence. Using population projections and standard rates of life expectancy they estimate that the average annual number of bequests of housing will increase consistently over the next forty years; the number will be more than twice as high in the period 2026–31 than in the period 1986–91. The projection is consistent with earlier estimates by Morgan Grenfell (1987) who forecast that by the end of this century the number of estates including residential property wealth would be in excess of 200 000 a year. Although the precise rate at which the level of annual bequests of residential property will rise is hard to forecast it is clear that in the longer term that rate must increase substantially. This is a direct implication of the increase in the rate of owner-occupation.

The long-run implications for the value of inheritances and for the rate of (non-housing) consumption of a greater stock of housing wealth being directly owned by the personal sector are potentially great. Consider a stylized example which brings out some of the longer-run effects of the changing pattern of home ownership through the twentieth century. In 1918 a typical British boy and girl would be born into households in rented accommodation. In 1948 these typical children are thirty, meet, get married, buy a new house and have children. (For simplicity let's assume they do all this in the same year, making 1948 rather hectic). By 1978 the mortgage has been paid off for some years and their own children are getting married and buying a house. Unlike their parents, however, these newly weds can expect between them to receive (as a bequest) a house unencumbered with a mortgage just before the end of the century (assuming an 80-year life span for their parents). The lifetime budget constraint of this second generation of home owners is different from that of their parents in the crucial respect that the total value of repayments of capital on their own mortgage is offset by the receipt (some fifteen years after their first mortgage payments are made) of an asset whose value is likely to be of the same order of magnitude. (House price inflation, the level of mortgage interest rates and the relative sizes of houses bought by the successive generations clearly influence the exact relation between the total value of mortgage repayments and the value of the inheritance; we shall analyse this more formally in Chapter 5.) Members of this first generation to inherit an (unmortgaged) house could spend the proceeds from its sale over the remainder of their life and still hand on a bequest to the next generation equal to the value of a home, since by the early part of the 21st century their own mortgage will be fully repaid.

The thing which makes the difference here is that only one generation of this dynasty — the one born just as the First World War ends — has to pay off a mortgage *without* receiving an unmortgaged house as a bequest. Lifetime consumption of non-housing goods by that generation must, other things (specifically net acquisition of non-housing wealth) equal, be lower by roughly the full value of a home. If that home was newly built in 1948 then the lower lifetime consumption of non-housing goods by that generation is the counterpart to the extra resources used to build the house. But all future generations have to do to keep the housing stock constant is to cover the depreciation.

One way to see the macroeconomic implications of this fable is to assume that the first generation of new households that were formed after the Second World War moved into newly built homes, but that once that generation was housed the stock of dwellings was in line with the population of households. Net investment in residential housing could be lower once this post-war generation was housed and could stay lower so long as the population of households was constant. The steady-state savings ratio — part of which is the counterpart to residential investment — would be lower or else investment in non-housing assets higher.

The simple example ignores numerous factors which are of great quantitative importance. We will consider some of these shortly. But fables are helpful and what this one shows is that the increase in owner-occupation over the twentieth century — a period of rising population and falling household size which, as Table 3.1 showed, has implied a sharp rise in the number of dwellings — has involved substantial household resources being devoted to accumulating housing equity. If the number of households were to grow by much smaller amounts in the next 50 years, then the national saving required to preserve a balance between the number of households and dwellings could fall (an issue to which I return below); in itself this is a good thing and one for which we should thank our parents and grandparents. For those countries which experienced devastating damage to their housing stocks during the war — Japan and Germany — the impact on national saving of emerging (but only after many decades) from a period when investment in housing needed to be great to rebuild the stock can be much higher.

A key point about these long-run trends in house building and in the accumulation of housing wealth is that the timescale of adjustment to disequilibria — in the stock of houses or in the composition of household wealth or in bequests — may be *very* long. The implications of a divergence between desired and actual housing wealth is transmitted from one generation to the next via its impact on bequests; it is the endogeneity of bequests which can make the effects of changes in housing markets stretch into the far future. The role of inheritances and the interaction between conditions in financial markets and the level of bequests is crucial in developed economies. We devote Chapter 5 to an investigation of the issues.

What the family fable brings out is that the saving done by the original generation of home buyers generates a tangible asset, the income from which (effectively the real return on housing, net of depreciation) can accrue to all future generations. But the benefits of that saving would fail to stretch far into the 21st century if the recipients of bequests spend the proceeds *and* fail to bequeath an unmortgaged house to their heirs. In the past in the UK that would have proved hard to do unless a household was prepared to move to the rented sector late in life and use the proceeds of the house sale to finance retirement consumption. But during the 1980s it became much easier in the UK for home owners to extract housing equity while remaining within the owner-occupied sector. Second mortgages, top-up mortgages, interest-only mortgages (which allow home owners to borrow against housing equity without necessarily accumulating net equity as the loan matures) and equity-release schemes have been widely marketed (Goodhart, 1986; Drake, 1991). If substantial amounts of housing equity are being extracted we should expect to see a sharp fall in the savings rate for the generation with housing wealth at the time credit restrictions are eased. Measuring the extent of equity extraction (or equity withdrawal), and assessing the uses to which equity extracted from the housing market is put, is therefore important.

3.4   MEASURING EQUITY WITHDRAWAL

Equity withdrawal is usually defined as the excess of net (of repayments) new lending for house purchase over all forms of investment in residential property (see, for example, Bank of England (1985)). Table 3.6 shows the nominal and real value of equity withdrawal on this definition, using a comprehensive measure of investment in the housing stock. Figure 3.3 shows the level of equity withdrawal relative to total consumption. The figure shows clearly that equity withdrawal increased dramatically in the 1980s; funds leaking from the housing market were more than 6% of total consumption in 1988. Between 1985 and 1990 around one third of total net new 'housing' lending each year was for purposes other than financing housing investment, repairs or home improvements. The scale of equity withdrawal over that period was greater than the size of the UK current account deficit and was, in a purely accounting sense, sufficient to account for the decline in the personal sector saving ratio in the second half of the 1980s from the level of the late 1970s and early 1980s. The personal sector saving rate fell from around 12% of income in the early 1980s to around 5.5% in 1988. Savings would have needed to have been just under £20 billion higher in 1988 to have generated a savings rate equal to the

Table 3.6   Equity withdrawal in the UK

	(1)	(2)	(3)	(4)	(5)	(6)
1963	571	640	164	−34	−199	−1 677
1964	751	769	175	−41	−152	−1 236
1965	701	828	187	−47	−267	−2 068
1966	721	837	205	−50	−271	−2 019
1967	981	931	226	−56	−120	−871
1968	1 022	1 089	269	−61	−275	−1 906
1969	838	1 079	271	−68	−444	−2 916
1970	1 250	1 069	294	−81	−32	−198
1971	1 827	1 422	325	−106	186	1 062
1972	2 777	1 748	381	−157	805	4 316
1973	2 831	2 133	448	−222	472	2 335
1974	2 423	2 310	543	−268	−162	−686
1975	3 613	2 725	650	−228	466	1 595
1976	3 884	3 151	730	−512	515	1 525
1977	4 262	3 452	863	−667	614	1 585
1978	5 441	4 091	1 073	−592	869	2 048
1979	6 516	5 312	1 305	−439	338	701
1980	7 368	6 115	1 594	−163	−177	−317
1981	9 483	6 174	1 800	177	1 331	2 136
1982	14 128	6 850	1 927	756	4 594	6 780
1983	14 525	7 757	2 230	−465	5 003	7 041
1984	17 069	9 186	2 459	−1 123	6 547	8 776
1985	19 118	9 683	2 822	−623	7 225	9 209
1986	27 183	11 526	3 416	−370	12 611	15 436
1987	29 573	13 333	3 847	−256	12 649	14 843
1988	40 111	17 601	4 474	588	17 448	19 501
1989	34 054	18 234	4 689	1 022	10 109	10 648
1990	33 164	16 530	4 760	−298	12 172	11 876
1991	26 785	14 467	5 046	−2 072	9 344	8 512
1992	18 488	15 152	5 209	−2 462	589	513

Column (1) = Net new loans for house purchase
Column (2) = Private fixed residential investment
Column (3) = Home improvements (DIY plus repairs)
Column (4) = Other*
Column (5) = Net cash withdrawal i.e. (1) − (2) − (3) − (4)
Column (6) = Net cash withdrawal at 1990 prices (using the consumption price deflator).

* This includes the value of dwellings sold by local authorities — government sector capital grants to the private sector for housing — slum clearance. (Slum clearance values have been estimated between 1963 and 1977).

average from the early part of that decade. The table reveals that equity extraction in 1988 was approximately equal to this 'savings gap'.

Prior to 1980 equity withdrawal was small. The massive expansion in withdrawal has coincided with the period in which borrowing for house purchase has, on a variety of measures — loan-to-value ratios, the length of mortgage queues,

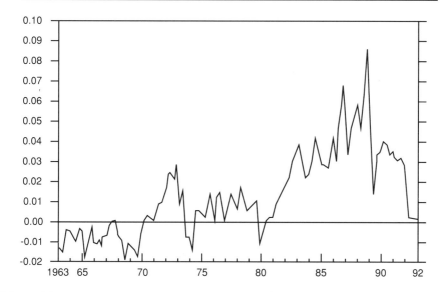

Figure 3.3   Real equity withdrawal relative to total consumption

availability of interest-only and second mortgages — become easier (see Bank of England, (1989)). It is natural to interpret the rise in borrowing and in equity withdrawal in the 1980s as a response to the easing of credit restrictions which allowed the personal sector to finance consumption, and that this was the driving force behind the decline in the savings ratio and its counterpart in the massive current-account deficits between 1985 and 1990. But the figures in Table 3.6 are consistent with many different stories. First, it is not clear what the personal sector has done with funds which have been raised on the back of housing collateral. One route for equity withdrawal is the sale of properties by the middle-aged which they have been left by their parents. If the buyers of this property finance the purchase with mortgage debt, and assuming the deceased left an unmortgaged home, measured equity withdrawal will rise by the value of the mortgage. Hamnett and his co-authors report that out of a sample of 295 households interviewed in 1988 who had inherited housing wealth, almost 70% sold the property more or less immediately, which is unsurprising since the overwhelming majority of beneficiaries were themselves home owners. They found that the most common initial use of sale proceeds was for financial investment. Around 50% of their sample used *most* of the funds released to acquire financial assets; only 24% used most of the funds to finance consumption. *If* it is through the sale of inherited property that most equity is released *and* if most of the proceeds are saved the implications of equity withdrawal of even £15 billion a year for consumption may not have been very significant.

But alternative means of equity withdrawal exist — e.g. second, or top-up, mortgages, mortgages for 'home improvement' and home equity plans. The propensity to consume out of equity withdrawn in these ways may be different from that on funds released through the sale of bequeathed property. The Hamnett evidence suggests a low short-run propensity to consume out of bequeathed housing wealth. But evidence reported in Maclennan (1990), who studied the uses to which a sample of households who had taken out further advances on their existing mortgages put the funds, suggests a high propensity to consume. His survey shows that only a relatively small proportion (between 25 and 50%) of funds borrowed for home repairs or improvements were used for that purpose; non-housing consumption was the main use of funds. Maclennan's findings suggest a high propensity to consume out of funds raised by second mortgages and are consistent with evidence from the US. Poterba and Manchester (1989) analyse the balance sheets of a large sample of US households who had taken out second mortgages; they estimate that the propensity to consume out of funds raised is around 80%. In Chapter 5 we will attempt to estimate the overall propensity to consume out of equity withdrawn — by whatever means — from the UK housing market. The strategy will be to assess the correlation between equity withdrawn from housing and that part of aggregate UK consumption which cannot be explained by a forecasting equation (estimated by Pesaran and Evans (1984)) which was constructed using data from a period when extracting equity had been difficult. As we shall see, that correlation implies a high propensity to consume out of equity withdrawn and that the contribution of credit liberalization in housing markets to the consumption boom of the 1980s was significant. The implied propensity to consume withdrawn equity will turn out to be almost exactly equal to the estimates made by Poterba and Manchester for the US.

These pieces of evidence suggest that a substantial proportion of the equity that has already been released from the housing market in the UK has financed consumption. An implication is that *if* credit restrictions have prevented households in other European countries from borrowing against accumulated housing wealth the impact on consumption of relaxing those constraints could be great; certainly the experience of the Scandinavian economies in the late 1980s — where bank lending skyrocketed and saving rates fell sharply — is consistent with this. But we really only have scraps of circumstantial evidence about what happened in the UK in the decade after credit conditions were relaxed in the early 1980s. We aim to consider the evidence more closely in Chapters 6 and 7.

The longer-term issue about the phenomenon of equity withdrawal and the uses to which that equity might be put is this: will a significant part of the wealth accumulated in housing over the past hundred years be used to finance a one-off rise in consumption for the current generation of home owners, who are now better able to borrow against the value of their homes and who are also the prime recipients of bequests of houses, *or* will the net value of housing wealth held by the personal sector be largely preserved for future generations? The question is hard to answer because there has been no other similar episode in UK history — the recent (relative to life expectancy) rise of mass home ownership makes the phenomenon of widespread property inheritance a new one. What is clear is that the level of equity withdrawn thus far is relatively small compared with the value of the owner-occupied housing stock. Even if we assume that as much as 80% of measured equity withdrawal since the early 1980s has been spent on non-durable consumer goods the implied reduction in net assets held by the personal sector as a proportion of the value of the owner-occupied housing stock is unlikely to exceed 10%. So *if* the slow-down in mortgage lending in the 1990s and the sharp decline in equity withdrawal marks the end of significant transformation of housing wealth into consumption it is clear that the net wealth in housing will not have been seriously diminished. Whether the recent declines in equity withdrawal will be reversed is the big question.

Although it is very hard to know what proportion of inherited housing wealth will be transformed into consumer goods we can at least think about what difference the answer would make. A decision by current households to use a significant part of housing equity to finance consumption clearly reduces the saving ratio. If domestic investment is financed, at the margin, predominantly from domestic savings the implications of this equity withdrawal is that the non-housing capital stock is reduced relative to what it would have been. In effect the release of excess accumulated wealth in housing, itself a product of the interaction of the benefits to owner-occupation and the past difficulty in financing consumption with mortgage debt, reduces the stock of other wealth. But in a small open economy which, like the UK, has no capital restrictions, it is more plausible that profitable investment can be financed relatively easily with overseas' savings. In this case a collective decision by UK households to liquidate part of its tangible housing wealth need have no effect on domestic investment and can succeed if the overseas sector is prepared to swap consumer goods for claims on houses. This process does not, of course, involve the transfer of houses across the Channel nor the direct purchase of UK homes by Germans, French or Japanese. The process whereby net housing wealth is exchanged for consumption is via equity withdrawal, whereby mortgage claims upon houses increase — the funding for extra lending coming from overseas' accumulation of claims upon UK banks and building societies which, in turn, is the capital account counterpart of the current-account flows generated by the extra net UK consumption.

The implication of this process is clear — if a substantial proportion of the current net housing equity held by UK households comes to be held by those who would like to transfer that wealth into current consumption, then given that financial liberalization has provided means for the release of excess equity in ways which have not previously been feasible, we might expect that housing equity will be reduced in a process which generates low savings and high current account deficits for a possibly prolonged transitional period. We will analyse in detail the mechanism by which this process works in Chapter 5, where we also consider the scope for equity withdrawal in those countries where borrowing against housing wealth has, so far, been less easy than in the US and UK.

Ultimately, the choices made by current home owners on the uses to which they put net housing wealth clearly depend upon their degree of benevolence to subsequent generations. If members of the first generation of home owners to receive substantial inheritances of housing equity from their parents aim to bequeath an equivalent amount of real housing to their heirs, the dramatic and sustained, but nonetheless *transitional*, decline in savings and increase in current-account deficits described above will not materialize. But as noted above *steady-state* savings might be reduced relative to the levels over the period when real housing wealth was accumulated. The scale of that effect will depend upon the future levels of gross investment in residential capital required to generate an equilibrium housing stock. Key determinants of that investment figure are trends in population and in the rate of household formation.

3.5   POPULATION AND HOUSEHOLD FORMATION IN THE NEXT 50 YEARS

The growth in the number of households over the next half century will be a major factor behind the scale of net new housing investment. Tables 3.7–9 bring together some key data relevant to the issue. Table 3.7 shows the rise in the stock of dwellings and the balance between dwellings and potential households in the 40-year period from the Second World War. Table 3.8 shows gross investment in residential dwellings relative to GDP through the century. Table 3.9 shows forecasts reported by John Ermisch (1991) and Adrian Coles (1991), based on Office of Population Census and Surveys projections and Department of the Environment forecasts, of changes in population and in the number of households over the next thirty years.

Table 3.7

	(1) Total dwellings (millions)	(2) Potential households (millions)	(3) Balance (2) − (1)
1939	11.50	12.00	−0.50
1945	11.10	13.40	−2.30
1951	12.33	14.19	−1.85
1961	14.54	15.42	−0.90
1971	17.00	17.14	−0.12
1981	19.1	18.68	+0.41

Source: Holmans (1987), Table IV.12

* Potential households equal separate households plus 'concealed' married couples plus 'concealed' one-parent families. Dwellings here are defined as 'structurally separate dwellings' a concept introduced in the 1921 census and one slightly different from that used in the Annual Abstract figures reported in Table 3.1, where in the period since the 1950s a wider definition is used. For exact definitions and sources see Chapter IV of Holmans (1987).

Table 3.8   Gross fixed investment in dwellings in the UK as a proportion of UK GDP

1889–1903	2.3
1921–23	2.0
1924–28	3.2
1929–32	3.1
1933–35	4.0
1936–38	3.6/3.2
1948–51	2.7
1952–55	3.6
1956–59	2.9
1960–64	3.3
1965–67	4.1
1970–74	4.0
1975–79	4.1
1980–85	3.4
1986–90	3.7
1991–92	2.5

Sources:
Feinstein, *National Income Expenditure and Output*, Tables 3, 39, 40, 62 and 63.
Holmans (1987), Table IV.16.
UK National Income Accounts (1993).

Pre-1936 figures expressed as % of GDP at *factor* price; post-1936 as % of GDP at *market* prices. Figures for 1936–38 are at factor *and* market prices respectively.

Table 3.9   Projections of housing demand

	Total population (lower variant) (000's)		Change in number of households	
			(A) male age 15–29 head of house	(B) male age 30–44 head of house
1987	55 355	1989–91	−25 000	−30 000
1997	56 198	1991–96	−26 000	−57 000
2007	56 251	1996–2001	−24 000	−16 000
2017	56 093	2001–06	−5 000	−36 000
2027	55 353	2006–11	+9 000	−54 000

Sources: Ermisch (1991) and Coles (1991)
The figures presented here are based on Department of Environment Forecasts and Office of Population and Census Surveys (OPCS) projections.

Several things emerge from these tables. First, that major investment in dwellings over the twentieth century in the UK has reflected two things: a significant trend increase in the number of households and the transition from a position, in 1945, of a major gap between the potential number of households and the stock of dwellings to one — by 1981 — when that gap had been, at least in aggregate, removed and when the number of dwellings exceeded the number of households. The projections reported by Ermisch and Coles also suggest that the net increase in new households over the next 40 years will fall steeply and be substantially lower than the average annual increases since the Second World War. Ermisch reports that predictable changes in the age distribution will in themselves lead to a slowing in the rate of annual net household formation from 160 000 to 40 000 over the next 15 years.

The implication of the tables is that whereas throughout most of the twentieth century there has been substantial net investment in housing in order to keep the number of dwellings from lagging too far behind the number of households (Tables 3.7 and 3.8), in the twenty-first century there is likely to be a substantially reduced requirement for new dwellings (Table 3.9). Provided that domestic ownership of the housing wealth that currently exists is not substantially reduced by a process of equity withdrawal of the sort which generates an increase of net overseas holdings of liabilities of UK financial institutions, the implication of a reduced level of net residential investment in new dwellings is that resources available for other purposes by UK residents are likely to be higher. Of course the demand to improve the size and quality of existing dwellings will still be a factor, so even if the number of new dwellings required to match the increase in households were to fall sharply, total net investment in the housing stock would fall by proportionately less. But we might still expect some decline in net residential investment. Consequently, investment in other assets can be higher or national saving can be lower.

3.6   HOUSE PRICES AND THE COST OF HOUSING SERVICES

We have looked back at the process whereby housing wealth has been accumulated and forward at the implications of that accumulation process for consumption and saving. One factor which is crucial to an understanding of both the past and future are trends in housing costs — both house prices and the user cost of housing. Two long-run issues are particularly important. First, to what extent do trends in house prices; the ways in which housing is taxed; and in interest rates help explain the tenure choices made over the century? Second, what is the cause of house price changes and what is the impact of changes in house prices upon the consumption choices faced by individuals?

From the model of household behaviour developed in Chapter 2 it emerged that the best way to evaluate how the tax system, financial markets and housing markets have combined to generate incentives to owner-occupation is to evaluate the user cost of owner-occupied housing. Figure 3.4 shows a measure of the ex-post user cost of housing, that is the cost of housing allowing for what actually happened to house prices rather than what might have been expected to happen when tenure decisions were made. The series measures the real resources which would have been used by an individual as a result of owning a typical home in each year. The formula used to construct the measure of the user cost of housing is based

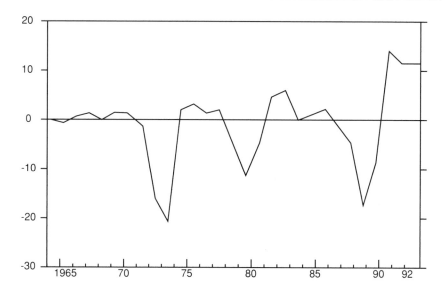

Figure 3.4 UK user cost of housing for 'average owner'

on the analysis of Chapter 2. In constructing the numbers we have initially taken
no account of the impact of binding credit restrictions and have ignored the risk
premium on housing; in terms of the notation of Chapter 2 we set $\sigma_{u\dot{p}} = \lambda = 0$.
   The resulting formula for the user cost is

$$uc_t = (p_t)[b_t r_{mt}\{\alpha_t(1 - t_{yt}) + (1 - \alpha_t)\} + (1 - b_t)r_{it} + \tau_{pt} + \delta + \mu_t - \dot{P_t}] \quad (3.4)$$

where
uc_t is the user cost of housing at time t
p_t is an index of the *real* price of houses at t; it is the ratio of the nominal house
price index (P) to an index of consumer goods prices (PC); $p_t \equiv P_t/PC_t$
b is the proportion of the house financed through mortgage debt
r_m is the *nominal* interest rate on mortgage debt
α is the proportion of mortgage interest repayments which are deductible against
income tax
t_y is the rate of income tax
r_i is the *nominal*, post-tax return on alternative investments, or the opportunity cost
of funds invested in home ownership
τ_p is the rate of property tax
δ is the rate of physical depreciation of housing
μ is maintenance and repairs as a proportion of the value of the home
$\dot{P}$ is the rate of increase in *nominal* house prices.
   Note that with this specification of the user cost we choose to measure interest
rates and house price appreciation ($\dot{P}$) both in *nominal* terms; in Chapter 2, where

we did not specify the tax treatment of loans for house purchase in detail, we dealt with real rates and real house-price inflation. Were the tax system neutral with respect to balanced inflation that would make no difference — in using nominal variables we should merely be adding consumer price inflation to the real cost of borrowing funds and adding it again to the real rate of house-price inflation. But because the tax system in many countries is not inflation-neutral it is essential to use nominal variables; in the UK and in the US it is nominal (rather than real) interest payments that are tax deductible, so a balanced increase in nominal rates and in consumer and house-price inflation, which leave the real price of houses and the pre-tax real interest rates constant, reduces the user cost.

The measure defined in (3.4) reflects the real purchase price of a home, the cost of financing the purchase (whether by mortgage or else by forfeiting the chance of holding financial assets which yield returns), taxes paid as a direct result of home ownership (e.g. rates but *not* a poll tax), repairs and maintenance, and depreciation. A data annex describes exactly how each of the components of the user cost is measured. The real house price (P_t / PC_t) is measured in index number form and is equal to unity in 1985; the user cost measure therefore represents an index of how many consumer goods needed to be given up in each year to enjoy the services of an owner-occupied home. If the user cost index is negative the real, ex-post capital gain on housing exceeded all the costs of home ownership so that owner-occupation, rather than requiring a commitment of real resources, yielded a real profit in that year.

Since the user cost varies with the way in which the house purchase is financed, as well as with the tax status of the home-owner, there is no unique measure of the user cost of housing. But if we consider the opportunity cost of wealth tied up in homes to be the net of tax return on building society deposits then variations in the proportion of the value of the home financed by mortgage have a small effect on the user cost. This is because for much of the period since the early 1960s a high proportion of mortgage interest payments have been tax deductible and the spread between the tax-adjusted mortgage interest rate and the net-of tax rate paid on deposits is relatively small. So whether we focus on those who bought houses financed primarily on mortgage (first time buyers) or those whose homes were financed largely by equity makes little difference. Figure 3.4 shows an 'average' measure of the ex-post user cost, where we use the average personal sector ratio of debt to home value as our measure of b. That measure is negative during the major house price booms of the early 1970s and late 1980s; over the whole period (1963–90) the average user cost is slightly negative (-0.9%).

Figure 3.4 seems to confirm the conventional view that housing has been a good investment in the UK — even for those that gained no benefit from the real services provided by home ownership. But the picture is not easily squared with the view that on average house price changes are forecast correctly, since if that were the case an equilibrium in which the *expected* user cost for home owners were negative would be implied — which is surely implausible. Furthermore, the rational expectations/efficient market hypothesis about the user cost implies that on average the ex-post user cost should be equal to the marginal value of the services from housing; proxying the latter as the market rent for a property of similar quality to the average owner-occupied home, and expressing that rent as a proportion of the average price of a house, tells us what the average user cost should be under the null hypothesis of efficiency/rationality.

Measuring the market price of the services from the typical owner-occupied home is hugely problematic since rented properties are generally smaller than owner-occupied homes and, more seriously, most recorded rents in the UK over the period since the 1960s are not free market prices. Hills (1991) uses estimates of the annual flow of real housing services of 3.5% of the value of the stock. This figure is almost exactly equal to the ratio of the average registered annual rent of furnished tenancies (excluding housing association rents) to the average value of houses over the past three years (*Housing Construction*, various issues, Table 1.14 Department of the Environment). Yet that ratio is almost certainly a substantial underestimate of the real services of owner-occupied houses, since furnished tenancies tend to be smaller than average houses *and* registered rents are not free market rents. An alternative means of estimating the value of the housing services consumed by owner-occupiers is to use the value of imputed rent to owner-occupiers reported in the national accounts. This figure is based upon assessment of the free market rent which owner-occupied houses could command. Over the past ten years the ratio of the CSO estimate of imputed rent to the value of the owner-occupied housing stock has averaged around 2.5%. However, that figure relies on estimates of ratable values made in the 1970s and is not likely to be a good guide to the real services provided by owner-occupied housing.

So either of these estimates — 3.5% or 2.5% — could conceivably be only one half of the true rental yield on owner-occupied housing. We therefore consider a conservative range for that yield to be 3–7%. Given the slightly negative average user cost in Figure 3.4 the implied average excess return on owner-occupied housing has therefore probably exceeded 5% per year over the past thirty years.

On the surface, then, our measure of the user cost of housing in the UK seems inconsistent with the model of rational, forward-looking agents and market clearing prices developed in the previous chapter. But by setting $\lambda_1 = \sigma_{u\dot{p}} = 0$ in deriving (3.4) from the first-order conditions of Chapter 2 we have ignored the influences of credit restrictions and of risk. Both of these are likely to be important. Consider the impact of risk. By taking the opportunity cost of own equity in housing (r_i) to be the return on virtually riskless building society deposits it is implicitly assumed that wealth invested in housing yields riskless returns. But clearly the investment which is made in housing wealth generates a return which is uncertain; a risk premium should be added to the cost of funds. Knowing the size of this premium is central to assessing whether the returns on housing have been excessive.

We consider two ways of estimating the required risk premium on housing. Both methods allow us to estimate the riskiness of housing wealth relative to the risk of a diversified portfolio of UK equities. The first method assumes that the Sharpe–Lintner Capital Asset Pricing Model (CAPM) is valid; the second assumes that the Consumption CAPM of Breeden (1979) is valid. In the Sharpe (1964) and Lintner (1965) model of asset pricing, risk premia on all assets are proportional to the covariance of the asset return with the returns on a portfolio composed of all risk assets. The balance sheets of the UK personal sector (Table S2, *Financial Statistics*, various issues) reveal that a very high proportion of aggregate net wealth can be split into three categories: the gross value of residential property (50%); equity in life assurance, pension funds, unit trusts and UK company securities (32%) and net liquid assets (14%). (Figures in brackets are 1991 proportions). If we assume that, at least over periods as short as one quarter, the return on net liquid assets is safe and that the return on funds with institutional investors and on directly held company securities closely follows the return on the UK stock market, then we can think of the portfolio of *risky* assets as comprising two assets: equities (in one shape or other) and houses. Denoting the share of risky assets in housing by x, so the share in equities is $(1 - x)$, we can then write the CAPM betas of houses and equities — which are a function of the conditional covariances of the returns on the assets with the returns on the whole portfolio — in the following way:

$$\beta_h = \frac{E\{[R_h - E(R_h)][x(R_h - E(R_h)) + (1 - x)(R_e - E(R_e))]\}}{x^2\sigma_h^2 + (1 - x)^2\sigma_e^2 + 2x(1 - x)\sigma_{eh}} \quad (3.5)$$

$$\beta_e = \frac{E\{[R_e - E(R_e)][x(R_h - E(R_h)) + (1 - x)(R_e - E(R_e)]\}}{x^2\sigma_h^2 + (1 - x)^2\sigma_e^2 + 2x(1 - x)\sigma_{eh}} \quad (3.6)$$

where $E(R_h)$ is the expected return on housing conditional on agents' information; $E(R_e)$ is the expected return on equities; σ_h^2 is the conditional variance of the return on housing; σ_e^2 is the conditional variance of the return on equities; and σ_{eh} is the conditional covariance in returns. We assume that theses conditional moments do not vary over time.

The numerator in equations (3.5) and (3.6) is the conditional covariance between the return on housing (equities) and on the whole portfolio of risk assets. The denominator in both 5 and 6 is the conditional variance of the return on the whole portfolio. The beta of each asset is the ratio of its conditional covariance with the portfolio of all risk assets to the conditional variance of the whole portfolio. The CAPM implies that the risk premia on housing and equities are proportional to these betas so we can write

$$E(R_h - R_f)/E(R_e - R_f) = \beta_h/\beta_e = (x\sigma_h^2 + (1 - x)\sigma_{eh})/((1 - x)\sigma_e^2 + x\sigma_{eh}) \quad (3.7)$$

where R_f is the safe rate (the return on liquid assets). $E(R_h - R_f)$ is the expected excess return on housing, which we call the risk premium.

Table 3.10 shows two sets of estimates of σ_h^2, σ_e^2 and σ_{eh}, based on quarter-to-quarter annualized percentage changes, and also on annual percentage changes, in UK house prices and in the FT industrial share price index. Raw data are from the period 1963 I to 1993 II. A comprehensive measure of the returns on housing

Table 3.10 Volatility of asset prices

	σ_h^2	σ_e^2	σ_{eh}
Quarter to quarter returns (annualized)	184	2291	−21
Quarter on lag 4 quarter	119	508	4

House prices are the mix-adjusted series described above and which were used to construct the user cost in Figure 3.4. The FT industrial share price index (the 500 index minus oil and gas) is used to calculate equity returns.

would also include the quarterly flow of real housing services, net of quarterly depreciation and maintenance, all relative to the house value; but our measures of those variables (which we used to construct the ex-post user cost of Figure 3.4) show so little variability relative to house prices that nothing is lost by using the simpler measure.

The figures suggest that the variability of returns on housing have been very much smaller than the volatility of equity returns, though by how much they differ depends heavily on the period over which returns are measured. Measured from quarter to quarter, housing returns have been less than one tenth as volatile as equities; but measured over four quarter periods those returns are almost one quarter as variable. Over both horizons covariability in returns is very small. Using a ratio of housing wealth to wealth in equity type assets of 5/3 (the 1991 value) equation (3.7) and Table 3.10 imply that the risk premium on housing is between 0.16 and 0.37 the size of the risk premium on equity. The average, excess return on UK equities over a safe rate of interest for the period 1919–1988 is approximately 8% (see Spackman (1991) and Office of Water Services (1991)). This suggests that we need to add a premium of between 1.3% (= 8(0.16)%) and 3.0% (= 8(0.37)%) to the user cost of funds to account for risk. These are not insignificant risk premia but are too small to wipe out the unadjusted, average excess return on housing of around 5–6% per annum implied by the numbers in Figure 3.4.

But the CAPM is a single-period model. In the context of the model developed in Chapter 2 the consumption CAPM, based on a general equilibrium where agents maximize utility which depends on current and future consumption, is a more attractive basis for measuring risk. Breeden (1979) shows that with time-additive utility functions, where consumption (*unlike* wealth) at any date is a sufficient statistic for marginal utility, the risk premium on all assets are proportional to the covariance of their return with the percentage change in real consumption (see also Breeden, 1989). Thus risk premia on assets are proportional to consumption betas which are the slope coefficients from an OLS regression of the asset returns on the percentage change in real consumption.

Table 3.11 shows the results of OLS regressions of the return on the FT index, and of the percentage change in house prices, on the percentage change in aggregate, real consumption expenditure. Once again the results are sensitive to the period

Table 3.11   Coefficients on consumption growth — OLS regressions

Dependent variable:		Coefficient on % change c (unadjusted t statistics in parentheses)
Equity return	(1) quarterly	0.30 (0.48)
	(2) annual	1.11 (1.58)
Housing return	(1) quarterly	0.58 (3.05)
	(2) annual	1.97 (7.74)

Period: 1963 II to 1993 II. Consumption is of durable and non-durable goods and is deflated by the RPI (Economic Trends; various issues). House prices and equity prices are as in Table 3.10. t statistics in parentheses.

over which returns are measured — one quarter or one year. The point estimate for the consumption beta on equities using quarterly returns is small and statistically insignificant. For housing, the beta is substantially larger and significant at the 5% level. With annual returns the point estimates of both betas are considerably higher (1.11 for equities and 1.97 for housing) though overlapping data makes standard errors unreliable.

Given the substantial average excess return on equities over a long period the implication of Table 3.11, where estimated housing betas are considerably larger than equity betas, is that risk premia on housing should be very large.

Clearly, the CAPM and consumption CAPM give very different estimates of appropriate risk premia for houses which range from 2% per annum to as much as 15%. Although the theory underlying the Consumption CAPM makes it a more attractive basis for measuring housing risk, recent studies (e.g. Mankiw and Shapiro, 1986) have found that the simple CAPM is better able to account for the time-series properties of asset prices. In the light of this one would want to discount rather heavily results which indicate that housing is a substantially more risky asset than equities and confine the range of plausible values for the relative riskiness to, say, 0.25–1.0. Using the 8% figure for the average risk premia on equities, this range for the relative riskiness of housing wealth implies that the housing risk premium might be in the range 2–8%.

With this range of premia, allowing for risk obviously has a significant impact on the user cost of housing. Adjusting the measure in Figure 4.3 for risk using the mid-point of the range (5%) would generate an average user cost over the period 1963–90 of just under 4%, which is close to our central estimate of the value of the services of houses.

What these results show is that measuring the appropriate opportunity cost of funds to use in a measure of the user cost of housing — which necessitates measuring the risk of housing — is extremely difficult. But central estimates of housing risk are substantial and once allowance is made for them the average return to housing in the period since the early 1960s no longer appears excessive.

This conclusion in no way suggests that the tax benefits to home ownership — the existence of mortgage tax relief and the zero tax rate on imputed rental income — are insignificant. Rather they imply that those benefits have been capitalized in house prices. *Given* the tax implications of home ownership, this is exactly what the forward-looking model of Chapter 2 suggests should happen; in an efficient market with rational agents house prices are driven up so that the tangible benefits of home ownership are priced so as to clear the market.

One implication of the capitalization argument is that tax breaks on owner-occupation may do little to help *potential* owner-occupiers since they are, in large part, reflected in buying prices. The real gainers from favourable tax treatment are those who bought property when the expected present value of tax concessions were lower than they subsequently became. Whether or not the gains enjoyed by these people really increased welfare or were instead merely paper profits is the issue to which we turn in the next chapter.

I think what emerges from our analysis of the user cost of housing is that uncertainty over an appropriate measure of the riskiness of investment in residential property is such that even over the post-war period, when real house prices have risen dramatically, it is far from clear that the returns to home ownership have been excessive. Attempting to adjust the user-cost measure of Figure 3.4 to account for the effects of liquidity constraints would further muddy the waters. Equation (2.8) showed that the impact of credit restrictions upon the true user cost of housing depends upon interest rates, expected house price inflation and the maximum loan-to-value ratio of lenders; even the *sign* of the net impact is unclear. The difficulty in measuring the impact of credit restrictions compounds the problem of assessing whether house values have been consistent with forward-looking, market-clearing models. A safe, though rather anaemic, conclusion would be that the spectacular rise in house prices over the past thirty years is *not* inconsistent with market efficiency.

There remains the question as to why real house prices have risen so dramatically over the century. It seems unlikely that productivity in house building should grow sufficiently less fast than productivity in the rest of the economy to explain the increase; Holmans (1990) shows that rising construction costs cannot account for much of the rise in the real cost of new houses. A natural answer is that the real value of the one non-renewable resource used in the construction of a new house — land — has risen rapidly. Real land values have indeed risen through the century, and at a pace considerably faster than house prices (Holmans, 1990). Over the period 1963–88 the average annual increase in the real price of new houses was 3.5% while the average increase in the real price of building land was 7.5%. These figures are consistent with the view that limits on the supply of building land due to planning restrictions have contributed to the rise in house prices; in no way does this imply that such restrictions are bad, merely that they have a significant impact on house values.

While deregulation of planning restrictions might cause substantial reductions in the price of houses deregulation of financial markets in the 1980s can plausibly be seen as one of the factors behind the sharp rise in prices over the decade. As we showed in Chapter 2, the availability of funds which can be borrowed using housing as collateral affects the demand for houses. Greater ability to borrow against housing wealth, and more specifically to extract equity, enhances the real value of housing because owner-occupied dwellings become a fungible source of wealth. It would not be surprising if a real, and probably permanent, improvement in one of the characteristics of an asset (i.e. its fungibility) should increase its value. Thus, part of the rise in the real value of houses in the 1980s may have been due to the process of financial liberalization, may prove to be permanent, and can be explained in a way quite consistent with rational behaviour, rather than speculative frenzy. Furthermore, the analysis of Chapter 2, and in particular Figure 2.2, suggests that the immediate impact upon house prices of a change in fungibility will be greater than the long-run effect; house prices should rise sharply in the immediate aftermath of unanticipated financial liberalization and then decline smoothly to a level which is above the previous equilibrium. In the UK in the mid-1980s, and a little later in the Scandinavian countries, house prices increased sharply at the same time as lending exploded; prices subsequently fell, though in all cases by less than they had risen. In qualitative terms these price changes are consistent with market efficiency, though the sharpness of the price falls in some areas is less easily squared with rational expectations.

3.7   CONCLUSIONS

The aim of this chapter has been to describe the housing market in the UK, to compare it with markets in other countries and to see how conditions have changed over the century. We have seen that in the UK a typical house has recently been worth between three and four years of average disposable income; in many other developed countries house prices are even higher. There has been substantial net investment in housing in all developed countries over the post-war period; the stock of residential property is a major component of national wealth, which yields a stream of benefits in the form of real housing services. In the UK the real resources that need to be devoted to preserving the stock of housing in line with the population of households may be lower in the next century than it has been over the last hundred years. This would represent a real gain to national welfare. But rises in the real price of houses, *per se*, may not contribute to national wealth; we consider the circumstances under which price rises do increase wealth in the next chapter. A significant proportion of the benefits of the slow accumulation of housing wealth through the century may be reaped by the current generation of home owners if they choose to pass on real bequests lower than those which they receive. The welfare implications of such a decision are unclear — the argument that it is undesirable implicitly assumes that the discount rate applied by the current generation to the welfare of future generations is too high; which is just a fancy way of saying that we don't care enough about our grandchildren. We consider these issues in Chapter 5 and analyse the evidence on the uses of equity withdrawal in Chapters 6 and 7.

REFERENCES

Ashton, P., Minford, P. and Peel, D. (1987) The Housing Morass, Hobart Paper, No. 25, Institute of Economic Affairs, London.

Bank of England (1985) The housing finance market: recent growth in perspective, *Bank of England Quarterly Bulletin*, March, 80–91.

Bank of England (1989) The housing market, *Bank of England Quarterly Bulletin*, February, 66–77.

Bank of England (1991) Housing finance — an international perspective, *Bank of England Quarterly Bulletin*, February, 56–66.

Bank of England (1992) House prices, arrears and re-possessions, *Bank of England Quarterly Bulletin*, May, 173–179.

Black, J. and Stafford, D. (1988) *Housing Policy and Finance*, Routledge, London.

Boleat, M. (1987) *National Housing Finance Systems — a Comparative Study*, Croom Helm, London.

Breeden, D. (1979) An intertemporal asset pricing model with stochastic consumption and investment opportunities, *Journal of Financial Economics*, 7, 265–96.

Breeden, D. (1989) Intertemporal portfolio theory and asset pricing, in *Finance: The New Palgrave*, edited by J. Eatwell, M. Milgate and P. Newman, Macmillan, London.

Coles, A. (1991) Household formation projections, in *Housing Finance*, no. 12, 24–31.

Coles, A. and Taylor, B. (1993) Trends in tenure preference, *Housing Finance*, no. 19, 22–25.

Congdon, T. and Turnbull, P. (1982) *The Coming Boom in Housing Credit*, Messels and Co., June.

Drake, L. (1991) *The Building Society Industry in Transition*, Macmillan, Basingstoke.

Ermisch, J. (1991) An ageing population, household formation and housing, *Housing Studies*, 6, 230–40.

Goodhart, C. (1986) Financial Innovation and Monetary Control:, *Oxford Review of Economic Policy*, 2, 79–99.

Hamnett, C., Harmer, M. and Williams, P. (1991) *Safe as Houses*, Paul Chapman Publishing, London.

Hayashi, F., Ito, T. and Slemrod, J. (1988) Housing finance, imperfections and national saving: a comparative simulation analysis of the US and Japan, *Journal of Japanese and International Economies*, 3.

Hills, J. (1991) *Unravelling Housing Finance*, Oxford University Press, Oxford.

Holmans, A. (1987) *Housing Policy in Britain*, Croom Helm, London.

Holmans, A. (1990) House Prices: Changes Through Time at the National and Sub-National Level, Government Economic Service Working Paper no. 110.

Inland Revenue (1990) *Inland Revenue Statistics*, HMSO, London.

International Housing Finance Factbook (1987), International Organisation for Housing Finance Institutions, London.

Lee, J. and Robinson, W. (1990) The fall in the savings ratio: the role of housing, *Fiscal Studies*, **11**, 36–52.

Lintner J. (1965) The valuation of risk assets and the selection of risky investments in stock portfolios and capital budgets, *Review of Economics and Statistics*, **47**, 13–37.

Maclellan, D. (1990) Paper presented at the first Conference of the LBS Housing Research Group, London, September.

Mankiw, G. and Shapiro, M. (1986) Risk and return, consumption beta versus market beta, *Review of Economics and Statistics*, **68**, 452–9.

Miles, D. (1990) Financial Liberalization, the Current Account and Housing Markets, Birkbeck College Discussion Paper in Financial Economics.

Miles, D. (1994) Fixed and floating rate finance, *Bank of England Quarterly Bulletin*, February.

Morgan Grenfell (1987) *Housing Inheritance and Wealth*, Economic Review no. 45, November.

Muellbauer, J. and Murphy, A. (1989) Why Has the UK Savings Ratio Collapsed? Credit Suisse First Boston Research Paper, July.

Muellbauer, J. and Murphy, A. (1990) Is the UK Balance of Payments Sustainable? *Economic Policy*, **11**, 345–83.

Office of Water Services (1991) *Cost of Capital: A Consultative Report*, July.

Pesaran, M. and Evans, R. (1984) Inflation, capital gains and UK personal savings 1953–1981, *Economic Journal*, **94**, 237–257.

Poterba, J. and Manchester J. (1989) Second Mortgages and Household Savings. NBER Discussion Paper No. 2853.

Sharpe, W. (1964) Capital asset prices: a theory of market equilibrium under conditions of risk, *Journal of Finance*, **19**, 425–42.

Spackman, M. (1991) Discount Rates and Rates of Return in the Public Sector: Economic Issues, UK Treasury Working Paper no. 58.

Takagi, S. (1988) Trends of Japanese Savings and Wealth and Recent Developments in National Accounts in Japan. In *The Global Role of the Japanese Economy with Affluent Savings and Accumulated Wealth*, Fifth International EPA Symposium, Economic Planning Agency, Tokyo.

Urban Housing Finance (1989), OECD, Paris.

NOTES

1. At the end of 1992 the average value of a house was in excess of three times the average annual earnings of those buying houses with a mortgage (*Housing Finance*, Tables 7 and 8).

2. CSO estimated annual depreciation on dwellings, at current replacement cost, is slightly less than 1% of the *market* value of dwellings.

3. Hills' (1991) estimate of the annual flow of real housing services of 3.5% of the value of the stock implies a value of around £40 billion for the benefits of home ownership in 1990 — over 10% of total personal disposable income.

4. At the start of the 1990s owner-occupied houses accounted for over 40% of the total net worth of the personal sector. 38% of the total net capital stock of the UK in 1990 was accounted for by dwellings (*UK National Income Accounts*, CSO, 1991).

5. The ratio of the average registered annual rent of furnished tenancies (excluding housing association rents) to the average value of houses was just under 3.5% over the period 1989–92 (*Housing Construction*, Table 1.14). This is almost certainly a substantial underestimate of the real rental services of owner-occupied houses since furnished tenancies tend to be smaller than average houses *and* registered rents are not free market rents. An alternative means of estimating the value of the housing services consumed by owner occupiers is to use the value of imputed rent to owner occupiers reported in the national accounts. This figure is based upon assessment of the free market rent which owner occupied houses could command. Over the period since 1979 the ratio of the CSO estimate of imputed rent to the value of the owner occupied housing stock has averaged around 2.5%. However, that figure relies on estimates of ratable values made in the 1970s and is a not likely to be a good guide to the real services provided by owner occupied housing. Either of these estimates — 3.5% or 2.5% — could conceivably be only one half or one third of the true rental yield on owner-occupied housing. In the main text we take a conservative, range for that yield to be 4–7%.

APPENDIX: MEASURING THE USER COST OF HOUSING

Variables used in the construction of the user cost of housing (uc_t, equation (3.4) in the text) are defined as follows:

P_t: mix adjusted house price index (collected by the Department of the Environment and the Building Societies Association: see *Economic Trends*, various issues) = 1.0 in 1985.

PC_t: Retail Price Index (*Economic Trends*) = 1.0 in 1985.

b_t: for the 'average' existing owner-occupier the proportion of the value of the home financed by debt is measured as the ratio of the total outstanding stock of mortgage debt held by the personal sector (*Financial Statistics*) to the value of the owner-occupied housing stock (*Financial Statistics Balance Sheets* of the personal sector: Table S2). For 'first time buyers' β is set equal to the loan to value ratio of first-time buyers reported in *Housing Finance*, various issues. Figure 1 only reports the average owner since the two series are close.

r_m: is the building societies average interest rate on mortgages through the year (*Financial Statistics*, various issues).

α, t_y: an estimate of the product of t_y and α is made by dividing the cost to the Inland Revenue of mortgage tax relief (which is the proportion of total interest paid on mortgage debt that is eligible for relief times the average marginal income tax rate of borrowers) by the total value of mortgage interest repayments. Total interest payments are calculated by multiplying the stock of outstanding mortgages (*Financial Statistics*, various issues) by r_m. Re-arranging the equation in the text reveals that only the product of t_y and α is needed to calculate the user cost of housing.

r_i: is the net return on building societies' shares.

τ_p: is the ratio of total payments by the personal sector of rates, sewerage and water charges as a proportion of the value of the housing stock (*National Income Accounts*, various issues).

δ: estimate of depreciation rate set at 1.0% (which is close to the recent ratio of CSO depreciation on the housing stock to the market value of that stock).

μ: total personal sector expenditure on home maintenance, repairs and DIY as proportion of value of housing stock (*National Income Accounts*, various issues).

CHAPTER 4

House-price shocks and consumption with forward-looking households

4.1 INTRODUCTION

We have argued that housing wealth is different from other components of the net worth of the personal sector. A house is a durable commodity which yields a flow of consumption services. But it is also a tangible asset whose worth constitutes a high proportion of the net wealth of most owner-occupiers. It is the importance of residential property in national balance sheets which makes changes in the housing market of macroeconomic significance. (See Hayashi, Ito and Slemrod (1988); Dekle (1989); Poterba and Manchester (1989); Muellbauer and Murphy (1990) for different analyses of the interaction between housing markets and the wider economy). In this chapter we analyse the impact of house-price shocks on the consumption and saving decisions of households, building on the theoretical framework developed in Chapter 2.

In view of the importance of housing wealth in the personal sector's portfolio of assets and the increasing use of wider definitions of wealth — which include residential property — in empirical models of consumption (Muellbauer and Murphy, 1990) the issue addressed in this chapter is central to understanding consumer behaviour. In Chapter 3 we saw that in the UK over the past century rises in the price of houses relative to those of a basket of consumer goods have been dramatic and are by far the most important factor in accounting for the rise in the value of the aggregate housing stock. Whether this part of the increase in the total value of residential property should be seen as contributing to national wealth is the real issue of this chapter.

Here we develop a theoretical model which suggests that, in the absence of credit restrictions, the effect of shocks to the level of house prices is likely to be small; shocks which change the growth rate of prices are likely to have a much bigger impact on saving. Empirical evidence is presented which is consistent with these results.

Changes in house prices simultaneously change the market value of the wealth of home owners and the cost of consuming housing services. The dual nature of houses, as commodities yielding utility and as personal sector assets, makes analysis of the effects of price changes complex. Such effects can be compared with the impact of changes in the value of assets which leave unchanged the price of all goods which directly enter utility functions; in the case of equities, for example, unanticipated increases in their price in itself has an unambiguous, positive wealth effect upon consumption for owners of stock since there is no simultaneous, offsetting increase in the price of some consumer goods. In contrast, if changes in the price of houses are more than transitory a rational, forward-looking household will consider the impact of price shocks on both the market value of current assets and on the future costs of housing services. Even for home owners there is no *a priori* reason why an unexpected increase in real house prices should be treated as a boost in real wealth. Indeed we will show that there are conditions under which the consumption and savings of home owners are independent of shocks to house prices. Not surprisingly, it turns out that the conditions under which changes in the market value of housing wealth do not effect consumption are very restrictive — more so than the conditions under which Ricardian equivalence holds and bonds should not count as part of net worth (Barro, 1974).

It is because of the crucial difference between housing and other tangible assets that the aggregation of all types of tangible and financial assets in empirical models of consumers' expenditure is not well grounded in theory. But the real issue is *not* one of inappropriate aggregation of assets which differ in their degree of marketability or fungibility, which has been commonly cited as a reason for not including housing wealth in the measure of wealth used in empirical models of consumption. In the theory developed below we abstract from differences in the liquidity of assets so as to bring out the real issues more clearly; housing wealth is assumed to be perfectly fungible and home owners are able to borrow against the current market value of their home to finance any type of expenditure.

Our aim in this chapter is to analyse the wealth effect of house price changes for agents unconstrained by credit restrictions. (Yoshikawa and Ohtake (1989) consider the effects of house-price changes in a model with borrowing restrictions for first-time buyers; they do not, however, consider the impact of price changes on existing owner-occupiers). In the theory section of this chapter we therefore ignore what may be an important mechanism in the transmission of house-price shocks to changes in consumption — that is the impact of enhanced collateral upon the ability to borrow. If that mechanism is powerful it should, however, be revealed by our empirical work where the impact of price shocks should be different from that implied by a theory based on perfect capital markets. By allowing the estimated impact of price changes to vary across decades we should be able to assess whether the credit mechanism is important. Credit effects should have been stronger in the

1980s when financial intermediaries were more willing to lend against rising house values than in earlier decades. We will return to the importance of credit effects and their role in explaining fluctuations in consumer saving in Chapters 5 and 6.

Our strategy is to use a simplified version of the model of household consumption decisions outlined in Chapter 2 and to derive the optimal response of spending and saving to various types of house-price shock as a function of household characteristics and housing-market conditions. We will show how the response of saving to house-price shocks is sensitive to the time horizon of the household, the degree of substitutability between housing and other consumption goods, the nature of the shock and the composition of household assets before the shock occurs. We use data on the consumption decisions of UK households and on UK real house prices to assess whether the model of rational, forward-looking agents is consistent with the time-series evidence on price shocks and consumption growth.

The plan of this chapter is this. In Section 4.2 we develop a model of the impact of various types of shocks on house prices. In Section 4.3 we use UK aggregate data to assess the scale of the impact of house-price shocks on saving. Conclusions are drawn in Section 4.4.

4.2   THE IMPACT OF CHANGES IN HOUSE PRICES ON CONSUMPTION: A SIMPLE FRAMEWORK

4.2.1   THE MODEL

Assume that an agent has a planning horizon of T periods and aims to maximize a utility function which depends upon consumption of a single non-housing good and of housing services in each period up to T. (Agents may expect to live for less than T periods in which case consumption of goods by others, most obviously their heirs, enters the utility function.) As before, we denote the consumption of the non-housing good in period t by c_t and let the number of units of housing owned by the agent (or their heirs) at time t be H_t. Units of housing are homogeneous and are assumed to depreciate at a constant per-period rate of δ. Let the market price, *measured in terms of the consumer good*, of a unit of housing at time t be p_t. We assume that all agents own the home in which they live; there is no rental market. We assume that agents are able to borrow or lend subject only to a single budget constraint over the T period horizon. This assumption implies that agents are able to borrow against the value of housing wealth provided that any loans can be repaid over the agent's life, or at least out of the value of the liquidation of gross assets at T. Thus, we aim to identify the impact of house price shocks on expenditure of unconstrained households; should the calculated effect on consumption of positive price shocks for owner-occupiers be small, that result could not then be attributed to the limited ability to smooth consumption due to borrowing restrictions.

We assume a constant real interest rate, measured in terms of the consumer good, of r. Agents lend or borrow at this rate. We make a simplifying assumption that the return on financial assets and the cost of debt is the same and, since we also ignore credit restrictions, we only need focus on the net financial position of households (unlike in the more general model of Chapter 2, where the mortgage rate was allowed to differ from the return on financial assets). We denote the value of *net* debt outstanding at t by M_t; agents with net financial assets have $M < 0$. (Notice that M here does not have the same meaning as in Chapter 2, where it denoted *gross* debt.) We ignore taxes. The evolution of wealth from one period to the next is given by

$$p_{t+1}H_{t+1} = y_{t+1} - c_{t+1} + (1 - \delta)P_{t+1}H_t + M_{t+1} - M_t(1 + r) \tag{4.1}$$

where y_{t+1} is labour income earned in period $t+1$, which we assume is independent of conditions in the housing market.

The market value of non-human wealth at t is given by

$$W_t \equiv p_t H_t - M_t \tag{4.2}$$

The only restriction upon the evolution of wealth is that $W_T > 0$. Using (4.1) and (4.2) we can write the single budget constraint at time $t = 0$:

$$\sum_{t=0}^{T} y_t/(1+r)^t + W_0 - W_T/(1+r)^T = \sum_{t=0}^{T} c_t/(1+r)^t + \sum_{t=0}^{T} (uc_t H_t)/(1+r)^t \tag{4.3}$$

where $uc_t \equiv p_t(1 + r - (1 - \delta)(1 + \dot{p}_t))/(1 + r)$ and $(1 + \dot{p}_t) \equiv p_{t+1}/p_t$. uc_t is the user cost of housing at time t. For small r, δ and $\dot{p}$ it is approximately equal to $p_t(r + \delta - \dot{p}_t)$.

The left-hand side of (4.3) is the present discounted value, at $t = 0$, of future labour income plus the difference between current (non-human) wealth and the present value of terminal wealth. W_0, current wealth, is measured at the beginning of the period just before decisions on period 0 consumption and housing are made and before period 0 income is received. The right-hand side of (4.3) is the present value of all future consumption of housing services and of the non-housing good. We use (4.3) to characterize the response of an agent at time $t = 0$ to a shock to house prices. For simplicity we will assume there is no uncertainty over future labour incomes and that the only uncertainty comes from a one-off shock to the current level and/or the future rate of change of house prices. At a point in time the rate of change of future house prices is assumed to be constant. (This merely simplifies the conditions derived below substantially; we could easily, but rather messily, allow the anticipated per-period rate of change of house prices to vary across future periods.)

We consider three types of shock to the path of house prices. The first shock hits the current level of real house prices but does not change agents' views of the growth of future real house prices. Here the effect of the shock to the level of p_0 persists into the future; we assume a unit root in the *level* of house prices. The second type of shock causes a revision to the future *growth* of real house prices, but has no effect on the current level of house prices. The third type of shock changes both the current level and the future growth of real house prices. Throughout we do not specify the cause of shocks — the aim in this chapter is not to model a general equilibrium in the housing market but rather to assess the impact of shocks on the individual household; it seems appropriate that a household would consider these shocks to be exogenous, which is all we require.

The issue we address is that of measuring the response of consumption of non-housing goods to an unexpected, but non-transitory, shock to house prices.

We denote the percentage size of a shock to the *level* of house prices at $t = 0$ by $100\,\varepsilon\%$ so that

$$\tilde{p}_0 = (1 + \varepsilon)p_0$$

where $\tilde{p}_0$ is the post-shock price. The change in W_0 induced by a level shock is $\varepsilon(p_0 H_0)$, so the market value of wealth, in terms of the consumer good, rises to an extent dependent on current real house prices and the size of the house.

We denote the rate of growth of future house prices before a *growth* shock by $\dot{p}$; after a growth shock house prices will rise at a per-period rate of $\tilde{\dot{p}}$.

Given that future labour income and the interest rate are assumed to be independent of house prices, we can use the budget constraint (4.3) to calculate the change in the present value of non-housing consumption induced by the house-price shock. Denoting the planned level of housing for period t, made before the price shock, as H_t and the post-shock demand as $\tilde{H}_t$, we have from (4.3) that the change in the present value of total non-housing consumption between $t = 0$ and $t = T$, denoted ∂C_{pv}, is

$$\partial C_{pv} \equiv \sum_{t=0}^{T}(\tilde{c}_t - c_t)/(1 + r)^t = \tilde{W}_0 - W_0 - (\tilde{W}_T - W_t)/(1 + r)^T$$

$$- \sum_{t=0}^{T}(\tilde{u}c_t\tilde{H}_t - uc_t H_t)/(1 + r)^t \qquad (4.4)$$

where $\tilde{c}_t - c_t$ is the change in planned c for period t due to the shock to house prices. (Variables with a tilde above them will always denote post-shock values.)

In order to evaluate (4.4) we assume that agents maximize the present discounted value of utility in all periods up to T, where in each period utility is additively separable in c_t and H_t. Denote this maximand U_0, which is:

$$\sum_{t=0}^{T}[U_c(c_t) + U_H(H_t)]/(1 + \rho)^t \qquad (4.5)$$

where $U_c(.)$ and $U_H(.)$ are the sub-utility functions for consumption and housing and ρ is the rate at which future utility is discounted. Separability between c and H is restrictive; whilst it is certainly inappropriate for some types of consumer goods (e.g. snooker tables!) aggregate evidence is consistent with separability between broadly defined categories of durable and non-durable goods (Bernanke, 1985). Maximization of U_0 subject to the budget constraint (4.3) yields the first-order conditions:

$$U'_c(c_0) = ((1+r)/(1+\rho))^t U'_c(c_t) \qquad \text{for } t = 1, 2, \ldots, T \qquad (4.6)$$

$$U'_H(H_t) = (uc_t)U'_c(c_t) \qquad \text{for } t = 0, 1, 2, \ldots, T \qquad (4.7)$$

where $U'_c(c_0) \equiv \partial U_c(c_0)/\partial c_0$, etc.
From (4.6) and (4.7),

$$U'_H(H_t)/U'_H(H_{t+1}) = (uc_t/uc_{t+1})(1+r)/(1+\rho)$$

Noting that prior to a growth shock $uc_t/uc_{t+1} = 1/(1+\dot{p})$ (since r, δ are assumed constant) and taking a first-order approximation to $U'_H(H_{t+1})$ of

$$U'_H(H_t) + U''_H(H_t g_{t+1})$$

where $g_{t+1} \equiv (H_{t+1} - H_t)/H_t$ we can write

$$g_{t+1} = [r - \rho - \dot{p} - \dot{p}\rho]/\{(1+r)\xi_h\} \qquad (4.8)$$

where $\xi_h \equiv -H[U''_H(H)/U'_H(H)]$ which we assume is a non-negative constant.
For small ρ, $\dot{p}$, we can write (4.8) as

$$g_{t+1} = (r - \dot{p} - \rho)/\xi_h \qquad (4.9)$$

which implies that optimal housing demand rises or falls at a constant rate since by assumption the right-hand side is constant. After a shock to the growth of house prices the new equilibrium rate of change of optimal house size will be

$$\tilde{g}_{t+1} = (r - \dot{\tilde{p}} - \rho)/\xi_h \qquad (4.10)$$

An analogous argument implies that the first-order condition (4.6) yields an optimal path for consumption which grows at a constant rate equal to

$$g_c = (r - \rho)/\xi_c \qquad (4.11)$$

where $\xi_c \equiv -c[U''_c(c)/U'_c(c)]$.

ξ_c is the inverse of the instantaneous elasticity of substitution of consumption. Notice that the rate at which consumption of non-housing goods rises does not depend upon either the level or rate of growth of house prices, though condition (4.7) implies that the ratio of house size to consumption at any time does since the user cost depends on both the level and rate of change of house prices. This is a useful result because it implies that the proportionate change in optimal consumption in each period following a shock of any sort to house prices at $t = 0$ is the same for all future periods. The change in optimal consumption t periods after a shock at time 0 can then be written $(\tilde{c}_0 - c_0)(1 + g_c)^t$.

We now write (4.4) as

$$\partial C_{pv} \equiv \sum_{t=0}^{T} (\tilde{c}_0 - c_0)(1 + g_c)^t/(1 + r)^t = (\tilde{W}_0 - W_0) - (\tilde{W}_T - W_T)/(1 + r)^T$$

$$- \sum_{t=0}^{T} (\tilde{u}c_t \tilde{H}_t - uc_t H_t)/(1 + r)^t \qquad (4.12)$$

Using the facts that

$$\tilde{W}_0 - W_0 = \varepsilon p_0 H_0$$

$$H_t = H_0(1 + g)^t$$

$$\tilde{H}_t = \tilde{H}_0(1 + \tilde{g})^t$$

(4.12) becomes

$$\sum_{t=0}^{T} (\tilde{c}_0 - c_0)(1 + g_c)^t/(1 + r)^t = \varepsilon p_0 H_0 - (\tilde{W}_T - W_T)/(1 + r)^T$$

$$- \left\{ (\tilde{H}_0 - H_0) \sum_{t=0}^{T} \tilde{u}c_t(1 + \tilde{g})^t/(1 + r)^t \right.$$

$$\left. + H_0 \sum_{t=0}^{T} [\tilde{u}c_t(1 + \tilde{g})^t - uc_t(1 + g)^t]/(1 + r)^t \right\} \qquad (4.13)$$

The term within braces on the second and third lines of (4.13) is the change in the present value of housing costs as a result of shocks to the level and/or the growth of house prices. This will depend upon the interest rate, the rate of increase and level of house prices before the shock, the elasticity of demand for housing services (itself a function of ξ_c and ξ_h) and the horizon over which the agent plans (T). The second term on the right-hand side of (4.13) is the change in the present value of the planned terminal value of wealth due to the house-price shock. If all agents whose consumption affects the utility of the agent are dead by T, then in a world of certainty $W_T = \tilde{W}_T = 0$, so this second term could be ignored. (Indeed it is helpful to interpret T not as the agent's expected time until death but rather the time until the last person whose utility affects the agent dies; we shall adopt this interpretation of the planning horizon T and from now on set $W_T = \tilde{W}_T = 0$.)

(4.13) then says that after a shock to real house prices the present value of consumption expenditure rises if the increase in the market value of the current home exceeds the present value of all the net increases in the future optimal expenditures on housing. It is this condition that we now use to derive an explicit formula for the change in consumption in terms of exogenous variables.

A second-order Taylor expansion of (4.7) implies

$$(\tilde{H}_0 - H_0)/H_0 = [1 - \tilde{u}c_0/uc_0]/\xi_h + (\tilde{u}c_0/uc_0)(\xi_c/\xi_h)[(\tilde{c}_0 - c_0)/c_0] \qquad (4.14)$$

Using (4.14) in (4.13) and rearranging yields

$$[\tilde{c}_0 - c_0] \left\{ \sum_{t=0}^{T} (1 + g_c)^t/(1 + r)^t + (H_0/c_0)(\tilde{u}c_0/uc_0)(\xi_c/\xi_h) \right.$$

$$\left. \times (\sum_{t=0}^{T} (\tilde{u}c_t(1 + \tilde{g}_t)^t/(1 + r)^t)) \right\} = \xi p_0 H_0 -$$

$$H_0 \left\{ \sum_{t=0}^{T} [(1 - (\tilde{u}c_0/uc_0))/\xi_h]\tilde{u}c_t(1 + \tilde{g})^t/(1 + r)^t \right.$$

$$\left. + \sum_{t=0}^{T} [\tilde{u}c_t(1 + \tilde{g})^t - uc_t(1 + g)^t]/(1 + r)^t \right\} \qquad (4.15)$$

Finally we note that

$$uc_t = p_t(1 + r - (1 - \delta)(1 + \dot{p}))/(1 + r)$$

$$= p_0(1 + \dot{p})^t(1 + r - (1 - \delta)(1 + \dot{p}))/(1 + r)$$

and

$$\tilde{u}c_t = \tilde{p}_t(1 + r - (1 - \delta)(1 + \dot{\tilde{p}}))/(1 + r)$$

$$= p_0(1 + \varepsilon)(1 + \dot{\tilde{p}})^t(1 + r - (1 - \delta)(1 + \dot{\tilde{p}}))/(1 + r)$$

Making the approximation: $(1 + r - (1 - \delta)(1 + \dot{p}))/(1 + r) \simeq (r + \delta - \dot{p})$ we may, after some tedious algebra, now write

$$[\tilde{c}_0 - c_0]/c_0 = [p_0 H_0/c_0]\{(\varepsilon + AB - CA + D)/(E + FA)\} \qquad (4.16)$$

where

$$A = (1 + r)/((1 + r) - (1 + \dot{\tilde{p}})(1 + \tilde{g}))$$

$$\times [1 - ((1 + \dot{\tilde{p}})(1 + \tilde{g})/(1 + r))^{T+1}] \qquad (4.17)$$

$$B = ((1 + \varepsilon)((r + \delta - \dot{\tilde{p}})/(r + \delta - \dot{p})) - 1)[(1 + \varepsilon)(r + \delta - \dot{\tilde{p}})]/\xi_h \qquad (4.18)$$

$$C = (1 + \varepsilon)(r + \delta - \dot{\tilde{p}}) \qquad (4.19)$$

$$D = (r + \delta - \dot{p})(1 + r)/((1 + r) - (1 + \dot{p})(1 + g))$$

$$\times [1 - ((1 + \dot{p})(1 + g)/(1 + r))^{T+1}] \qquad (4.20)$$

$$E = ((1 + r)/(r - g_c))\{1 - [(1 + g_c)/(1 + r)]^{T+1}\} \qquad (4.21)$$

$$F = [(1 + \varepsilon)^2(r + \delta - \dot{\tilde{p}})^2/(r + \delta - \dot{p})](\xi_c/\xi_H)(P H_0/c_0) \qquad (4.22)$$

Since g; $\tilde{g}$; and g_c are functions of $\dot{p}$, $\dot{\tilde{p}}$, r, ξ_h, ξ_c, and ρ we can use (4.16)–(4.22) to write the induced percentage change in current consumption from a shock to house prices as an explicit function of: preference parameters (ρ, ξ_h, ξ_c, T); exogenous housing market variables $(\delta, p_0, r, \dot{p})$; predetermined (at the time of the shock) choice variables (H_0) and the parameters of the exogenous shock $(\varepsilon, (\dot{\tilde{p}} - \dot{p}))$. Our strategy is to use central estimates of the key parameters and to calculate how various house price shocks influence consumption for households with various characteristics.

4.2.2   CALIBRATING THE IMPACT OF PRICE SHOCKS ON CONSUMPTION

First we consider some special cases. When the demand for housing is perfectly inelastic ($\xi_H = \infty$) $B = F = 0$ and, from (4.9), $g = 0$. In this case if we consider the effect of just a level shock ($\dot{p} = \dot{\tilde{p}}$) for households with an infinite time horizon we get some clear results; provided $r > g_c$ and $r > \dot{p}$ then with $T = \infty$ the impact of a level shock on consumption is

$$[\tilde{c}_0 - c_0]/c_0 = [p_0 H_0/c_0]\varepsilon\{1 - (1+r)(r+\delta - \dot{p})/(r - \dot{p})\}(r - g_c)/(1+r) \quad (4.23)$$

$[\tilde{c}_0 - c_0]/c_0$ becomes insignificant as $\delta \to 0$. (More accurately the condition is that the effect on consumption is close to zero if the *increase* in the real cost (in consumer goods) of depreciation each year resulting from a higher real cost of houses is zero.) The intuition behind this result is clear. If households have infinitely inelastic demand they will not substitute away from housing in response to a price increases; if they also have long planning horizons then the increased future user cost of housing offsets the increase in the market value of wealth.

A second special case is where $\xi_H = T = \infty$ and we have a pure growth shock (i.e. $\varepsilon = 0$). Provided $r > g_c$; $(1+r) > (1+\dot{p})(1+g)$ and $(1+r) > (1+\dot{\tilde{p}})(1+\tilde{g})$, then:

$$[\tilde{c}_0 - c_0]/c_0 = [p_0 H_0/c_0](r - g_c)\{(r+\delta - \dot{p})/(r - \dot{p}) - (r+\delta - \dot{\tilde{p}})/(r - \dot{\tilde{p}})\} \quad (4.24)$$

Once again $[\tilde{c}_0 - c_0]/c_0 \to 0$ as $\delta \to 0$.

Aside from these special cases the impact of shocks on consumption will not be neutral. Tables 4.1–6 report the results of using (4.16) to calculate the percentage change in current consumption caused by different types of house-price shocks for various types of household. In each table we show the impact for households with different planning horizons and with varying degrees of substitutability between housing and other goods. For the first four tables we consider a household which is already an owner-occupier when the shock occurs; we take a household for whom the pre-shock ratio of the value of the house to planned annual consumption is 3 (i.e. $[p_0 H_0/c_0] = 3$). For the US the ratio of average house value to average disposable income is probably close to this figure. In the period 1985–90 the average ratio of the median value of US owner occupied housing units to median disposable income was around 2.8 (*Statistical Abstract of the US*); with a savings rate of around 5% for that period the implied ratio of house value to consumption is almost exactly 3. A ratio of 3 also comes close to matching the UK long-run average; the mean ratio of UK average disposable income to average house price between 1960 and 1990 is around 3.5; assuming the average number of earners per household is 1.3 and taking the average savings ratio out of disposable income for that period (10%) generates a house-price/consumption ratio of around 3.

Using this value of $[p_0 H_0/c_0]$ allows us to estimate the impact of price shocks on the average owner-occupier. We use values of the other parameters which match the average aggregate figures for the UK over the past thirty years. (In most cases the figures would be little different for the US.) Specifically, we assume: $r = 3\%$; $\delta = 1\%$; $\dot{p} = 1\%$. We use a value of ξ_c of 1.25, implying an elasticity of substitution of consumption of 0.8 (see Mankiw, Rotemberg and Summers (1985), Blanchard and Fischer (1989) and references therein for evidence that the elasticity of substitution is likely to be slightly less than unity). Per capita, real consumption in the UK has on average grown by around 2% per annum over the past thirty years; setting $g_c = 2\%$ implies, by (4.11) that the discount rate, ρ, is 0.5%. Using that value of ρ for each value of ξ_H we can then use (4.9) to calculate $g(\tilde{g})$ as a function of $\dot{p}(\tilde{\dot{p}})$.

Thus we use values of r; ξ_c; ρ; to solve for g and $\tilde{g}$ for various values of ξ_H, $\dot{p}$ and $\tilde{\dot{p}}$. We then use (4.16)–(4.22) to solve for the percentage change in consumption as a function of T and for a value of $[P_0 H_0/c_0]$ which for owner-occupiers equals 3.

Table 4.1 considers a pure level shock to house prices; we set the steady-state growth of real house prices at 1% both pre- and post-shock. A 1% growth figure is marginally lower than the average growth in UK real house prices over the post-Second World War period (see Holmans (1990) and Chapter 3). The level

Table 4.1 Percentage change in consumption of non-housing good for 1% shock to *level* of house prices

T	ξ_h	∞	2	1.5	1	0.7
1		1.418	1.383	1.373	1.353	1.328
5		0.424	0.443	0.449	0.460	0.473
10		0.200	0.229	0.239	0.257	0.280
15		0.118	0.149	0.160	0.181	0.208
20		0.075	0.108	0.119	0.141	0.171
30		0.033	0.065	0.076	0.100	0.133
50		0.002	0.030	0.041	0.067	0.104
70		−0.01	0.016	0.027	0.052	0.094
100		−0.01	0.006	0.016	0.042	0.089
∞		−0.02	−0.01	0.0	0.025	0.243

The figures reported are derived from equation (4.16). As explained in the text (4.16) can be solved for the percentage change in consumption as a function of T, ξ_h, ξ_c, r, ρ, δ, $\dot{p}$, ε and $(\tilde{\dot{p}} - \dot{p})$. We use the following values: $r = 3\%$; $\xi_c = 1.25$; $\dot{p} = 1\%$. For $g_c = 2\%$ these figures imply $\rho = 0.5\%$, which is the value used to derive g and $\tilde{g}$ from (4.9).

shock is set at 1% and the table shows the induced percentage change in current period consumption, i.e. the elasticity of consumption with respect to the level of house prices. The results show that for a value of ξ_H of 2, which implies a user cost elasticity of housing demand of around -0.5, existing home owners with very long planning horizons reduce consumption, but to an insignificant extent, in response to an unanticipated increase in the level of prices. For agents with planning horizons of between 20 and 100 years the impact on consumption is positive, though not large; even with a planning horizon of 15 years the elasticity of consumption to the house price level is only around 0.15. With very short time horizons the effects are much larger as the capital gain more than offsets the higher cost of future housing when agents are nearer the ends of their 'lives'. For a two-year horizon the elasticity of consumption is slightly less than unity.

When ξ_H is unity, implying a higher price elasticity of housing demand and one greater than that suggested by either UK research (King, 1980) or US work (Poterba, 1984), the results are slightly different. First the impact is positive at all horizons — though once again for agents with all but the shortest horizons the effect on consumption is small. For agents with long time horizons the greater substitutability out of housing generates a slightly larger consumption effect than when the user cost elasticity of housing is only one half. Note, however, that for households with a very short time horizon the effect of a level shock on consumption is slightly higher the lower is the substitutability between housing and consumption. The reason that greater substitutability does not generate higher consumption effects at all time horizons is that lower ξ_H (higher substitutability) means higher planned growth of house size; households who had planned to trade up to larger houses increase consumption less after a positive house-price shock. But greater substitutability *per se* goes in the opposite direction and will generate higher consumption effects. These two effects have different relative strengths for households with different time horizons.

When the price elasticity of housing demand is zero ($\xi_H = \infty$) then for households with all but the shortest time horizons the consumption effects of a price level shock are small, both absolutely and relative to when substitutability is higher; when the time horizon exceeds 55 years the impact on consumption is negative.

Tables 4.2 and 4.3 show that in contrast to the effect of price-*level* shocks, the effects of growth shocks are significant for households with long- *and* short-time horizons. The tables show the percentage change in current consumption when there is no change to the level of house prices but a permanent change in the rate of increase. Notice that with a positive growth shock there is an initial fall, but eventual rise, in the user cost of housing; this arises because the higher growth rate of prices immediately reduces the user cost, but as time passes and higher growth drives the level of prices sufficiently high the user cost ($p_t(r + \delta - \dot{p})$) eventually rises. (We can write the ratio of post- to pre-shock user cost for period t as $[(1 + \dot{\tilde{p}})/(1 + \dot{p})]^t \{(r + \delta - \dot{\tilde{p}})/(r + \delta - \dot{p})\}$; for $r + \delta > \dot{\tilde{p}} > \dot{p}$ this ratio is < 1 for small t and > 1 for sufficiently large t).

Table 4.2   Percentage change in consumption for a change in *growth* of real house prices from 1% to 1.5%

T	ξ_h	∞	2	1.5	1	0.7
1		1.474	0.832	0.627	0.232	−0.250
5		1.375	0.790	0.601	0.235	−0.219
10		1.256	0.739	0.570	0.237	−0.180
15		1.147	0.690	0.539	0.240	−0.138
20		1.043	0.641	0.508	0.242	−0.094
30		0.853	0.548	0.447	0.248	0.000
50		0.538	0.374	0.329	0.259	0.216
70		0.292	0.219	0.218	0.269	0.469
100		0.024	0.015	0.064	0.284	0.927
∞		−0.50	−0.91	−0.97	0.444	$+\infty$

The figures reported are derived from equation (4.16). As explained in the text (4.16) can be solved for the percentage change in consumption as a function of T, ξ_h, ξ_c, r, ρ, δ, $\dot{p}$, ε and $(\dot{\tilde{p}} - \dot{p})$. We use the following values: $r = 3\%$; $\xi_c = 1.25$; $\dot{p} = 1\%$. For $g_c = 2\%$ these figures imply $\rho = 0.5\%$, which is the value used to derive g and $\tilde{g}$ from (4.9).

Table 4.3   Percentage change in consumption for a change in *growth* of real house prices from 1% to 2.0%

T	ξ_h	∞	2	1.5	1	0.7
1		2.956	1.932	1.601	0.955	0.152
5		2.785	1.857	1.556	0.965	0.226
10		2.580	1.765	1.499	0.977	0.323
15		2.385	1.674	1.443	0.989	0.424
20		2.200	1.585	1.387	1.001	0.529
30		1.853	1.411	1.276	1.026	0.751
50		1.257	1.082	1.059	1.075	1.247
70		0.766	0.778	0.849	1.124	1.814
100		0.190	0.365	0.549	1.195	2.809
∞		−1.50	−2.08	−1.92	2.024	$+\infty$

The figures reported are derived from equation (4.16). As explained in the text (4.16) can be solved for the percentage change in consumption as a function of T, ξ_h, ξ_c, r, ρ, δ, $\dot{p}$, ε and $(\dot{\tilde{p}} - \dot{p})$. We use the following values: $r = 3\%$; $\xi_c = 1.25$; $\dot{p} = 1\%$. For $g_c = 2\%$ these figures imply $\rho = 0.5\%$, which is the value used to derive g and $\tilde{g}$ from (4.9).

We take the pre-shock rate of increase of house prices as 1% and the post-shock rate first as 1.5% (Table 4.2) and then as 2% (Table 4.3). The tables reveal two things; first for $\xi_H > 1$ the impact of the growth shock on consumption decreases with the agents' planning horizons but remains substantial even for horizons of 60 years. Second, for price elasticities of housing demand in this range (which includes the values which most empirical studies tend to generate) the impact on consumption of a growth shock is negative if the planning horizon is sufficiently long. For a household which looks far enough ahead the long-run tendency of the user cost to rise more than offsets the immediate fall in the user cost and causes the optimal non-housing consumption path to fall.

Table 4.2 shows that when the degree of substitutability between housing and consumption is high ($\xi_H = 0.7$) the impact of growth shocks on consumption is lower (indeed negative) for households with relatively short time horizons but becomes positive and increasingly large for households with planning horizons exceeding 30 years. These households had planned to increase the size of their house significantly through time and so their scope to trade down in the future is great, as is the substitutability between housing and consumption.

Table 4.3 shows how sensitive the effects of changes in the permanent rate of growth of real house prices are to the size of the shock. When growth doubles (1% $\rightarrow$ 2%) the impact on consumption for relatively low levels of substitutability is roughly twice as high as when growth rises from 1% to 1.5%. But at high levels of substitutability ($\xi_H = 0.7$) the results are substantially different. Now the impact on consumption is positive at all time horizons; a household with a time horizon of 30 years — for whom an unanticipated increase in the rate of growth of house prices from 1% to 1.5% was neutral on consumption — increases consumption by 0.75% when the growth rate doubles.

Table 4.4 shows the effects of combining house price level and rate of growth shocks. The natural experiment here is to consider a shock of 1% to the level of real prices which also causes agents to expect prices to consistently rise by 1% higher a year; again we take a base rate of growth of real prices of 1%. In most cases the result is that consumption rises most strongly for agents with the shortest time horizons, though the extent to which the impact falls with the time horizon is quite limited. But once again for agents for whom substitutability is highest ($\xi_H = 0.7$) the results are rather different; here simultaneous positive shocks to house price levels and rates of change have their greatest effect on households with short (two years or less) or fairly long (50 years or more) time horizons; but the

Table 4.4 Percentage change in consumption for a change in the level of house prices (+1%) *and* a change in the growth of real house prices from 1% to 2.0%

T	ξ_h	∞	2	1.5	1	0.7
1		4.403	3.352	3.013	2.350	1.527
5		3.237	2.307	2.005	1.413	0.674
10		2.806	1.994	1.729	1.209	0.559
15		2.526	1.820	1.591	1.141	0.580
20		2.296	1.687	1.491	1.110	0.643
30		1.905	1.469	1.336	1.091	0.822
50		1.271	1.103	1.081	1.102	1.279
70		0.764	0.782	0.855	1.133	1.829
100		0.176	0.356	0.542	1.191	2.808
∞		-1.53	-2.12	-1.96	1.973	$+\infty$

The figures reported are derived from equation (4.16). As explained in the text (4.16) can be solved for the percentage change in consumption as a function of T, ξ_h, ξ_c, r, ρ, δ, $\dot{p}$, ε and $(\dot{\tilde{p}} - \dot{p})$. We use the following values: $r = 3\%$; $\xi_c = 1.25$; $\dot{p} = 1\%$. For $g_c = 2\%$ these figures imply $\rho = 0.5\%$, which is the value used to derive g and $\tilde{g}$ from (4.9).

change in consumption is less than 1% for agents with time horizons in the range 5–35 years.

Tables 4.5 and 4.6 describe the reactions of agents who do not yet own a house at the time of the house-price shock. Here we use the results derived above but set $W_0 = -M_0$ (equation (4.2)) so that $\tilde{W}_0 = W_0$ and the market value of assets is unchanged by the price shock. We assume that these agents had been about to buy a house at the time of the house price shock and that their first home would have cost three times planned consumption. For these simulations all we need do

Table 4.5 Percentage change in consumption for first time buyer from a change in the *level* of house prices (+1%)

T	ξ_h	∞	2	1.5	1	0.7
1		−0.090	−0.042	−0.027	0	0.034
5		−0.090	−0.042	−0.027	0	0.035
10		−0.086	−0.042	−0.027	0	0.036
15		−0.084	−0.041	−0.027	0	0.037
20		−0.082	−0.041	−0.027	0	0.038
30		−0.079	−0.041	−0.027	0	0.039
50		−0.073	−0.040	−0.027	0	0.043
70		−0.068	−0.039	−0.027	0	0.050
100		−0.062	−0.038	−0.027	0	0.053
∞		−0.045	−0.034	−0.028	0	0.243

The figures reported are derived from equation (4.16). As explained in the text (4.16) can be solved for the percentage change in consumption as a function of T, ξ_h, ξ_c, r, ρ, δ, $\dot{p}$, ε and $(\dot{\tilde{p}} - \dot{p})$. We use the following values: $r = 3\%$; $\xi_c = 1.25$; $\dot{p} = 1\%$. For $g_c = 2\%$ these figures imply $\rho = 0.5\%$, which is the value used to derive g and $\tilde{g}$ from (4.9).

Table 4.6 Percentage change in consumption for first-time buyer from a change in the *growth* of house prices (1% to 1.5%)

T	ξ_h	∞	2	1.5	1	0.7
1		1.474	0.832	0.627	0.232	−0.250
5		1.375	0.790	0.602	0.234	−0.219
10		1.257	0.739	0.570	0.237	−0.180
15		1.147	0.689	0.539	0.240	−0.138
20		1.043	0.641	0.508	0.243	−0.093
30		0.853	0.548	0.447	0.248	0.0
50		0.538	0.374	0.329	0.259	0.216
70		0.292	0.219	0.218	0.270	0.469
100		0.024	0.014	0.064	0.284	0.927
∞		−0.50	−0.91	−0.97	0.444	$+\infty$

The figures reported are derived from equation (4.16). As explained in the text (4.16) can be solved for the percentage change in consumption as a function of T, ξ_h, ξ_c, r, ρ, δ, $\dot{p}$, ε and $(\dot{\tilde{p}} - \dot{p})$. We use the following values: $r = 3\%$; $\xi_c = 1.25$; $\dot{p} = 1\%$. For $g_c = 2\%$ these figures imply $\rho = 0.5\%$, which is the value used to derive g and $\tilde{g}$ from (4.9).

is amend (4.16) to

$$[\tilde{c}_0 - c_0]/c_0 = [p_0 H_0/c_0]\{(AB - CA + D)/E + FA)\} \qquad (4.25)$$

where $[p_0 H_0/c_0]$ must now be interpreted as the planned ratio of the value of the house about to be purchased to consumption on the eve of the shock.

Table 4.5 shows the impact of a 1% unanticipated increase in the level of house prices. When the degree of price sensitivity of housing demand is relatively low ($\xi_H > 1$) the effect of the shock on consumption of non-housing goods is negative, though fairly small. The impact is also insensitive to the time horizon of the agents. The intuition behind this is clear: since there is no existing housing wealth, households with short horizons do not enjoy an unanticipated capital gain which they spend over a short period, which is the cause of large consumption effects for home owners who look only a few years ahead. Now the only effect on consumption is the reaction to a higher user cost of housing, which is negative if substitutability between housing and other goods is low. Empirical evidence suggests that for most agents there is a less than unit user cost elasticity of housing demand so a negative impact on consumption is to be expected. If the elasticity is unity (which here implies $\xi_H = 1$) the effect on consumption is neutral since total expenditure on housing is unchanged after the shock to the level of house prices. If the elasticity is higher ($\xi_H = 0.7$) there is a positive effect on consumption which rises with the time horizon of households as the present value of future economies on housing expenditure are larger the longer the planning horizon.

The impact of pure growth shocks is shown in Table 4.6; here we increase the anticipated growth of house prices from 1% a year to 1.5%. The effects on the consumption plans of (about to be) first-time buyers are very different from the impact of level shocks. Unless the price sensitivity of housing demand is very high ($\xi_H = 0.7$) we now see a significant *positive* impact on consumption which is higher the less sensitive is demand to cost. The explanation is straightforward: if ξ_H is very high then from (4.9) the planned growth in optimal house size after the first house is bought is very small; in the limit ($1/\xi_H = 0$) the household will never plan to move to a larger home. In that case since there is no shock to the *level* of house prices the household is able to buy the home it had planned at no extra cost and does not suffer from the larger costs of having to trade up in future at higher prices than had been anticipated. But even for a household that never moves to a larger house there remains the gain from the terminal value of the house being higher; since we assume that agents are able to borrow against future tangible wealth they will increase consumption today. The table shows that this effect is significant. For agents with completely price-inelastic demand for housing the growth shock increases current non-housing consumption by around 1.25% if the planning horizon is 10 years, and by around 0.85% if the planning horizon is 30 years.

If price sensitivity were high ($\xi_H = 0.7$) the household had planned to trade up over its life; the pre-shock planned growth of consumption of housing services would have been $(r - \rho - \dot{p})/\xi_H = 2.1\%$ and after the shock the planned growth of house size would still be substantial (1.4% pa). Now the impact of the growth shock on consumption is negative unless the planning horizon exceeds 30 years.

Tables 4.1–4.6 imply that the consumption effects of house-price shocks are very different depending on whether those shocks affect the level or the growth rate of real house prices. The results also show that for a given type of shock the impact can be highly sensitive to the agent's price elasticity of demand for housing services and to the agent's planning horizon. In general the effect of level shocks are quite small, both absolutely and relative to the effect of growth rate shocks.

Since we are interested in the macroeconomic impact of house price shocks it would be helpful to have a feel for the aggregate impact upon consumption. A crude strategy is to assume a representative household with average characteristics which I will take to be: $\xi_H = 2.0$ (King (1980), using household data, estimates values of price elasticity of demand for housing in the range $-0.5 \rightarrow -0.7$ (Table 3, pp 156); this implies a value of ξ_H in the range $2 \rightarrow 1.5$); $T = 50$; and $(p_0 H_0/c_0)$ (ratio of house value to consumption) = 3 (see above).

At these values Table 4.1 implies a consumption response to a 1% shock to the *level* of house prices of only around 0.03%; thus, a sudden, unanticipated shock of 10% to real house prices which was expected to persist would add less than $\frac{1}{3}\%$ to consumption. But a shock which increased the rate of *growth* of house prices from 1% to 2% would increase consumption by just over 1%.

These results are derived from a model where consumers have point expectations of future incomes and prices; an alternative interpretation is that utility functions imply certainty equivalence. In reality there is obviously major uncertainty over future earnings and prices, while certainty equivalence is an unpalatable assumption (Deaton, 1991, 1992). Both intuition, and also analytical results from Caballero (1990) and Skinner (1988), suggest that uncertainty tends to dampen the response of agents to shocks. The figures in the tables, although fairly low (especially for shocks to house price levels), are therefore likely to be upper bounds on the true response. This conclusion is, of course, conditional on our assumption of forward-looking behaviour.

In the next section we estimate the shocks to UK real house prices over the past thirty years in order to assess whether agents should rationally have altered their views on the growth, or merely on the level, of house prices. We then use these shocks in a model of consumption growth to assess the scale of response in order to see if it is consistent with the simulation results reported here.

4.3 EMPIRICAL EVIDENCE

4.3.1 THE STRATEGY

Ideally we should like to develop a model in which house prices are endogenously determined and the exogenous source of shocks to house prices could be specified.

(Poterba (1984) shows how this might be done in a rational expectations/efficient market setting.) In such a model the source of the shock to house prices, which we do not specify, is likely to be crucial; unexpected changes in the tax treatment of housing, unexpected changes in the availability of land for residential development and unanticipated changes in the relative productivity of the construction sector are all likely to affect the level, and perhaps the rate of change, of equilibrium house prices, but they may have very different effects on behaviour. In the model developed in Chapter 2 we noted that the dynamic response of house prices to these types of shock will differ. But although the transition paths are different for various shocks, in that model there was a static steady state; all shocks can only have long-run effects on the level, and cannot permanently change the growth rate, of house prices.

What we do here is generate a simple time-series model of house-price changes and estimate the impact of unexpected price movements (equation residuals) on consumption. We use seasonally unadjusted, quarterly, aggregate data on the consumption, housing wealth and incomes of the UK personal sector. In the simple model developed in Section 4.2 we assumed that future labour incomes and real interest were known. In any empirical test of the impact of house-price shocks we need to allow for the stochastic nature of interest rates and labour incomes; assessing the impact of income shocks on consumption is essential in this exercise because income shocks are likely to influence house prices, so a failure to allow for the direct influence of such shocks on the growth in consumption will bias any estimates of pure house-price effects.

4.3.2   DATA ISSUES

The basic data we use are constructed as follows:

Consumption (c). This is either total per capita consumer expenditure, or per capita non-durable consumption plus services expenditure, deflated by the appropriate (either total consumption or non-durable consumption) price index. (Source: *Economic Trends*, various issues). The non-durable series excludes consumption of housing services and may therefore be more appropriate; but that series also excludes other components of non-housing consumption which might be expected to have a large wealth elasticity of demand. We use both measures of consumption, but only report in detail results for non-durable consumption.

Labour income (y). This is total, per capita personal sector disposable income minus gross capital income, plus an estimate of the tax paid on capital income. In constructing disposable income National Insurance contributions and income tax are deducted from pre-tax labour incomes; transfer payments (National Insurance benefits and other current grants) are added. The resulting income series is deflated by the appropriate consumer price deflator. (Source: *Economic Trends*, various issues).

Interest rate (r). The nominal rate used to construct r is the quarterly average of the building society mortgage rate (*Financial Statistics*, various issues). In constructing a measure of the *real* rate we will proxy expectations of price changes with an average of past inflation rates with estimated weights.

Nominal house prices (*H P*). These are the Department of Environment mix-adjusted series (see Holmans (1990); source: *Housing Finance*). This series is an index of the market price of all residential properties and is adjusted for changes through time in the size of houses.

Housing wealth. This is the value of residential property owned by the personal sector as reported in the Balance Sheets of the Personal Sector (*Financial Statistics*, various issues). The series is measured per capita and relative to the appropriate consumption price deflator.

Figures 4.1–3 show time series of the variables of interest. Figure 4.1 shows that (unadjusted) per capita real labour income and consumption are, as is well known, seasonal, trending and in the long run move together. Figure 4.2 shows that *changes* in aggregate consumption and in labour income are also highly correlated. Figure 4.3 illustrates how house prices have risen relative to the price of non-durable goods over the past thirty years.

Table 4.7 shows some summary statistics of the time-series properties of the data. Real per capita labour income and both total and non-durable consumption appear to be integrated of order 1 ($I(1)$). Real house prices also appear $I(1)$. These results imply that shocks to incomes and house prices have permanent effects on

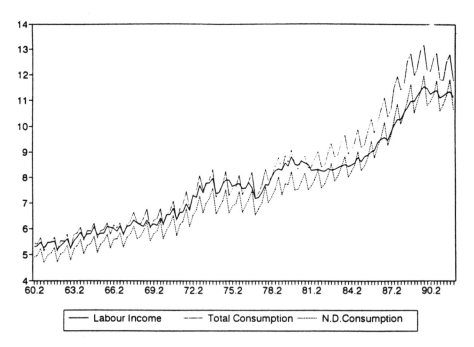

Figure 4.1 Consumption and labour income (real, per capita)

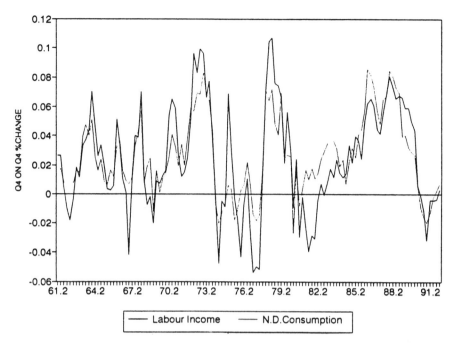

Figure 4.2   Growth of labour income and non-durable consumption (real, per capita)

the levels of the variables; but we can reject the hypothesis that shocks to prices lead to permanent changes in the growth of prices since there is no unit root in the change in (log) real prices. Given that house prices appear to be $I(1)$ then shocks to the level of prices appear to have a permanent effect and correspond to the level shocks analysed in Section 4.2. (See Engle and Granger (1991) for detailed discussion of orders of integration).

Our test involves regressing the change in log consumption on anticipated and unanticipated components of the growth of labour incomes and of real house prices. In constructing the anticipated component of labour income growth we use the fact, noted by Campbell and Deaton (1989), that if consumption smoothing is possible for at least some households savings should help predict changes in future labour income. The predictable component of labour income growth is the fitted value from a regression of income growth on three lags of income growth, two lags of the savings rate and seasonal dummies; further lags proved to be statistically insignificant. As one would expect saving is negatively correlated with subsequent labour income growth (Campbell, 1987).

The predictable component of real house-price changes is based on a regression where the explanatory variables include lags of real house-price changes, lags of real income growth, the lagged mortgage interest rate, and the level of income and of real prices four quarters earlier. Both these prediction equations are shown in

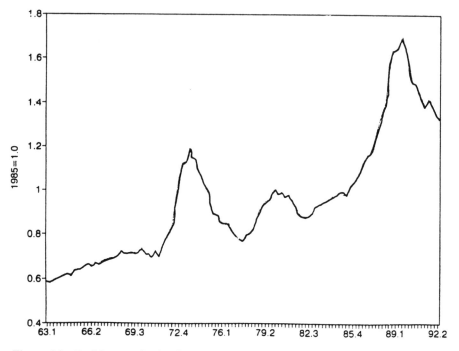

Figure 4.3   Real house-price level

Table 4.8. The fitted values from these regressions are interpreted as the anticipated component of growth. In the case of house prices any effects on consumption of either anticipated or unanticipated components of price changes will depend upon the level of real housing wealth held by the personal sector, so in the consumption equations fitted values and residuals from the house-price regression are scaled by the (lag of) the ratio of gross housing wealth to labour income.

The inclusion of generated regressors in the structural equation for consumption growth and the estimation of that equation by OLS in general creates biased standard errors and inefficient parameter estimates. But as Pagan (1984) shows, under the identifying assumption that the residuals from the prediction equations are uncorrelated with the errors from the structural equation of interest the parameters on shocks are efficiently estimated and the standard errors consistent. Furthermore, under the null hypothesis that anticipated growth in house prices and in incomes have no effect on consumption, all the coefficients and standard errors are consistent. Since we are unable to reject that null, even with standard errors which under the alternative are downwards biased and would therefore make rejection more *likely*, the use of uncorrected standard errors is justifiable. But as a check on this we also estimated the consumption, income and house-price equations as a system imposing, and testing, the non-linear cross-equation restrictions implied by the

Table 4.7 Time-series properties of raw variables

	Const	Number of lags	Sum of lag coeffs.	Level term −1	SE	DW	L4	Period	Mean	Reject unit root at 95% ?
DLY	−0.019 (1.08)	3	−0.18	−0.001 (0.13)	0.020	1.9	7.0	61.2− 92.1	0.0061	no
DDLY	−0.021 (4.62)	2	0.26	−1.179 (7.21)	0.020	1.9	7.0	61.2− 92.1	0.0002	yes
DCN	−0.036 (2.13)	9	0.24	0.0002 (0.04)	0.014	2.0	5.2	62.4− 92.1	0.0063	no
DDCN	−0.036 (2.89)	8	0.21	−0.860 (3.38)	0.014	2.0	5.2	62.4− 92.1	−0.0001	yes
DC	−0.028 (1.4)	10	−0.13	−0.001 (0.11)	0.020	2.0	6.4	63.1− 92.1	0.0061	no
DDC	−0.023 (1.9)	10	3.52	−1.419 (4.12)	0.020	1.9	6.5	63.2− 92.1	0.0001	yes
DPH	0.001 (0.25)	5	0.62	−0.011 (1.27)	0.023	2.0	2.7	64.3− 92.2	0.0071	no
DDPH	0.002 (0.41)	4	0.51	−0.394 (4.30)	0.023	2.0	2.8	64.3− 92.2	−0.0003	yes

All data are seasonally unadjusted; seasonal dummies were included in each regression but are not reported. *DLY* is the first difference of the log of per capita, real labour income. *DCN* is the first difference of the log of real per capita non-durable consumption. *DC* is the first difference of log real, per capita total consumption. *DPH* is the first difference of the log of the real house-price index (the ratio of the mix-adjusted price index to the non-durable consumer price deflator). *DDLY* is the *second* difference of the log of labour income; the same naming convention is used for the other variables. For each regression to determine the order of integration of variables we included sufficient lags of the dependent variable to remove signs of serial correlation in the residuals. The number of lags used is reported in the second column and the sum of their coefficients in the third. 'Level term −1' is the first lag of the dependent variable at one *lower* level of difference: for *DLY* 'level term −1' is LY_{-1}; for *DDLY* it is DLY_{-1} etc. Figures in parentheses beneath parameter estimates are *t* ratios. With 110 degrees of freedom, which is slightly fewer than we have with most of the regressions reported here, the 95% critical value of the *t* statistic on the level term for the rejection of the unit root hypothesis is approximately 3.0 (Mackinnon, 1990).

DW is the Durbin Watson statistic; *L4* is a Lagrange multiplier statistic for testing for serial correlation of up to fourth order, distributed; χ_4^2 under the null; *SE* is the equation standard error.

theory. (We used an iterative SUR estimator which, with the cross-equation restrictions, is asymptotically full-information maximum likelihood). While the system estimation proved feasible for the whole sample, there were convergence problems for the subsamples; we therefore use the system estimates just as a check on the validity of making inferences from the two-step procedure. (In Chapter 6 we consider these econometric problems in more detail and present an alternative means of generating unbiased estimates.)

Table 4.9 shows the (non-durable) consumption growth equation for the whole period and for sub-periods. Unlike in the model of Section 4.2 we do not assume here that expected real interest rates have been constant; we handle variability in ex ante real rates in an ad hoc way by including the lag of the (end of period)

Table 4.8 Income growth and real house-price inflation forecasting equations

			Dependent variable DLY			
	const	DLY_{-1}	DLY_{-2}	DLY_{-3}	SY_{-1}	SY_{-2}
ols	0.012	−0.218	0.178	−0.244	−0.153	−0.186
	(1.41)	(2.39)	(2.15)	(2.88)	(1.85)	(2.15)
sur	0.006	−0.127	0.176	−0.231	−0.264	−0.062
	(0.79)	(1.61)	(2.49)	(3.13)	(3.70)	(0.88)

OLS statistics $R^2 = 0.62$; $SE = 0.0185$; $L4 = 7.59$; $DW = 1.85$;
Period: 1961.2–1992.1; Norm = 0.29; Hetero = 0.61

					Dependent variable DPH						
const	DPH_{-1}	DPH_{-2}	DPH_{-3}	DPH_{-4}	DLY_{-1}	DLY_{-2}	DLY_{-3}	DLY_{-4}	r_{-1}	LY_{-4}	PH_{-4}

ols
−0.354	0.187	0.091	0.031	0.151	0.242	0.234	0.153	−0.165	−1.39	0.18	−0.126
(4.0)	(1.8)	(0.9)	(0.3)	(1.5)	(1.9)	(1.8)	(1.2)	(1.3)	(1.7)	(3.8)	(4.2)

sur
−0.347	0.164	0.074	0.021	0.156	0.262	0.253	0.176	−0.155	−1.51	0.18	−0.122
(4.3)	(1.7)	(0.8)	(0.2)	(1.7)	(2.2)	(2.1)	(1.5)	(1.3)	(2.0)	(4.1)	(4.5)

OLS statistics $R_2 = 0.58$; $SE = 0.023$; $L4 = 14.49$; $DW = 1.84$;
Period: 1964.2–1992.2; Norm = 4.40; Hetero = 14.40

Seasonal dummies were included in both specifications but are not reported. Regressions reported here are the result of a search over specifications which initially included four lags of all variables. SY_{-1} is the first lag of the ratio of a simple measure of aggregate saving (total personal sector disposable income net of total consumption) to labour income. r_{-1} is the lag value of the nominal interest rate on mortgages; LY_{-4} is the fourth lag of the log of labour income; PH_{-4} is the fourth lag of the log real house price index. Norm is the test statistic suggested by Bera and Jarque (1981) for testing the normality of errors assumption; distributed χ_2^2 under the null. Hetero is a test for the independence of squared residuals from squared values and cross-products of the explanatory variables; distributed χ_2^2 under the null of homoscedastic disturbances.

Other variables and statistics are defined in Table 4.7. sur estimates are from the simultaneous estimation of the house price, income and consumption equations reported in Table 4.9; non-linear cross-equation restrictions are imposed.

nominal interest rate and four lags of consumer price inflation; if households use a simple time-series model to predict next-period inflation this specification will allow for changes in ex ante real interest rates.

The table reveals that neither anticipated nor unexpected elements of real house-price changes seem to have had a clear impact on consumption before the 1980s; the estimated effect of house prices is somewhat clearer in the latest period, though still only at the margins of statistical significance. Moreover, the impact of our measure of anticipated house-price changes seems to be little different from the effect of shocks — a result consistent with the theory developed in Section 4.2 only when all house-price changes are unanticipated. An alternative explanation of this finding is that price changes enhance the ability of home owners to borrow and thereby relax binding constraints; if this mechanism were at work anticipated and unanticipated changes in prices would have the same impact on consumption.

Table 4.9 Excess sensitivity and shocks to house prices and incomes

	Dependent variable: Change in Log of Per Capita, Real Non-Durable Consumption				
	64.2–92.1	(sur)	64.2–69.4	70.1–79.4	80.1–92.1
Constant	−0.100	−0.101	−0.14	−0.07	−0.10
	(15.9)	(15.9)	(1.7)	(4.3)	(6.0)
UDLY	0.471	0.475	0.618	0.352	0.497
	(7.0)	(7.8)	(2.4)	(3.9)	(4.7)
ADLY	0.069	−0.023	−0.330	0.103	0.053
	(0.5)	(0.17)	(0.4)	(0.7)	(0.3)
UDPH	0.007	0.006	0.019	−0.010	0.008
	(1.2)	(1.1)	(0.3)	(1.0)	(1.7)
ADPH	0.009	0.009	0.004	0.024	0.011
	(1.4)	(1.4)	(0.2)	(1.8)	(1.4)
r_{-1}	−0.042	−0.064	1.954	−2.17	0.405
	(0.2)	(0.3)	(0.5)	(2.7)	(0.8)
DCP_{-1}	0.078	0.0410	0.397	0.026	−0.157
	(0.9)	(0.5)	(0.6)	(0.2)	(1.0)
DCP_{-2}	−0.168	−0.185	−0.122	0.392	−0.103
	(1.6)	(1.9)	(0.3)	(1.9)	(1.0)
DCP_{-3}	0.134	0.148	−0.027	0.003	−0.057
	(1.5)	(1.6)	(0.1)	(0.1)	(0.7)
DCP_{-4}	−0.124	−0.127	0.020	0.109	0.014
	(1.4)	(1.6)	(0.1)	(0.7)	(0.1)
R^2	0.970	0.972	0.977	0.987	0.991
SE	0.012	0.013	0.014	0.010	0.007
L4	34.72		16.17	7.08	5.85
DW	2.6	2.5	2.8	2.5	2.6
Mean	0.0067	0.0067	0.0098	0.0067	0.0053
Norm	2.70		0.23	12.90	0.41
Hetero	0.01		0.22	0.02	0.26

Data are seasonally unadjusted; seasonal dummies included but not reported. *UDLY* is the residual from the labour income growth equation of Table 4.8 (unanticipated income growth); *ADLY* is the fitted value from that regression (anticipated income growth). *UDPH* is the residual from the real house-price growth equation of Table 4.8, scaled by the lagged ratio of housing wealth to labour income; *ADPH* is the fitted value scaled in the same way. r_{-1} is the lag nominal mortgage interest rate. DCP_{-i} is ith lag of the log difference of the non-durable price deflator. Other notes as above.

The elasticity of consumption with respect to unanticipated house-price shocks implied by the coefficients in Table 4.9 is small. At 1990 levels of housing wealth the effect of a 1% rise in real house prices is to add slightly less than 1/10% to consumption. If we take an estimate of 2 for ξ_H the simulations reported in Section 4.2 suggest that an elasticity of 1/10% of consumption to a permanent shock to the level house prices is consistent with a planning horizon of 20 years.

The full sample coefficients from systems estimation of the consumption, income and house-prices equations are close to the two-step estimates. The two-step standard errors on coefficients are, as Pagan showed, biased relative to the consistent systems estimates, though the size of the bias revealed by Tables 4.8 and 4.9 is small.

Re-estimating the system without imposing the cross-equation restrictions (that variables in the house-price and income equations only influence consumption through their impact on expectations) allowed us to compute a likelihood ratio test of the restrictions. Without making a small-sample correction the test statistic, distributed χ^2_{10} under the null, is 26.3, suggesting rejection of the 10 cross-equation restrictions. But the effective degrees of freedom in the unrestricted system, where 47 parameters are estimated, is only 65; a small-sample correction to the test statistic would reduce the test statistic to 15.1, at which level the restrictions could not be rejected even at the 90% level.

Repeating the regressions using total consumption expenditure revealed that the small impact of house-price shocks was robust to the inclusion of consumption of durables.

4.4   CONCLUSIONS

In this chapter we have shown that the aggregate impact upon consumption of shocks to the *level* of house prices is likely to be small if existing home owners have long time horizons and consider the implications of shocks on the consumption possibilities of their future selves and heirs. If there are permanent shocks to the *growth* of house prices, the effects on consumption are likely to be far higher. But the time-series properties of real house prices suggest that permanent shocks to the level of prices are more likely than permanent shocks to the growth rate. Indeed if we go back to the model of equilibrium in the housing market developed in Chapter 2 all of the shocks considered there — unanticipated changes in the tax treatment of houses and of housing loans, unexpected changes in interest rates, changes in the maximum loan-to-value ratio set by lenders, shifts in the supply of land for construction — affected the steady-state *level* of prices.

Analysis of aggregate UK consumption data seems to confirm the simulation result that house-price shocks have had a relatively small impact on non-housing consumption. The effect is, however, higher in the 1980s than earlier and both anticipated and unanticipated components of price changes seem to influence consumption; these results seem more consistent with a collateral enhancement, or credit-based, effect than with a pure wealth effect.

Of course if agents are either myopic or are not concerned about their heirs, consumption will be more responsive to house-price level shocks. But myopia and/or lack of benevolence to future generations means that the cost of higher consumption by todays' home owners will be paid by their future selves, by the young and by the unborn. *If* consumption effects are substantial it is therefore likely that they will eventually be reversed and it is doubtful whether they should be labelled wealth effects.

One implication of these conclusions is that aggregation of housing wealth with other assets in models of consumer expenditure is unlikely to be valid and liable to generate seriously misleading forecasts of the impact of changes in house prices on the wider economy. A second implication is that it may be the enhanced scope to borrow against housing wealth, arising from financial deregulation and also from increases in the value of collateral against which loans are made (the most important cause of which is rising house prices), that is the key to the importance of housing market conditions for aggregate consumption. In the next chapter we consider such credit effects in more detail.

REFERENCES

Barro, R. (1974) Are government bonds net wealth?, *Journal of Political Economy*, **81**, 1095–1117.

Bera, A. and Jarque, C. (1981) An Efficient Large Sample Test for Normality of Observations and Regression Residuals. Australian National University Working Papers in Econometrics, No 40, Canberra.

Bernanke, B. (1985) Adjustment costs, durables and aggregate consumption, *Journal of Monetary Economics*, **15**, 41–68.

Blanchard, O. and Fischer, S. (1989) *Lectures on Macroeconomics*, MIT Press, Cambridge, Mass.

Caballero, R. (1990) Consumption puzzles and precautionary saving, *Journal of Monetary Economics*, **25**, 113–36.

Campbell, J. (1987) Does saving anticipate declining labour income? An alternative test of the permanent income hypothesis, *Econometrica*, **55**, 1249–73.

Campbell, J. and Deaton, A. (1989) Why is consumption so smooth? *Review of Economic Studies*, **56**, 357–74.

Chow, G. (1960) Tests of equality between sets of coefficients in two linear regressions, *Econometrica*, **28**, 591–605.

Deaton, A. (1991) Saving and liquidity constraints, *Econometrica*, **59**, 1221–48.

Deaton, A. (1992) *Understanding Consumption*, Clarendon Press, Oxford.

Dekle, R. (1989) A simulation model of saving, residential choice and bequests of the Japanese elderly, *Economic Letters*, **29**, 129–33.

Engle, R. and Granger, C. (1991) *Long-Run Economic Relationships*, Oxford University Press, Oxford.

Goodhart, C. (1986) Financial innovation and monetary control, *Oxford Review of Economic Policy*, **2**(4), 79–99.

Hayashi, F., Ito, T. and Slemrod, J. (1988) Housing finance, imperfections and national saving: a comparative simulation analysis of the US and Japan, *Journal of Japanese and International Economies*, **3**.

Holmans, A. (1990) House Prices: Changes Through Time at the National and Sub-National Level. Government Economic Service Working Paper no. 110.

King, M. (1980) An econometric model of tenure choice and demand for housing as a joint decision, *Journal of Public Economics*, **14**, 137–159.

MacKinnon, J. (1990) Critical Values for Cointegration Tests. UC San Diego Discussion Paper, 90–4.

Mankiw, G., Rotemberg, J. and Summers, L. (1985) Intertemporal substitution in macroeconomics, *Quarterly Journal of Economics*, February, 225–51.

Muellbauer, J. and Murphy, A. (1990) Is the UK balance of payments sustainable, *Economic Policy*, **11**, 345–83.

Pagan, A. (1984) Econometric issues in the analysis of regressions with generated regressors, *International Economic Review*, **25**(1), 221–47.

Poterba, J. (1984) Tax subsidies to owner-occupied housing: an asset-market approach, *Quarterly Journal of Economics*, November, 729–752.

Poterba, J. and Manchester, J. (1989) Second Mortgages and Household Savings NBER Discussion Paper No. 2853.

Skinner, J. (1988) Risky income, life cycle consumption and precautionary savings, *Journal of Monetary Economics*, **22**, 237–55.

Yoshikawa, H. and Ohtake, F. (1989) An analysis of female labour supply, housing demand and the saving rate in Japan, *European Economic Review*, **33**, 997–1030.

CHAPTER 5

Housing wealth, bequests and financial liberalization in the major economies; the theory of economies in transition

5.1 INTRODUCTION

In most developed economies the value of the stock of housing exceeds, often substantially, annual GDP; the aggregate implications of changes in the fungibility of that stock are therefore great. We saw in Chapter 3 that housing markets differ significantly between countries. Levels of owner-occupation, ratios of house prices to income and the value of the stock of outstanding mortgage debt are markedly different across economies which in other respects (per capita GDP, population) are similar. In part this reflects variations in regulations on the rental sector, differences in the tax treatment of owner-occupied housing and mortgage debt, and cultural factors which mould attitudes to home ownership (Boleat, 1987). Differences across countries in the ability of households to borrow against housing collateral is also likely to be an important factor and one with implications for aggregate saving as well as for home ownership and house prices. Yoshikawa and Ohtake (1989), for example, argue that the much higher deposit required by Japanese households to buy a house (at least relative to households in the UK and in the US) is a major factor in accounting for that country's high saving rate. In this chapter we consider the implications of possible future convergence in national systems of housing finance.

There are several reasons for believing that the structure of housing finance systems — and in particular the availability of credit — are important. First, and most obviously, the fact that houses cost several times annual income makes the timing and size of house purchase dependent upon the availability of mortgage debt. As a result the price of houses, the level of owner-occupation and also the saving rate are likely to depend upon limitations in the availability of credit. (Hayashi, Ito and Slemrod, 1988; Thurow, 1969; Ranney, 1981; Russell, 1974). Second, those countries in which there were changes in the availability of housing credit during the 1980s, most notably the US, the UK and the Scandinavian countries, experienced unusually rapid growth in consumption, low personal sector savings rates and rapid real house-price inflation (Muellbauer and Murphy, 1989, 1990; Manchester and Poterba, 1989; Summers and Carrol, 1987; Kennedy and Anderson, 1994). This is at least *prima-facie* evidence for the macroeconomic significance of changes in mortgage market conditions. Third, the systems of financing house purchase within Europe may be significantly affected by the abolition of capital controls and the creation of a single financial market. The implementation of EC directives on banking will mean that institutions permitted to offer mortgage products in one country will be able to offer services in all EC countries. Given the huge variation in the type of mortgages currently on offer in different EC countries this expansion in the range of products may have profound implications for savings rates and consumption — at least in those countries where the limited range of mortgage products currently on offer constrains house-purchase decisions. Estimating the extent to which households in the major economies where mortgage debt is relatively low have faced credit restrictions is therefore crucial to an assessment of the implications of greater choice in mortgage products. It is one of our aims in this chapter to gauge the size of pent-up demand for mortgage debt by owner-occupiers in various economies. (In Chapter 8 we will return to the subject of the integration of the markets for household credit within Europe.)

The plan of this chapter is as follows. Section 5.2 reviews some key facts on housing markets in the major economies and briefly describes the systems of housing finance. Section 5.3 presents a simple theoretical model showing the short- and long-run implications of relaxing credit restrictions (and in particular of increasing the fungibility of housing wealth). Section 5.4 presents evidence that in the US and UK the type of credit liberalization analysed in Section 5.3 has taken place. Section 5.5 presents simulation results designed to analyse the extent to which the limited range of mortgage products on offer in most OECD countries constitutes a binding constraint on households. Section 5.6 briefly discusses the implications of possible convergence of housing finance systems on those of the US and UK.

5.2   HOUSING MARKETS IN THE MAJOR ECONOMIES

Tables 3.4 and 3.5 showed levels of home-ownership in various countries. While it is clear from those tables that there is significant variability in owner-occupation rates across countries, no simple hypothesis can account for the differences. Countries of similar size (in terms of population and GDP) display great variability in ownership rates — for example France (54%), Germany (42%) and the UK (68%). A more formal test confirms the absence of any simple link between the standard of living and the pattern of housing tenure. Using data on the 33 most developed economies for 1981 (the last year for which ownership rates were available for all these countries) an OLS regression of owner-occupation levels on GNP per capita gave the following results:

$$OWN = 69.63 \quad -0.0011GNP$$
$$(12.9) \quad (-1.02)$$

$\bar{R}^2 = 0.002$ No of observations=33.

t statistics in parenthesis.

OWN = % owner-occupation rate in 1981.

GNP = 1981 GNP per capita in US dollars.

If anything there is a negative correlation between owner-occupation and income, though the relationship is statistically insignificant and explains virtually none of the variability in ownership rates.

Table 3.4 also showed the ratio of outstanding mortgage debt to income for various countries. Not only is cross-country variability far greater than for owner-ship rates but any link between owner-occupation and the stock of mortgage debt is weak — Italy, with owner-occupation of around 2/3, has a negligible stock of mortgages; Switzerland has the lowest rate of owner-occupation in the developed world but one of the highest levels of mortgage debt. (It is worth noting here that Switzerland is one of the few countries where interest-only mortgages, where none of the outstanding capital is repaid over the life of the mortgage, are widely available (Boleat 1987). Assessing the impact of greater availability of debt with limited repayments through the life of the contract is one of the aims of this chapter.)

Despite great variability in the rates of ownership and in levels of indebtedness, the net housing equity of the personal sector is substantial in all economies. Table 5.1 below reproduces the estimates of the housing equity in various countries from Chapter 3 and also shows some recent, alternative estimates from the BIS (Kennedy and Anderson, 1994); the table also shows estimates of house prices relative to incomes. Both sets of estimates are subject to a wide margin of error because data on the value of houses is not easily available for many countries. But the finding that net wealth in houses accounts for a large proportion of the worth of the personal sectors in the major economies — 70% in Japan (Takagi, 1988), and around 50% in both the US and UK (Takayana et al. 1988; CSO National Income and Expenditure; 1990) — is robust to even substantial errors in measuring house prices.

The average price of new houses in relation to per capita GDP are shown for those countries where reliable estimates can be made (figures for Japan are hard to find because although land value data is available the value of residential buildings is difficult to estimate with any confidence). Again the numbers have to be treated

Table 5.1   International comparisons of housing wealth and house prices

Personal sector net equity in housing relative to GDP		
UK	1.68	(1989)
US	0.73	(1989)
Germany	1.22	(1989)
Japan	2.20	(1986)
France	0.91	(1984)

BIS Estimates of the ratio of net housing wealth to annual household income*

	1980	1990
Australia	2.5	2.9
Belguim	1.8	1.3
Canada	0.5	0.6
Denmark	1.2	0.4
Finland	1.2	2.3
France	1.8	1.9
Germany	2.0	2.2
Japan	2.6	4.9
UK	1.8	2.3
US	1.2	0.8

*Source: Kennedy and Andersen (1994).

Estimates of the average price of new house as proportion of per capita GDP

	1981	end of 1980s	BIS estimate Kennedy and Andersen (1994)
UK	6.4	6.8 (1990)	6.6 (1990)
US	6.3	5.6 (1990)	5.4 (1990)
France	7.6	5.0 (1989)	5.3 (1990)
Germany	10.2	8.7 (1989)	10.6 (1990)
Netherlands	6.4	5.1 (1988)	4.8 (1990)
Sweden	6.2	—	4.1 (1990)
Japan	—	17.9 (1990)	9.2 (1990)
Italy	—	5.8 (1989)	5.7 (1990)
Canada	—	—	5.9 (1990)

Sources: Equity figures in the top panel are from Table 3.5. Figures for 1981 house prices in the bottom panel are all from Holmans (1990) who went to great lengths to construct comparable figures for each country; the estimates for house prices for 1990 and 1989 from the same panel in the table are from various sources and are not always comparable to the 1981 figures, nor to each other. The UK figure for 1990 is the average price of houses bought on mortgage (*Housing Finance*) relative to per capita GDP. The US figure is based on the median price of *new*, one family houses (*US Census Bureau*). The Japanese figure is also based on the average price of *new* properties constructed in Metropolitan areas (data kindly made available by the Real Estate Economic Research Institute in Tokyo); the figure is certainly an overestimate of the price of the average Japanese property since prices in rural areas are much lower than in the cities (the BIS figure for Japan is likely to be more reliable). The figures for prices in Germany, Italy and the Netherlands at the end of the 1980s are based on indices of national prices in Holmans (1991). The French figure for 1989 is based upon estimates in the *Journal of Housing Research*, **3**(1), special issue on housing finance in developed countries

with great caution, though it is clear that an average house represents several years income to a typical household in all of these countries.

As noted, no simple hypothesis can account for the pattern of ownership and mortgage indebtedness revealed in the tables. Numerous factors are relevant to the housing tenure/financing decision, including:

- the tax treatment of capital gains on, and imputed income from, housing;
- the tax deductibility of interest repayments on debt;
- restrictions on the rental sector;
- demographic factors.

These factors differ substantially across countries. For example, at least part of the reason for the high levels of owner-occupation in the UK compared with Germany is the history there of relatively generous tax treatment of mortgage-financed owner-occupation and restrictions on the rental sector (Bank of England, 1991). Restrictions on the rented sectors are also significant in Italy and Japan (Ito, 1988).

One determinant of housing-tenure patterns has been the subject of much research and is the focus of this chapter: the availability of mortgage finance. While it is hard to identify the extent to which the availability of housing finance determines housing-tenure decisions it is clear that actual financing patterns differ greatly between countries. Whether these differences simply reveal differences in the unconstrained demand of households in various countries for different forms of tenure or reflect supply restrictions which themselves determine ownership patterns is the subject of Section 5.4. But first the facts.

First, loan-to-value ratios vary greatly across countries. In the UK and US first-time borrowers have recently been able to finance close to 100% of the purchase price of homes (Bank of England, 1991, Table E, page 61.) In Italy and Germany, in contrast, loans rarely cover more than 50–60% of the value of the house. In Japan down-payment rates of 40% on first-time purchases are usual (Hayashi, Ito and Slemrod, 1988). In France loans can only be made up to a maximum of 80% if they are to be eligible for refinancing on the secondary market.

Second, typical loan maturities are shorter in France (15 years), Germany (Baus-parkassen loans are usually only available up to 12 years), Italy (10–25 years) and Spain (10–15 years) than in the UK and US where 25–30 year loans are common.

Finally, there is far greater scope for explicit equity withdrawal — that is borrowing backed by the collateral of a house which is used for purposes other than house purchase and results in a reduction in the net housing equity — in the US and UK. In the 1980s, for the first time, mortgage products were offered in these countries which have been designed to allow households to consume part of their housing equity. Second mortgages of this type have not been easily available — or at least have not been widely supplied — in most other countries.

In short, people are able to borrow more, and for longer, in the US and UK than in the major continental European countries and in Japan. Furthermore, during the

1980s there came to exist the scope for home owners in the US and UK to take out further loans backed by the collateral in their housing without moving house. I argue in the next two sections that the availability of these forms of debt contract constitutes the most important form of credit liberalization for the personal sectors in these countries and that the implications of this have been, and will continue to be, great. In Section 5.5 I consider the impact that the availability of such loan contracts might have in continental Europe and Japan.

5.3   A MODEL OF CREDIT LIBERALIZATION

5.3.1   PRELIMINARY DISCUSSION

In this section we develop a simple model of the impact of credit restrictions in the market for home loans which allows us to analyse the impact of financial liberalization. We use a similar framework to that developed in Chapter 2 but here we explicitly model bequests of wealth. We do so in order to trace through the implications of greater availability of mortgage debt both for current home owners and for future generations. With such a model we can analyse the time scale over which adjustments to new equilibria are reached after financial liberalization.

There are several types of borrowing restriction which have been analysed in the literature. Hayashi, Ito and Slemrod (1988) present simulations which show the impact on savings and housing tenure decisions of limits on the minimum down-payment for a first-time house purchase in the US and Japan. Dolde (1978) also develops a model to show how lifetime expenditure plans are distorted by the need to build up a down-payment early in the life cycle. But Hayashi, Ito and Slemrod (1988) find that this type of restriction is unable to account for much of the difference in the savings rates of Japanese and US households.

Here we focus on a rather different restriction — namely limits on the ability of households to borrow against *accumulated* housing equity. If such restrictions exist they may constrain owner-occupying households who do not move to a (smaller) house to accumulate substantial housing equity by paying off their first mortgage. Even with lending restrictions such households can release equity, however, by moving to the rented sector or by 'trading down' (i.e. moving to a less valuable house). But either option involves potential costs — moving to a less valuable home forces the household to alter consumption of housing services while benefits stemming from home ownership (security of tenure and capital gains on housing) are forfeited if the decision is made to rent.

The primary reason to focus on limits to equity withdrawal is that in the two countries where liberalization in housing finance came early and has gone furthest — the US and UK — these restrictions are likely to have been substantially reduced. In the US Home Equity Lines of Credit, which allow households to borrow against housing equity when they want to were offered in the 1980s and taken up on a substantial scale. Canner, Fergus and Lucket (1988) report that in 1987 3 million US households had such accounts, the vast majority of which had been taken out within the previous five years. Manchester and Poterba (1989) report that while the real value of first mortgage debt grew at an annual rate of 4.3% between 1980 and 1987, second mortgage debt grew by 23.3% a year. At the end of 1987 second mortgages accounted for 10.8% of the total stock of mortgages. The dramatic growth in such mortgages does not, of course, imply that binding restrictions have been relaxed; it is possible that US households never found it hard to borrow against housing wealth but did not wish to release equity before the 1980s. Zeldes (1989), however, presents evidence that prior to the 1980s households with substantial financial assets behaved in a way consistent with a life cycle/permanent income model of consumption whilst the behaviour of households with substantial housing equity, but relatively low financial assets, was not consistent with the unconstrained maximization of lifetime utility. Zeldes notes that an explanation of his findings was limited ability to borrow against net housing wealth. In the UK banks and building societies offered second mortgages, or top-up loans, in the 1980s. Before 1980 — when the mortgage market was dominated by the building societies and when rationing of loans had been prevalent — such products had not been offered. (For evidence of credit restrictions in the UK prior to 1980 see Meen (1989), Anderson and Hendry (1984), Buckley and Ermish (1983) and Wilcox (1985). For details of the credit liberalization in the 1980s, and on the importance of the abolition of the 'Corset' which limited the growth of bank lending, see Bank of England (1985)).

It is plausible that for some households the demand to release equity in housing in the UK is, and has been, significant; in the past most of this demand would have been frustrated by the limited range of types of mortgage on offer. In the past building societies rationed mortgages, partly as a result of explicit government requests to limit the growth of mortgage debt which were formalized in so-called 'memoranda of agreement'. (Such agreements were allowed to lapse after the election of the Conservative government in late 1979.) Preference for the limited funds available was given by building societies to first-time buyers taking out standard loan contracts; societies considered it their primary duty to provide funds for new buyers to finance house purchase rather than to enable equity withdrawal from the housing market (Boleat, 1986). One effect of this was that the great majority of people who had been owner-occupiers for many years came to hold a large proportion of their wealth as equity in their own homes. This may have reflected the difficulty of unlocking that equity which could generally only be released by moving house and incurring the associated transactions costs. The difficulty of extracting equity was exacerbated by the reluctance of many financial institutions to lend to people nearing retirement. As Goodhart (1986) puts it, 'Prior to 1981/82 the limited, and rationed, availability of mortgages meant that the existence of a huge hoard of excellent personal sector collateral, in the form of unencumbered house values, went unutilized ...'.

The changes in the housing finance market in the US and the UK may have given people substantially greater flexibility over financing house purchase. US and UK households are now in a better position to make decisions on house purchase and on the size of their mortgages as part of a wider portfolio decision, rather than something solely to do with picking a space to live. The repercussions of this are great. Once the level of mortgage gearing on a house becomes a choice variable which is at least partly independent of the real decision about where to live, the options for lifetime consumption and saving look very different. Decisions on the level of bequest left by a household can, for example, be made independently of housing tenure if financial institutions are willing to let people top up mortgages in old age. Given the importance of bequests as a determinant of total savings the effects of greater flexibility in financing are potentially large. (Kotlikoff and Summers (1981) estimate that at least 70% of wealth in the US is attributable to bequests rather than life-cycle savings.) It is the repercussions of a greater degree of independence between these real and financial decisions which is the subject of this chapter.

5.3.2   THE MODEL

We use a similar set-up to that introduced in Chapter 2, but adapt it in several ways. We will abstract from the complexities of the tax system and also assume that there is a single interest rate, but we explicitly model bequests to future generations and inheritances from previous ones. Households last for period T and are indexed by i, $i = 1, \ldots, I$. Household utility depends upon consumption of housing services, consumption of other goods (c) and bequests. Bequests equal terminal net wealth (W_T). Consumption goods are the numeraire with a price of unity; they can be bought from domestic or overseas firms. Units of housing (assumed perfectly divisible) can be bought at a price of p. Consumption of housing services in any period is proportional to the number of units of housing held (H). Households receive labour income from the provision of a fixed amount of labour per interval of time at a constant real wage of w; all output from work is paid out as wages so w is the average productivity of labour in the economy. There are no profits. Households receive, or pay, interest at rate r on (gross of mortgage debt) financial wealth (S_t). Households receive a non-negative bequest (denoted W_{T-1}) from the previous generation of the dynasty L periods from the end of the household's life and leave a non-negative bequest for their heirs (W_T) at time T. Thus, successive generations of the same family line overlap by $T - L$. (One could think of individuals in the economy living for 75 years — the first 25 years as part of their parents household, the remaining 50 years as part of their 'own' household; thus $L = 25$; $T = 50$ and people are born as their great-grandparents die and set up home at the time of their grandparents' funeral). The utility derived from terminal wealth reflects concern for the welfare of the next generation. Some households may derive no utility from leaving bequests.

Each household makes a decision on its housing at the date of that household's formation, 0. (Thus 0 is specific to households though it is the same for households within a particular cohort; where confusion can be avoided household-specific subscripts will be omitted.) We assume for the moment that there is no rented sector and all households make a once and for all decision on house purchase at 0. (The simulation exercise of Section 5.5 is designed to estimate the degree to which restrictions on equity withdrawal bite in various countries; in some of these countries (most notably Germany) rental markets are relatively unrestricted and in Section 5.5 the option to rent is considered). We assume, for simplicity, that houses do not depreciate and require no maintenance; it would not be hard to allow for these factors.

The type of credit liberalization we analyse is one which changes the fungibility of housing wealth; more specifically we consider an increase in the amount of debt that an *existing* home-owner can have. We do not model changes in the availability of debt to first-time buyers; there are no changes in the required deposit of house buyers. We focus on restrictions to established households, the easing of which is likely to have greater effects on bequests than are changes in the availability of credit to first-time buyers. We shall, in fact, assume that buyers are able to borrow up to the full value of a house. Initial household financial wealth is zero and a mortgage (denoted M) for the full value of the house is taken out at 0. Repayments on the mortgage are made each period (m_t); these are the sum of interest on the outstanding loan $(M_t r)$ and any repayment of principal.

Depending on conditions in the market for housing finance, households may have some flexibility over the size of mortgage debt which is outstanding at time T. When there are no credit restrictions in the market for housing finance, households are able to choose how much capital to repay over the life of the mortgage. Households wishing to reach their terminal date, T, with a level of equity in their homes less than 100% (i.e. $M_T > 0$) are allowed to do so. To be specific, when there are no restrictions in the mortgage market we allow households to arrange a mortgage contract with a financial intermediary such that mortgage payments made over the life of the household leave an outstanding balance at T of any amount up to the value of the house. When credit restrictions are in place there will be an upper limit to the outstanding balance on a mortgage at time T; in such cases there is effectively a lower limit to housing equity held by the household at T. For some households this will be a binding constraint and will affect the level of bequest and the size of house purchased.

We assume throughout that there are no taxes. All agents have perfect certainty over future incomes, prices and the time of death. The population of households is assumed constant at I; the number of households buying a house for the first time within any period is therefore proportional to I and equals the number of houses coming on to the market from the liquidation of the estates of households who have reached the end of their lives.

In continuous time household i's maximization problem can be written

$$\max \quad U_i = \int_{t=0}^{T} e^{-\rho t} U(H, c_t) \, dt + e^{-\rho T} \phi(W_T, p_T) \qquad (5.1)$$

subject to

$$S_T \geq 0 \qquad (5.2)$$

$$M_T \leq \beta(p_T H) \qquad\qquad 0 \leq \beta \leq 1 \qquad (5.3)$$

where
$$\left. \begin{array}{l} W_T = S_T + p_T H - M_T \\[4pt] \dot{S}_t = rS_t + w - c_t - m_t \\[4pt] S_{T-L} = \int_{t=0}^{T-L} \dot{S} \, dt + W_{T-1} \end{array} \right\} \quad (\text{for } t \neq T - L)$$

$$(5.4)$$
$$(5.5)$$

$$M_0 = p_0 H \qquad (5.6)$$

$$m_t = (M_0 - M_T)\tilde{r} + M_T r \qquad (5.7)$$

$$\tilde{r} = r/(1 - e^{-rT}) \qquad (5.8)$$

$U(H, c_t)$ is the instantaneous, time-separable and time-invariant utility function describing preferences over consumption of housing services and of consumption goods. U is assumed to be increasing, twice differentiable and concave in its arguments. We assume that demands for housing services and for the consumption good are normal. $\phi(W_T, p_T)$ is the utility of terminal wealth (or bequest). The utility derived from a bequest of size W_T is assumed to depend upon the real value of that wealth at T, which is a function of the relative cost of housing to consumption goods (p_T). ρ is the discount rate. Equation (5.4) defines terminal wealth; the sum of financial wealth and housing equity (the value of the house net of any outstanding mortgage). Equation (5.5) describes the evolution of gross financial saving, taking into account the receipt of any bequest from the previous generation at $T - L$. Equations (5.7) and (5.8) define the constant-repayment schedule which pays off the original loan, minus any terminal balance, over the life of the household — households face a choice between paying off a high proportion of the principal when alive (low M_T, high m_t) or paying off a significant part of the mortgage out of the estate (high M_T, low m_t). Notice from (5.3), (5.6) and (5.7) that if β is large enough and if p_T exceeds p_0 by a significant amount m_t could be negative; if households can keep borrowing against rising housing wealth and house values appreciate significantly, then home owners could liquidate their capital gains through time and use their home as a source of income. Financial wealth and housing equity at T have to be non-negative. On top of these restrictions credit limits may constrain households to repay more of their mortgage out of lifetime earnings than they would wish (equation (5.3)). In this model credit restrictions are varied through changes in the limits on the householder's terminal mortgage — i.e. through variations in β. This seems the most natural way to vary households' flexibility in accumulating housing equity.

The financial sector comprises intermediaries who take deposits from households and from overseas and lend the proceeds. Aggregate net overseas deposits with the domestic financial sector are denoted S_F. We assume that each financial intermediary can always raise deposits at the world rate of interest, r. Competition drives the loan rate to r. Aggregating across financial intermediaries and domestic households we have the balance sheet of the financial sector:

$$\sum_{i=1}^{I} M_{it} = \sum_{i=1}^{I} S_{it} + S_{Ft} \qquad (5.9)$$

If the stock of mortgages outstanding at t, $\sum_{i=1}^{I} M_{it}$, is greater than domestic savings, $\sum_{i=1}^{I} S_{it}$, then net deposits of the overseas (or foreign) sector with domestic financial intermediaries, S_{Ft}, are positive. If total domestic financial savings exceed total mortgages, domestic financial intermediaries are holders of net deposits with overseas financial intermediaries on behalf of the domestic personal sector ($S_{Ft} < 0$). These deposits earn the world rate of interest r.

Using the equation describing the evolution of household saving, (5.5), and the balance sheet of the financial sector, (5.9), we can show the relation between financial flows and the balance of payments.

From (5.4), (5.5) (5.6) and (5.9), and letting the repayment of mortgage debt of established households equal the excess of m_t over $r M_t$, we can derive

$$I w - \sum_{i=1}^{I} c_{it} - p_t \dot{\bar{H}}_t = r S_{Ft} - \dot{S}_{Ft} \qquad (5.10)$$

where the total stock of housing is denoted $\bar{H}$ and the number of new houses built at t is $\dot{\bar{H}}_t$. (We will focus below on the simplest case where the supply of houses is completely inelastic, i.e. $\dot{\bar{H}} = 0$.) Equation (5.10) says that the total of domestic production (which is simply total household income of $I w$), *minus* consumption expenditure and the value of new houses built, equals net accumulation of claims on the rest of the world ($-\dot{S}_{Ft}$) plus interest paid (or minus interest received) on outstanding indebtedness to the overseas sector. The left-hand side of (5.10) is just the balance on the trade account which must equal the net interest due abroad plus net accumulation of overseas assets.

Equilibrium with and without Credit Rationing

We begin by characterizing equilibrium with no rationing in the market for housing finance in Section (5.3.3), then consider the effects of limits on the size of mortgages (i.e. $\beta < 1$) in Section 5.3.4, and finally analyse the transition path from a constrained to an unrestricted economy (Section 5.3.5).

5.3.3   EQUILIBRIUM WITH NO RATIONING

The first-order conditions for a household facing no mortgage restrictions are straightforward:

$$\dot{c}_t = [r - \rho]/\varepsilon_t \tag{5.11}$$

where $\varepsilon_t = -U_c''(C_t, H)/U_c'(C_t, H)$;

$$U_c'(c_T, H) \geq \phi_W'(W_T, p_T) \tag{5.12}$$

with equality if $W_T > 0$;

$$\int_0^T U_H'(c_t, H) e^{(T-t)\rho} \, dt = U_c'(c_T, H)[p_0 e^{rT} - p_T] \tag{5.13}$$

Equation (5.11) implies that consumption is rising (falling) throughout the household's life if $r > \rho$ ($r < \rho$). Equation (5.12) says that a household which leaves a bequest, in the absence of binding credit restrictions which constrain it to have more wealth at T than is desired, equates the marginal utility of final period consumption with the marginal utility of bequest. Equation (5.13) characterizes the optimal house purchase. The condition is that the marginal lifetime benefit from the services flowing from an extra unit of housing equals the utility from the consumption foregone through spending more of lifetime wealth on housing. The cost of a marginal unit of housing is expressed in terms of final period spending power foregone $[p_0 e^{rT} - p_T]$; this cost depends upon the purchase price of housing units (p_0), the selling price (p_T) and the interest rate. In static equilibrium, with no capital gain or loss on housing, the cost of housing in terms of final period spending power is simply $p(e^{rT} - 1)$. (This is, effectively, the user cost of housing in our model where taxes, depreciation and uncertainty are ignored.)

It is very hard to derive any results on the nature of general equilibria for the economy without further strong assumptions. A key question we wish to address is the way in which credit restrictions in the market for housing finance have different effects on households with different preferences over housing and bequests. We therefore allow households to have different preferences, but we make the strong assumption that different generations of the same family line, or dynasty, share their ancestors' preferences. This assumption means that if, at unchanging house prices, one generation chooses to bequeath to its heirs a level of wealth equal to that which it received, then the next generation—facing the same prices—exactly reproduces the same lifetime expenditure plan. (See A.1 of the Appendix for conditions under which such an equilibrium exists. Atkinson (1974) derives conditions under which a much simpler economy will have a static equilibrium of bequests; his results depend on specific forms for utility functions.) If a reproducing equilibrium does exist we can use the first-order conditions derived above to characterize various types of household behaviour which would exist in it. It is useful to describe three, mutually exclusive and exhaustive, types of dynasty: (1) those that receive and

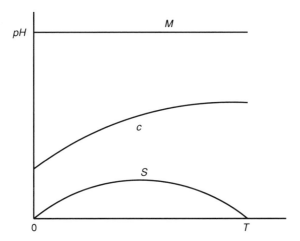

Figure 5.1   No bequest dynasty

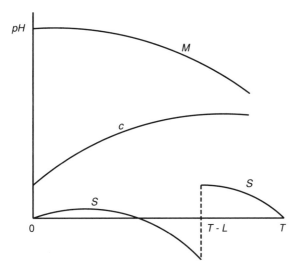

Figure 5.2   Positive bequest dynasty

choose to leave no bequest; (2) those that receive and choose to leave a positive bequest which is less than the value of their house; (3) those that receive and choose to leave a bequest which exceeds the value of their house. The lifetime spending plans of a typical household of each of these three types of dynasty are shown in Figures 5.1, 5.2 and 5.3, which show plans for households with $r > \rho$. (See Section A.2 of the Appendix for proofs that for dynasties in equilibrium the evolution of consumption must be as in one of these figures.)

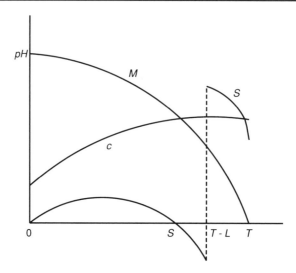

Figure 5.3 Dynasty with bequest greater than house value

5.3.4 EQUILIBRIUM WITH RATIONING

The equilibrium expenditure plans depicted in Figures 5.1–5.3 are for an economy with no credit restrictions. We can derive similar expenditure patterns for a credit-restricted economy. The first-order conditions for households in a credit-restricted economy will differ from those above. With an upper limit of $\beta(< 1)$ on the proportion of the value of a house which can be mortgaged at T the optimal lifetime plan satisfies

$$\int_0^T U'_H(c_t, H) e^{(T-t)\rho} dt = U'_c(c_T, H) p_0 e^{rT} - p_T [\beta U'_c(c_T, H)$$
$$+ (1 - \beta)\phi'_W(W_T, p_T)] \tag{5.14}$$

$$U'_c(c_T, H) \geq \phi'_W(W_T, p_T) \tag{5.15}$$

equation 5.15 holds, with equality only if the credit constraint does not bite.

For households for whom the restriction does not bite this condition is as before since $U'_c(c_T, H) = \phi'_W(W_T, p_T)$. But for households who would otherwise prefer to leave a bequest less than $(1-\beta)$ of the terminal value of their house, the effective user cost of housing changes. Comparing the right-hand sides of equations (5.13) and (5.14) reveals that a binding credit constraint increases the effective user cost of housing because $U'_c(c_T, H) > \phi'_W(W_T, p_T)$ for the credit-restricted. Other things (in particular bequests received) equal households for whom credit restrictions bite will therefore demand smaller houses. The same argument can be used to show that the effect of easing credit conditions is to increase the demand for housing. (See Section A.3 of the Appendix for proofs.) Notice that the perfectly

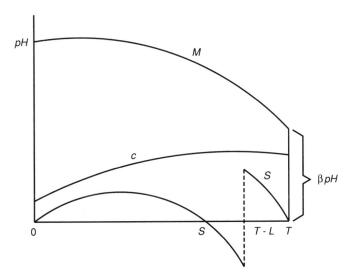

Figure 5.4   Credit restricted dynasty

foreseen limitation on equity withdrawal affects housing purchase at the start of the household's life and influences consumption throughout the household's life; it is not only housing and consumption decisions in old age that are affected by limits on β.

This simple argument is clearly partial in nature since it compares housing demand in a credit-restricted world with the household's unrestricted demand holding constant house prices and the bequest received. But if credit restrictions had been in force, bequests, and possibly house prices, would have been different. The first-order conditions (5.11), (5.14) and (5.15) would still hold and can be used to characterize optimal expenditure plans. Indeed we can consider an economy in credit-restricted reproducing equilibrium and characterize lifetime plans for households in different types of dynasties. As before there will be three types of dynasty — those wishing to bequeath more than the value of their home will follow plans as depicted in Figure 5.3; households bequeathing less than the value of a home but for whom the credit restriction does not bite behave as in Figure 5.2; restricted households follow a plan as shown in Figure 5.4. (See Section A.4 in the Appendix.)

5.3.5   THE TRANSITION PHASE

We analyse transitional and long-run effects of easing credit conditions using the model developed above. We assume that restrictions are *unexpectedly* and *completely* removed at a particular date; furthermore we assume that restrictions had been in place for long enough for a credit-restricted equilibrium of the type described above to exist.

We characterize the transition path by first considering the demand for houses from the first generation of households to be formed in the new, liberalized credit regime. The supply of existing houses to this generation is fixed, being equal to the stock of houses owned by the oldest generation. At unchanged house prices the total demand for housing from the new generation exceeds sales by the oldest generation since new households from dynasties which had been credit restricted have higher demands than their ancestors. The nature of the transition depends on how house prices react to this excess demand, i.e. upon the elasticity of supply of new houses. We consider the simplest case where the supply of housing is fixed. (For an analysis of the case where housing is in elastic supply see Miles (1990)).

The demand for housing of new households who would have been credit-rationed rises when restrictions are removed. But with a fixed supply of houses coming on to the market each period the price must rise to reduce the demand from new households for whom restrictions would not have been binding. The increase in the price of housing has an immediate implication: the lifetime plans of *all* new households and of many established households will now change as a result of the removal of restrictions. All established households will find that the real value of planned bequests — in terms of consumption goods — will rise when house prices increase unless planned terminal savings (S_T) are changed. Households who had intended to leave a bequest greater than the value of their home will be able to compensate by reducing S_T. These households will certainly find it optimal to increase consumption over the remainder of their lives since their heirs do not need to be fully compensated for changes in the price of housing. Concavity of the cost function implies that some of the capital gain on housing can be spent by the existing household while passing on a bequest which gives their heirs no lower utility. The greater is substitutability between housing and consumption goods, the greater will be this increase in consumption. Note that householders who had purchased a house just before the easing of restrictions, who we can think of as being in their twenties or thirties, will increase consumption smoothly over the rest of their lives.

The dynamic adjustment for the various types of dynasty following the easing in credit conditions when the supply of housing is fixed are particularly rich. The overall adjustment for the economy will generally have the following features:

(1)   An immediate increase in house prices to clear the market for first-time buyers.

(2)   An increase in the stock of mortgages outstanding which, given a fixed stock of housing, constitutes equity withdrawal.

(3)   A prolonged reduction in the stock of financial savings held by established households who had already owned a house when restrictions are eased and who had intended to bequeath more than the value of their house. This effect

lasts for $T - L$ periods, i.e. until the last household formed in the restricted credit regime dies.

(4) An immediate and sustained deterioration in the trade account. The deficit is the counterpart to the increased consumer spending of established households who consume some of their capital gain and to the new-found ability of the credit-hungry to have mortgages with low capital repayment schedules. Thus most of the extra spending comes from households who are a long way from the end of their lives.

(5) During the (lengthy) transition period following the removal of restrictions the housing stock becomes more concentrated in the hands of those who tend to have a lower preference for bequests — these types of household being those whose predecessors found credit restrictions binding and under-consumed housing. The demand for the *services* of housing of these households is high relative to their desire to hold houses as *assets* to bequeath to their heirs. Consequently average mortgage gearing for these households is high.

(6) The total stock of houses is fixed but there is a redistribution in home owner-ship away from those who, in the absence of financial liberalization, would not have been credit-restricted anyway. There is a corresponding rise in the average size of houses owned by the first generation of households from previously credit-restricted dynasties. After a period of length L new gener-ations from these dynasties may demand smaller houses as the bequests they receive are lower. As a consequence the path of house prices through time is quite possibly non-monotonic. (See A.5 of the Appendix for proofs of these transition effects.)

In effect the domestic economy emerges from the credit-restricted era with the scope to liquidate part of its portfolio of housing wealth but without having to cut back on its consumption of housing services. Since the equity in housing had been forced to high levels by credit restrictions it is not surprising that credit liberalization causes housing equity to fall — but the only way that housing equity for the aggregate economy can be reduced is via trade deficits (or a reduction in surpluses) which are the means by which housing units are transformed into consumer goods. Financial intermediaries facilitate this transformation of assets by allowing the overseas sector to indirectly build up its stake in the housing sector by financing the increased demand for mortgages of domestic residents. Effectively domestic residents have sold part of their houses for foreign cars, videos and exotic holidays while continuing to live in their homes.

5.4 EQUITY WITHDRAWAL AND CONSUMER SPENDING IN THE UK AND US

The model developed in the previous section shows the implications of removing binding restrictions on households' ability to withdraw housing equity. I argued in

Section 5.2 that in the 1980s households in the US and UK became able to withdraw equity more easily. If restrictions had been binding prior to that, we should expect equity withdrawal to have increased and household savings to have fallen as excess housing equity was liquidated and was used to finance extra consumption. In this section I present some preliminary evidence that this occurred in the 1980s. In chapters 6 and 7 we consider how to test this hypothesis more formally. I consider first the UK.

Table 3.6 showed the value of equity withdrawal — the difference between net lending for house purchase and net expenditure on housing. The equity withdrawal figure is simply derived from an identity which takes the aggregate of net new lending backed by housing collateral and subtracts actual expenditure on residential housing. There is nothing behavioural here; equity withdrawal simply measures funds which are raised from mortgage lending and are not used to finance residential investment or home improvements. That table showed that net new lending rose sharply in the 1980s. More significantly, in the second half of the 1980s equity withdrawal was about a third of total new lending and from 1986 was greater than £10 billion a year. This extraction of funds from the housing market was, in an accounting sense, more than enough to account for the decline in the personal sector saving ratio and about the size of the current account deficits which were sustained in 1987, 1988 and 1989.

Although consistent with the process described in Section 5.3 no clear link is established by these trends. Only if a high proportion of the funds which leaked out of the housing market was used to finance consumption, rather than to acquire financial assets or to pay off other forms of debt, can the fall in the savings rate be accounted for. A more direct test of the model is to assess whether funds raised by the personal sector in the housing finance market, in excess of new investment, were used to finance consumption. What we need to measure is the proportion of equity withdrawn which gets spent — the propensity to spend from withdrawn equity.

Adapting the consumption function estimated by Pesaran and Evans (1984, hereafter PE) to allow for the effects of credit liberalization in the housing market allows us to assess this propensity. The PE model, which was estimated on UK data up to 1981, was designed to allow for the effects of credit constraints; the size of the coefficient on current income in an equation explaining total consumption was rationalized in terms of credit constraints which made a specification in terms of lifetime resources inappropriate. Furthermore, the model outperformed the specifications preferred by Deaton (1977); Davidson *et al.* (1978); Ungern-Sternberg (1981) and Muellbauer (1983) — see Section 5.5 of PE.

Table 5.2 shows four versions of the PE model. (I am grateful to Christopher Stewart for these regressions.) In all cases the dependent variable is (the quasi-difference of) savings out of personal income — a transformation of total consumption expenditure. (Variables are exactly as in PE where data construction and sources are described). The first column shows the results from OLS estimation of the basic model using PE's original data. (This is equation (10), p. 245 in PE).

Table 5.2   Explaining UK household saving* (t statistics in parenthesis)

	(1)	(2)	(3)	(4)
Current income	0.468	0.419	0.275	0.340
	(10.9)	(8.2)	(3.8)	(5.3)
Intercept	−27 208	−67 520	−34 873	−46 354
	(−6.9)	(−5.3)	(−1.9)	(−2.9)
Real financial	−0.0465	−0.0437	−0.0459	−0.0444
asset	(−4.0)	(−3.2)	(−2.3)	(−2.5)
Real capital gains:				
on equities	−0.0306	−0.0282	−0.0323	−0.0301
	(−4.3)	(−3.5)	(−2.6)	(−2.8)
on gilts	0.0147	0.0249	0.0067	−0.0060
	(0.3)	(0.4)	(0.1)	(−0.1)
on money	−0.098	−0.121	−0.136	−0.016
	(−0.7)	(−0.8)	(−0.6)	(−0.1)
Equity withdrawal				−0.785
				(−3.5)
Standard error	0.0059	0.0065	0.0101	0.0087
Period	1953–81	1953–81	1953–88	1953–88
LM test for first order residual				
autocorrelation; under null $\approx \chi_1^2$			2.90	0.063

*Dependent variable is the quasi-difference of savings out of personal income. (See Pesaran and Evans (1984) for exact details.)

The second column is an identical specification but using the latest official data for the original period. Only the intercept is significantly different; this mainly reflects the rescaling of variables due to the change to 1985 price data. (Diagnostic statistics for the re-estimated equation are similar to those for the original PE equation which are reported at length in their paper.) Column (3) is the result of re-estimating the model of column (2) using an extra eight years of data so as to cover the period of low savings and the peak years of equity withdrawal. Column (4) simply includes equity withdrawal in the PE specification. We set this variable to zero prior to 1978 on the grounds that the uses to which households were able to put funds borrowed against housing equity was then limited; the propensity to consume out of measured equity withdrawal is therefore likely to have been small and, more importantly, different from in the later period.

If binding credit restrictions were *not* eased in the early 1980s there is no reason for the equity withdrawal variable to be significant and the specification which PE found adequate to explain consumption up to 1981 should stand the test of time. We should stress that no claim is made here that measured equity withdrawal is an exogenous variable; clearly consumption and financing decisions are simultaneous. The aim of including the withdrawal variable is to answer a specific and rather narrow question — namely what was mortgage lending which was not used to finance housing expenditure used for. (One can view the strategy as taking the residuals from the PE equation — consumption not explained by their credit-restricted specification — and seeing if this extra spending tracks equity withdrawal.) Two alternative hypotheses to the story outlined in the previous section would imply that the link between extra consumption and equity withdrawal should be weak: (1) equity withdrawal is used to pay off more expensive debt; (2) withdrawn equity is used to accumulate financial assets, possibly to increase future transfers to offspring so that they can buy a house despite rising real house prices. (If this last hypothesis were true, one should only expect equity withdrawal adjusted for house-price changes — i.e. our measure minus the change in the value in the housing stock — to influence consumption; given the rapid rise in UK house prices in the 1980s one should then expect the marginal propensity to spend out of our measure of equity withdrawal to be negligible.)

Columns (3) and (4) reveal two things. First, there was a significant reduction in the goodness of fit in the PE specification after 1981; the equation consistently overpredicted savings in the 1980s and there are signs of serial correlation in residuals. Second, the equity withdrawal variable is significant in the extended specification, substantially improving the fit of the equation and implying that almost 80% of measured equity withdrawal directly increased consumers' aggregate spending. There are no signs of error autocorrelation with specification (4). If 80% of equity withdrawal was spent on consumption, the impact of liberalization in 1988 (when the personal sector saving rate was at its lowest) was such as to account for the fall in savings from the levels of the late 1970s.

For the US, Manchester and Poterba (1989) address the same question — what are the uses to which extra loans backed by housing collateral have been put — but in a rather different way. They use micro data on household balance sheets to assess where second mortgage debt went. This question has particular relevance in the US since one explanation for the dramatic rise in second mortgage debt is that the 1986 Tax Reform Act caused a switch from tax-exempt borrowing to tax-sheltered mortgage debt. If true this would undermine the argument that the growth in second mortgages accounts for part of the decline in the US savings ratio. In fact, Manchester and Poterba present evidence that is consistent with the results reported above for the UK. They directly estimate how much of the funds raised by households in the 1980s from taking out second mortgages contributes to a decline in household net worth. Using a large sample of household data they find that 75% of second mortgage lending contributes to a reduction in net worth. This figure is close to the estimated propensity to consume (78%) out of equity withdrawn implied by the UK aggregate, time-series regression in Table 5.5. If greater use of second mortgages in the mid-1980s did *not* represent a response to credit liberalization that had limited household consumption there would be no link between this particular type of extra borrowing and reductions in net worth.

Finally, we note that an influential argument *against* the hypothesis that in the past many US households had faced binding constraints on releasing housing equity, has limited force against the story outlined in the previous section. Venti and Wise (1990) present evidence that elderly US households rarely trade down in old age to release housing wealth and that those that do move house do not move to cheaper homes. Their interpretation is that the demand to release equity is low. But an alternative interpretation is that limited house moves by the elderly tells us something about the costs, both financial and psychic, of moving from a home in old age. Indeed the story outlined in Section 5.4 *assumes* that the trading-down route to equity withdrawal is prohibitively costly; if this is a reasonable hypothesis Venti and Wise's results are exactly as one should expect.

5.5   ESTIMATING THE IMPACT OF CREDIT LIBERALIZATION IN EUROPE AND JAPAN

In this section I aim to estimate the impact that greater ease of withdrawing equity from the housing market might have upon households with substantial net housing wealth in continental Europe and in Japan. To do so it is necessary to estimate what proportion of home owners in those countries find current limitations on the ability to raise second mortgages binding. Clearly if there are no costs in moving to the rented sector in old age, or if the desired bequests of households are in excess of housing equity, constraints on the availability of second mortgages will not bind. I attempt to gauge how many households are affected by limited availability of second mortgages by simulating a discrete time, calibrated model which uses a particular functional form for household utility consistent with the model of Section 5.3. The use of simulations to gauge the extent of credit restrictions in housing markets has become popular in recent years (see Hayashi, Ito and Slemrod (1988) and, in particular, Dekle (1989)).

We focus on households who are current owner-occupiers and who have paid off any mortgage on their home. Such households are likely to be nearing the end of their working lives. Furthermore, owner-occupation rates amongst households nearing the end of their working lives are substantially higher in most countries than amongst the generality of households so that the question I address is relevant for a high proportion of elderly agents. (Dekle (1989) reports that in Japan the owner-occupation rate amongst the over-60s is 85%; in France the owner-occupation rate amongst 50–64 year olds was 65% in 1984 compared with average owner-occupation rates of 51% (Holmans 1990); in Germany around 55% of households with heads in the age range 50–60 are owner-occupiers).

The questions I ask are these: What types of household with 100% home equity would wish to take out a second mortgage? In the absence of a market for second mortgages, what types of household would move to the rented sector and use part of the proceeds from house sale for present consumption?

The optimization problem facing the household is similar to that analysed in Dekle (1989) and is to maximize at time t a rest-of-life utility function of the form:

$$U_t = c^{1-a}/(1-a) + (sH)^{1-a}/(1-a) + \theta(W_T/p_T)^{1-a}/(1-a)$$

where

c is rest of life consumption of non-housing goods

H are units of housing

s is a parameter converting units of housing into a flow of housing services

W_T/p_T is the level of bequest measured in terms of housing, i.e. period T total net worth deflated by the real price of housing p_T.

$T - t$ is the remaining life of the household

θ is a parameter reflecting the degree of benevolence to heirs

a is the reciprocal of the elasticity of substitution.

Households are assumed to have 20 years left to live and own an average size (and value) house at t when decisions are made. Households then make a once-and-for-all decision on rest-of-life housing tenure. Households face three options as regards housing — they may stay in the current home and (credit markets allowing) take out a new mortgage to be repaid out of the value of the estate in 20 years time; they may move to a similar home in the rented sector; or they may remain in the family home without taking out a new mortgage. I assume that if households choose the rented option the utility they receive from the housing services is the same as if they owned the home. (This assumption almost certainly biases the results *against* finding binding credit restrictions.) Note that by making the utility of the bequest depend on the value of the estate in terms of housing we assume households consider the implications for their heirs of changes in real house prices.

The budget constraint facing the household 20 years from death is :

$$Y = c + (S - M)/(1 + r) \qquad \text{if the household remain}$$

$$W_T = S + p_T H - M \qquad \text{owner-occupiers}$$

$$Y + p_t H - \text{RENT} = c + S/(1 + r) \qquad \text{if the household moves}$$

$$W_T = S \qquad \text{to the rented sector}$$

where

Y is the present value at t of all *non*-housing wealth plus the present value of future income

p_t is the value of a unit of housing in terms of consumer goods at t

S is gross *financial* wealth at $t + 20$ $(t + 20 = T)$

M is the size of any mortgage outstanding at T

r is the rest-of-life interest rate (if the annual interest rate is 2.5% with 20 years left to live $r = 0.64$)

RENT is the present value at t of annual rental payments over $T - t$ of the real interest rate times the start-of-year value of the rented house.

Assuming that the rental rate is the real rate of interest in terms of consumer goods implies that the rent charged does not fall when real house price inflation increases; owners of rented buildings do not pass on the gains from appreciating house values to renters. Given the tax treatment of real (in consumer goods) capital gains on non-owner-occupied housing in most countries it would be inconsistent to have all the benefits of capital gains passed on to renters in lower rent; we make the rather extreme, simplifying assumption that none of the pre-tax benefits are passed on by landlords. The key point here is that provided at least some of the capital gain is not passed on it will always be preferable to release equity by taking out a mortgage rather than move to the rented sector if house prices are rising.

The mortgage at t is allowed to be as great as $p_T H/(1 + r)$; if a household had a maximum mortgage and accumulated no other financial assets by T this would generate $S_T = 0$; $M = P_T H$ and the bequest would be 0. *Second mortgages thus allow households to leave zero bequest without moving into the rented sector.*

For given values of the parameters, of the interest rate and given a rate of real house-price inflation we can calculate maximum utility from renting and owner occupying, both with and without the option of a second mortgage. Household pick housing tenure to maximize utility subject to the constraints.

We take as our base case a value of $\theta = 2$, which is that used by Dekle, who notes that for a 20-year real interest rate of unity (an annual rate of around 3.5%) this value is consistent with leaving a bequest such that all future generations could use it to consume indefinitely the same level of non-housing goods as the current household. This represents a high level of benevolence. We take a base value for the elasticity of substitution of 0.25 ($a = 4$) but experiment with higher values of 0.50 ($a = 2$) and 1.0 ($a = 1$). (Campbell and Mankiw (1989) estimate the elasticity of substitution to be much nearer 0 than 1).

Table 5.3 shows the housing tenure and mortgage decisions for householders with various levels of non-housing wealth for our base case of $\theta = 2$, $a = 4$, and with an annual real interest rate (in terms of consumption goods) of 2.5%. We use a 2.5% increase in real house prices as our base; this is the average annual real increase in house prices of Japan, Germany, UK, US and Italy in the 1980s (Bank of England (1991), p. 63, Table H). This figure of 2.5% is also the average annual increase in the real price of UK housing over the period 1945–90 (see Table 3.3).

We measure Y in terms of the proportion of the value of the house which the period t net present value of all other (human and financial) wealth represents. For

Table 5.3   Base case: interest rate = rate of house price inflation = 2.5% pa; $\theta = 2$; $a = 4$

Y	Mortgage available			No mortgage available
	Tenure	Remortgage?	Mortgage	
0.2	owner occ	yes	45%	rent
0.4	owner occ	yes	36%	rent
0.5	owner occ	yes	31%	own
0.8	owner occ	yes	18%	own
1.1	owner occ	yes	4%	own
1.2	owner occ	no	—	own
2	owner occ	no	—	own
3	owner occ	no	—	own

example, if the house price to average economy earnings ratio were 4, a retired householder with 20 years of retirement pension equal to 30% of average earnings whose real value grew at the real rate of interest would have $Y = 1.5$.

The table reveals that only householders with non-housing wealth of 1.2 times the value of their home, or less, would want to take out a second mortgage. A householder with $Y = 0.5$ would want to take out a second mortgage of 31% of the value of their home. If second mortgages were not available householders with Y less than 0.5 would choose to move to the rented sector.

To know how many householders would want to remortgage requires information on the distribution of income amongst elderly householders. For the US we can get some idea by using data on the median income of retired householders relative to average earnings. Summers and Carrol (1987) report a figure of around 40% for 1980. The ratio of the median value of recently purchased US homes to median annual household income at the start of the 1990s was around 4 (*US Annual Abstract of Statistics*). Thus a *very* crude measure of average Y is $(20* 0.4)/4.0 = 2.0$. Table 5.3 shows that householders with less than 60% of this value of Y would want to remortgage.

Note that if there were no restriction on second mortgages no householders would want to move to the rented sector because the real cost of housing for owner occupiers is always lower than the cost of renting if the real price of housing rises. Given our assumption that the rental cost of housing is equal to the real interest rate, then only if the real price of houses is constant are households indifferent between renting and owner-occupying.

Table 5.4 shows the impact of lower real interest rates. If real house prices rise at an annual rate of 2.5% while real interest rates are 1% all households with $Y < 1.3$ remortgage. Householders also take out larger mortgages; if $Y = 0.5$ the householder now mortgages 40% of the home. If real interest rates fall to zero all householders with $Y < 1.35$ take out mortgages. But with real interest rates as high as 3% and with a constant real house price only householders with $Y < 0.6$ remortgage.

Table 5.4 Annual real interest rate = 1%; rate of house price inflation = 2.5% pa

Y	Mortgage available			No mortgage available
	Tenure	Remortgage?	Mortgage	
0.2	owner occ	yes	55%	rent
0.4	owner occ	yes	45%	rent
0.5	owner occ	yes	40%	rent
0.8	owner occ	yes	25%	own
1.1	owner occ	yes	9%	own
1.2	owner occ	yes	4%	own
2	owner occ	no	—	own
3	owner occ	no	—	own

If the benevolence parameter is halved to 1/4, and with the interest rate equal to the rate of increase in real house prices of 2.5% per annum, all householders with $Y < 1.4$ take out second mortgages; if second mortgages are not available households with $Y < 0.7$ move to the rented sector. Varying the elasticity parameter has a significant effect on the results. With other parameters at their base values but with a higher elasticity of substitution of $\frac{1}{2}(a = 2)$ the critical value of Y beyond which households would not want to remortgage rises from 1.2 to 1.4; the size of second mortgages also rises; at $Y = 0.5$ the mortgage rises from 31% to 38%. If utility is logarithmic ($a = 1$) all householders with $Y < 2.0$ remortgage.

Finally Table 5.5 shows the impact of higher rates of real house-price inflation. With 4% appreciation, and other parameters at base values, all households with $Y < 1.35$ take out mortgages. Because of substantial capital gains only the poorest households ($Y < 0.3$) would choose to move to the rented sector if second mortgages were not available.

What do these simulation results tell us about the potential demand for second mortgages in Europe and Japan? First, for nearly all parameter values households with a level of non-housing wealth below 70% of the value of their home would want to remortgage unless moving to the rented sector were costless. (Note that non-housing wealth includes the present value of all future incomes, including pension rights.) The higher are house prices in terms of other wealth the greater proportion of households fall into this group. Second, the demand for remortgages is somewhat sensitive to expected real house-price inflation. Both in Japan and the UK annual real house-price increases exceeded 4% per annum over 1980–89; in both countries real house prices subsequently fell. If there were a return to expectations of high real house-price inflation — say at 4% — then our results imply that households with non-housing wealth worth less than 130% of their house would want to remortgage. If house prices were four times average annual incomes (almost certainly an underestimate for Japan, where Horioka (1988) estimated the average price of a house as between 4.5 and 9 times average household income for 1987, before the explosion of land prices of the late 1980s) then even highly benevolent

Table 5.5   Interest rate = 2.5%; rate of house price inflation = 4.0% pa

Y	Mortgage available			No mortgage available
	Tenure	Remortgage?	Mortgage	
0.2	owner occ	yes	62%	rent
0.4	owner occ	yes	51%	own
0.5	owner occ	yes	46%	own
0.8	owner occ	yes	30%	own
1.1	owner occ	yes	13%	own
1.2	owner occ	yes	8%	own
1.3	owner occ	yes	2%	own
2	owner occ	no	—	own
3	owner occ	no	—	own

($\theta = 2$) households in retirement in these countries would need annual retirement income more than a third of average working wages *not* to remortgage. Any retired couple relying solely on a UK government pension, which was worth about 25% of average male earnings in 1990, would want to take out a second mortgage in this situation.

But in countries where expected real house-price inflation were low only the poorest households would want to remortgage. Real house prices in Germany, for example, fell slightly in the 1980s whilst Italian house prices are estimated to have risen at only 0.9% per annum (Bank of England, 1991). The simulations suggest that the cut-off level of non-housing wealth beneath which households in these countries want to remortgage might be around two-thirds the level in Japan or the UK. For example, with no real capital gain and an interest rate of 2.5% then with a house price/average income ratio of 4 only retired households with beneath 20% of average earned income would remortgage.

Data on the replacement ratio of retired households — that is the average value of retirement income relative to average earnings of all households — suggest that very few elderly households in Germany and France would want to remortgage given our simulation results. Ratios of state old-age pensions for retired couples to average manufacturing wages in France and Germany were 75% and 49% (in 1980) respectively (Aldrich, 1982). Adding in private pensions increases the average replacement ratio for Germany to around 80% (*Luxembourg Income Study Data File*, 1988). For households with no other source of income who had 20 years left to live that ratio would imply a level of non-housing wealth of 16 years in terms of manufacturing wages. A ratio of house prices to average annual manufacturing wages as high as 6 would then imply a value of Y of 2.7 — well in excess of the cut-off point below which non-housing wealth is low enough to make remortgaging desirable. But in Japan replacement ratios are lower and the value of a typical house higher. Aldrich (1982) estimates replacement ratios for an average Japanese couple relying on a state pension at 61%. Only 9% of Japanese receive regular income from private pension schemes in addition to their public pension. Using a 61% replacement ratio and a ratio of house prices to average manufacturing earnings of 8 (towards the upper end of Horioka's range of estimates for 1987) gives an average value of Y for Japan of 1.5. This is only slightly higher than the cut-off value of 1.3 implied by our base-case parameters and using an expected rate of house price inflation of 4%.

5.6 CONCLUSIONS

The theoretical model developed in this chapter suggests that the effects of allowing equity withdrawal from the housing market upon saving, consumption, bequests and house prices may be both substantial and prolonged. We presented preliminary evidence that in those countries where borrowing for existing owner-occupiers against the value of housing has become easier — the US and UK — there has been a significant impact upon saving. Finally, we addressed the issue of the possible implications of the greater availability of housing credit upon households in countries where financial liberalization has furthest to go. Countries with high house values and where expectations of rising real house prices may be deeply embedded — e.g. Japan — are likely to feel the greatest impact of liberalization. But in Germany and Italy (where real house prices were broadly flat in the 1980s) and in France (where, as in Italy, the state pension of the elderly is substantial relative to average earnings) the absence of second mortgages may constitute a binding credit restriction for only a small number of households. The extent to which further credit liberalization in housing finance markets in continental Europe, which allows existing owner-occupiers to borrow against accumulated equity, boosts consumption may not be substantial.

Changes in the down-payment requirements on first-time buyers, however, might have quite different effects. This is an issue to which we will return in Chapter 8. In the meantime we take a closer look at the evidence from countries where credit restrictions have already been eased. In the next two chapters we shall first use aggregate, and then household, data to analyse more closely the links between house values, credit flows and saving.

REFERENCES

Aldrich, D. (1982) The earnings replacement rate of old age benefits in 12 countries 1969–1980, *Social Security Bulletin*, November, 3–11.

Anderson, G. and Hendry, D. (1984) An econometric model of United Kingdom building societies, *Oxford Review of Economics and Statistics*, **46**(3), 185–210.

'Atkinson, A. (1974)' — Review of Economic Studies, Vol 14, No. 1.

Bank of England (1985) The housing finance market: recent growth in perspective, *Bank of England Quarterly Bulletin*, March, 80–91.

Bank of England (1989) The housing market, *Bank of England Quarterly Bulletin*, February, 66–77.

Bank of England (1991) Housing finance — an international perspective, *Bank of England Quarterly Bulletin*, February, 56–66.

Boleat, M. (1986) *The Building Society Industry*, 2nd edition, London, Allen and Unwin.

Boleat, M. (1987) *National Housing Finance Systems — a Comparative Study*, Croom Helm, London.

Buckley, R. and Ermisch, J. (1983) Theory and empiricism in the econometric modelling of house prices, *Urban Studies*, **20**, 83–90.

Campbell, J. and Mankiw, G. (1989) Consumption, Income and Interest Rates: Reinterpreting the Time-series Evidence. NBER Discussion Paper, No. 2924.

Canner, G. Fergus, J. and Luckett, C. (1988) Home equity lines of credit, *Federal Reserve Board Bulletin*, June, 361–73.

CSO (1993) *Financial Statistics*, HMSO.

Daily, L. and Turner, J. (1990) Private Pensions in 9 Countries 1970–1988. In *Pension Policy: An Alternative Perspective*, US Department of Labour, Washington.

Davidson, J. Hendry, D. Srba, F. and Yeo, S. (1978) Econometric modelling of the aggregate time-series relationship between consumers' expenditure and income in the UK, *Economic Journal*, **88**, 661–92.

Deaton, A. (1977) Involuntary saving through unanticipated inflation, *American Economic Review*, **67**, 899–910.

Dekle, R. (1989) A simulation model of saving, residential choice and bequests of the Japanese elderly, *Economic Letters*, **29**, 129–33.

Dolde, W. (1978) Capital markets and short-run behaviour of life cycle savers, *Journal of Finance*, **33**, 413–28.

Goodhart, C. (1986) Financial innovation and monetary control, *Oxford Review of Economic Policy*, **2**(4), 79–99.

Hayashi, F., Ito, T. and Slemrod, J. (1988) Housing finance, imperfections and private saving: a comparative simulation of the US and Japan, *Journal of Japanese and International Economies*, **3**(2), 289–304.

Holmans, A. (1990) House Prices: Changes Through Time at National and Sub-national Level. Government Economic Service Working Paper no. 110.

Holmans, A. (1991) House Prices, Land Prices, The Housing Market, Housing Purchase, Debt and Personal Savings in Britain and Other Countries. Department of the Environment, London.

Horioka, C. (1988) Saving for house purchase in Japan. In *Global Role of the Japanese Economy with Affluent Savings and Accumulated Wealth*, Fifth International EPA Symposium, Economic Planning Agency, Tokyo.

International Housing Finance Factbook (1987), International Organisation for Housing Finance Institutions, London.

Ito, T. (1988) Comments on Horioka (1988) in *Global Role of the Japanese Economy with Affluent Savings and Accumulated Wealth*, Fifth International EPA Symposium, Economic Planning Agency, Tokyo.

Kennedy, N. and Andersen, P. (1994) Household Saving and Real House Prices: an International Perspective. BIS Discussion Paper No. 20, January.

Kotlikoff, L. and Summers, L. (1981) The role of intergenerational transfers in aggregate capital formation, *Journal of Political Economy*, **89**(4), 706–32.

Manchester, J. and Poterba, J. (1989) Second Mortgages and Household Savings, NBER Discussion Paper No 2853.

Meen, G. (1989) The ending of mortgage rationing and its effects on the housing market: a simulation study, *Urban Studies*, **26**, 240–52.

Miles, D. (1990) Financial Liberalisation, the Current Account and Housing Markets, Birkbeck College Discussion Paper in Financial Economics.

Muellbauer, J. and Murphy, A. (1989) Why Has UK Personal Savings Collapsed? Credit Suisse First Boston Research Paper, July.

Muellbauer, J. and Murphy, A. (1990) Is the UK Balance of Payments Sustainable? *Economic Policy*, **11**, 345–383.

Pesaran, M. and Evans, R. (1984) Inflation, capital gains and UK personal savings: 1953–1981, *Economic Journal*, **94**, 237–57.

Ranney, S. (1981) The future prices of houses, mortgage market conditions and the returns to home ownership, *American Economic Review*, **71**, 323–33.

Russell, T. (1974) The effect of improvement in the consumer loan market, *Journal of Economic Theory*, **9**, 327–39.

Summers, L. and Carrol, C. (1987) Why is US saving so low? *Brookings Papers on Economic Activity*, **1**, 607–35.

Takagi, S. (1988) Trends of Japanese savings and wealth and recent developments in national accounts in Japan. In *Global Role of the Japanese Economy with Affluent Savings and Accumulated Wealth*, Fifth International EPA Symposium, Economic Planning Agency, Tokyo.

Takayama, N. *et al.* (1988) Household asset holdings and the saving rate in Japan. In *Global Role of the Japanese Economy with Affluent Savings and Accumulated Wealth*, Fifth International EPA Symposium, Economic Planning Agency, Tokyo.

Thurow, L. (1969) The optimal lifetime distribution of consumption expenditures, *American Economic Review*, **59**, 324–30.

Ungern-Sternberg, T. von (1981) Inflation and savings: international evidence on inflation induced income losses, *Economic Journal*, **91**, 961–76.

Urban Housing Finance (1988), OECD, Paris.

Venti, S. and Wise, D. (1989) Aging, moving and housing wealth. In *The Economics of Aging*, edited by D. Wise, Chicago University Press, Chicago.

Wilcox, J. (1985) A Model of the Building Society Sector. Bank of England Discussion Paper No. 23.

Yoshikawa, H. and Ohtake, F. (1989) An analysis of female labour supply, housing demand and the saving rate in Japan, *European Economic Review*, **33**, 997–1030

Zeldes, S. (1989) Consumption and Liquidity Constraints: an empirical investigation, *Journal of Political Economy*, **97**, 305–335.

APPENDIX

In this appendix we prove several results stated in the text.

A1   EXISTENCE OF A REPRODUCING EQUILIBRIUM

The lifetime utility of a household depends upon the bequest received (W_{T-1}), the wage earned (w), the interest rate (r), the price of housing at 0 and T (p_0, p_T), and (for some households) on credit conditions in the housing market (β). Housing demand, consumption in any period and the bequest left to the next generation will depend upon these exogenous (to the household) variables. We can write the bequest left by a household as

$$W_T = G(W_{T-1}, w, r, p_0, p_T, \beta)$$

Since different generations of the same family are assumed to have the same preferences this function will have the same form for different households, or generations,
of the same dynasty. For given values of the other exogenous variables the bequest
left can be written as a function of the bequest received:

$$W_T = G(W_{T-1})$$

We seek conditions under which an equilibrium in bequests exists, i.e. conditions
under which there exists for each dynasty a W_T^* such that

$$W_T^* = G(W_T^*).$$

With no interest paid on savings ($r = 0$) and unchanging house prices, the assumption that demands for housing and for the consumption good are normal is sufficient
to guarantee a unique, stable equilibrium for each dynasty, and therefore for the
economy; households would always choose to spend some, but not all, of an increment to lifetime wealth on their own consumption, and $G'(W) < 1$ everywhere.
In general provided the $G(W)$ function cuts a 45° line from above, a stable equilibrium exists (Figure A5.1); but the assumption that housing and consumption are
normal goods is not sufficient to ensure this — if r is positive it is always possible

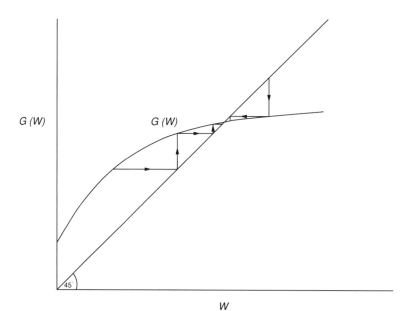

Figure A5.1   Stable bequest equilibrium

for households to use some of an increased bequest received to increase lifetime expenditure whilst passing on at least 100% of the higher inheritance. What we require is that the marginal utility of bequest should, beyond some level of bequest, fall sufficiently relative to the utility from lifetime expenditure that any increase in inheritance received is less than fully passed on. For plausible values of the real return on saving this seems a reasonable condition.

Note that we assume, but have not proved, that the price of houses is unchanging around an equilibrium. What we can show is that if a bequest equilibrium is reached and there is a large number of households then house prices are unchanging: the supply of houses coming on to the market in any period reflects house purchases by the cohort of oldest households T periods before. Since the population is stable and the characteristics of new cohorts will, in aggregate, match those of earlier cohorts, demand for new houses will match supply at the same prices as T periods before, *provided* that bequests received by the new households are the same as for their ancestors. In a bequest equilibrium this final condition holds by definition.

A2   LIFETIME EXPENDITURE PLANS FOR AN ECONOMY WITH NO MORTGAGE RESTRICTIONS

We show that expenditure and bequest plans for a household with $\rho < r$ are as depicted in Figures 5.1, 5.2 or 5.3 in the text. Households fall into one of three categories:

$$(1) \; W_T^* = 0; \qquad (2) \; 0 < W_T^* < pH^*; \qquad (3) \; pH^* < W_T^*$$

where $*$ denotes the optimal value of a variable.

Case (1). $W_T = 0$ implies that $S_T = (pH - M_T) = 0$ since plans must satisfy $S_T \geq 0; M_T \leq pH$. It follows immediately that households never repay any capital on their mortgage. Because households of this type receive no bequest and have constant earned income it also follows that $S_t > 0$ for all t, where $0 < t < T$, since otherwise the first-order condition that requires consumption to rise through time (equation (5.11)) could not hold. Expenditure plans are therefore as in Figure 5.1.

Case (2). $W_T < pH$ implies that either $pH - M_T = W_T$ and $S_T = 0$ or $pH - M_T < W_T$ and $S_T > 0$. Since the interest paid on mortgages equals the interest received on savings households are indifferent between these; we assume for simplicity that other things being equal, households will pay off mortgage debt, so $W_T = pH - M_T$ and $S_T = 0$. Since $M_T > 0$ households pay off some, but not all, of the capital on their mortgages over their lives. Households will receive an inheritance at $T - L$ equal to their terminal wealth. To ensure $S_T = 0$ this inheritance will be spent by T; for a large inheritance, or if L is small, this means that the optimal consumption plan will involve negative financial assets ($S < 0$) just before $T - L$, as depicted in Figure 5.2.

Case (3). $W_T > pH$ implies $S_T > 0$ and $M_T = 0$ (assuming again that, other things being equal, households pay off mortgage debt). Households pay off all their mortgage and hold financial assets at T. They will receive a large (relative to the size of their home) bequest at $T - L$. As with Case (2) households, if L is small this will usually generate $S < 0$ just before $T - L$, which is the case shown in Figure 5.3.

A3   THE IMPACT OF MORTGAGE RESTRICTIONS ON HOUSING DEMAND

We prove that the demand for housing is, other things being equal, lower for a household facing a binding mortgage restriction. Let the unrationed optimal house size for a household receiving a given bequest be H_u and the bequest handed on by the unrationed household be $W_{Tu}(< pH_u)$. H_u and W_{Tu} satisfy (5.12) and (5.13) above. Holding the bequest received fixed, imposes a binding mortgage restriction on the household. Such a restriction implies that $(1 - \beta)p_T H_u > W_{Tu}$. There are two effects of the restriction: first it requires a reduction in lifetime expenditure by the household to finance the higher bequest (a wealth effect); second there is a relative price effect since the restriction only relates to finance of housing and not to consumption (a substitution effect). The relative price effect can be measured by evaluating the right-hand side of (5.14) with and without mortgage restrictions. The right-hand side of (5.14), divided by $U'_c(c_T, H)$, is the relative cost of housing in terms of (final period) consumption. With no credit restrictions $\phi'_W(W_T, p_T) = U'_c(c_T, H)$ and the relative price is $(p_0 e^{rT} - p_T)$; with credit restrictions the relative price is

$$p_0 e^{rT} - p_T[\beta + ((1 - \beta)\phi'_W(W_T, p_T)/U'_c(c_T, H))]$$

Since $U'_c(c_T, H) > \phi'_W(W_T, p_T)$ the relative price of housing rises. Assuming the demand for housing services is normal, both wealth and substitution effects go in the same direction and the demand for housing services falls.

A4   LIFETIME EXPENDITURE PLANS FOR THE CREDIT-RESTRICTED HOUSEHOLD

A household for whom mortgage restrictions bite is forced to bequeath at least $(1 - \beta)pH$, where β is the lowest proportion of an initial mortgage (assumed to be of size pH) which can be outstanding at T. Since the restriction is binding $S_T = 0$. In reproducing equilibrium credit-restricted households will receive an inheritance of $(1 - \beta)pH$ at $T - L$. If either β or L is small, households will tend to have negative financial assets just before $T - L$. These debts will be paid off out of the inheritance, leaving positive financial wealth at $T - L$, which are run down over the remaining L years (Figure 5.4).

A5   PROPERTIES OF THE TRANSITION PATH — FIXED SUPPLY OF HOUSING

We show conditions under which the transition path has features (1)–(6) described in Section 5.3.5

(1) We showed above that after mortgage restrictions are removed the first generation of households from dynasties that had been credit restricted have higher demand for housing services. At unchanged house prices all other households have unchanged demand. With a fixed stock of housing the supply of housing units coming onto the market in any period is predetermined and equal to the housing owned by the dying generations. It follows that the price of housing has to rise to clear the market when mortgage restrictions are removed.

(2) The stock of mortgages rises after restrictions are removed as the value of new mortgages granted (which equals the value of first time purchases) rises in line with house prices whilst repayments on existing mortgages are unchanged.

(3) Established households who had intended to bequeath more than the value of their house increase consumption when mortgage restrictions are removed. Suppose not. The value of the bequest left would then be $p_T^{\uparrow} H + \bar{S}_T$ where $p_T^{\uparrow}$ is the (perfectly foreseen) post-restriction price of housing units at the time the household dies; $\bar{S}_T$ is the stock of terminal savings on an unchanged consumption plan. This bequest differs from the restricted equilibrium bequest because mortgage restrictions are unexpectedly removed and $p_T^{\uparrow}$ is different from the restricted price of housing. By concavity of the cost function the utility of any future generation of the dynasty which receives a fully indexed (against changes in the relative price of housing) bequest rises if prices vary. We showed that prices will vary when restrictions are removed; it follows that if the current generation leaves $\bar{S}_T$ the utility value of the bequest to the heirs rises. Concavity of the bequest function implies that the marginal utility of bequest to the established household would then fall; with $S_T > 0$ condition (5.15) implies that consumption over the remainder of the household's life must rise as a consequence. It follows that $S_T < \bar{S}_T$.

(4) With a fixed housing stock equation (5.10) shows that the trade balance will deteriorate if aggregate consumption rises when restrictions are removed. We therefore consider the consumption of all the possible types of householders who exist when restrictions are removed and show that aggregate consumption will generally rise: By A.5 (3), we know that established households with planned $S_T > 0$ increase consumption when restrictions are removed.

Established households with planned $S_T = 0$ will only reduce consumption if they plan to leave a higher bequest, in terms of units of housing, when house prices rise. This is only optimal if housing demand is inelastic and if the bequest fell significantly short of the value of the home; otherwise heirs would be made better off, which is not consistent with lower consumption for the established household. As $\beta \rightarrow 0$ a greater proportion of established households will respond to the removal of credit restrictions by increasing consumption, since the value of the bequest becomes close to the value of the house and concavity of the cost function implies less than full compensation to future generations for changes in house prices. In the UK it is plausible that β had been close to zero before credit liberalization in the 1980s; we conclude that the removal of mortgage restrictions will have increased the consumption of virtually all households already established at that time.

It remains to consider the consumption of new households.

New households for whom credit restrictions would not have been binding substitute away from housing whose price rises to clear the market. The bequest they will receive in future is sufficient to keep their lifetime utility from falling as a result of credit liberalization (otherwise their parents would not be in a bequest equilibrium). It follows that with a positive substitution effect in favour of consumption and no offsetting income effect consumption for these new households is higher.

The new households for whom credit restrictions are eased demand larger houses but are able to pass on lower bequests to their heirs — consumption for this group is not unambiguously higher. The closer β was to 0 in the restricted regime the greater was the restriction and the higher is the bequest they receive. The ability to spend this bequest in itself boosts lifetime consumption. Since a value of β close to 0 is plausible this wealth effect on the new households is large; wealth effects upon consumption are therefore likely to exceed negative substitution effects for the first generation of households in the new regime.

We have shown that the consumption of some types of household in the wake of the removal of credit restrictions is unambiguously higher; for other groups, low values of β (which are plausible) make increases in consumption likely. It follows that the trade balance generally deteriorates, and for a prolonged period, when credit conditions are eased.

(V, VI) The aggregate demand for housing from new households of credit-restricted dynasties is unambiguously higher after restrictions are removed. Bequests received by subsequent generations of these dynasties will be lower and housing demand functions will fall. This effect may be sufficient to cause a subsequent fall in house prices, the perfectly foreseen prospect of which will have influenced demand in the immediate wake of credit liberalization and dampened the initial rise in house prices.

CHAPTER 6

Assessing the impact of financial liberalization and income shocks on consumption; evidence from aggregate data

6.1 INTRODUCTION

The model developed in Chapter 5 showed that if a substantial proportion of house-holds have faced binding credit restrictions, financial liberalization which makes borrowing easier will have boosted aggregate consumption. If a substantial propor-tion of households have *not* faced binding credit restrictions favourable changes in expectations of future incomes will have increased consumption. It is far from clear what the relative importance of these two factors — easing of credit restric-tions and changing expectations of future disposable incomes — is in accounting for the sharp fall in the savings rate in many developed countries in the 1980s. The aim of this chapter is to develop a framework for discriminating between these two influences on consumption and to use it to analyse the dramatic fall in savings which occurred in the UK in the late 1980s. This chapter builds on the substantial literature that now exists for testing for liquidity constraints. (For good discussions of the issues involved in using various types of data in testing for liquidity constraints see Hayashi (1985), Zeldes (1989), Jappelli and Pagano (1989) and Campbell and Mankiw (1990)).

We try to assess how the personal sector in the UK responded to greater availability of housing credit. In Chapter 3 we showed that households certainly increased their mortgage debt sharply during the 1980s; and estimates of equity withdrawal imply that a high proportion of this flow of credit was used for purposes besides house purchases or improvements. But these facts do not imply that credit liberalization was the cause of the boom in consumption — while the figures are consistent with the mechanism described in the previous chapter there are other interpretations of the facts. In Chapter 1, for example, we described how positive shocks to incomes which cause a substantial change in households' estimates of human capital should, in the absence of any change in credit conditions, increase consumption, reduce saving, boost house prices and cause the demand for lending backed by housing collateral to rise sharply.

In this chapter we adapt the model of household intertemporal optimization introduced in Chapter 2 to analyse the differences in the time-series properties of income and consumption when the driving force behind lower saving is shocks to income, rather than easier credit conditions. We try to discriminate between the view that changes in the flow of housing finance to the personal sector have been a causal, rather than passive, factor in consumer spending. More specifically, we design tests to discriminate between those accounts of recent history which make deregulation, particularly in the market for housing finance, central to changes in UK savings (e.g. Muellbauer and Murphy, 1989, 1990) and those which place more emphasis on changes in expectations of future incomes (King, 1990; Pagano, 1990; Attanasio and Weber, 1992). Discriminating between these stories is important; if what now (in the 1990s) looks to have been an unsustainable rise in debt for many UK households was due to changes in the availability of credit the causes of financial liberalization need to be analysed. We need to consider whether the lending criteria used by financial intermediaries may have changed in a way which reduced welfare; since Stiglitz and Weiss (1981) it has been clear that borrowing restrictions may be an equilibrium response to information problems in credit markets, so it is not obvious that the relaxation of these restrictions leads to a better allocation of resources.

But if the level of household debt came to be excessive because expectations of income growth proved to be unwarranted different issues arise. Households may find it hard to discriminate temporary from permanent shocks to disposable incomes while governments, because of more information on the medium-term fiscal position, may find it easier. But governments may also have incentives not to reveal some of this information. These considerations suggest that issues of credibility and time-consistency in macroeconomic policy, rather than microeconomic factors in the design of lending criteria, are central to the build up of personal sector debt.

In assessing the impact upon households of changes in the lending criteria used by financial intermediaries, in this chapter we aim to shed further light on the transmission mechanism from changes in house values to consumption. Recent US evidence on the links between home ownership and saving (Bosworth, Burtles and Sebelhaus, 1991; Skinner, 1993) suggest a significant, positive relation between consumption and housing wealth at times when house values rise. Bosworth *et al.* show that the average saving rate of home owners fell by around 6% over the period from the mid-1960s to the early 1980s — a period when real house prices rose substantially—while the average saving rate of non-home owners was little changed. But in Chapter 4 we argued that the scale of pure wealth effects was likely to be small. In this chapter we aim to test whether a collateral enhancement story—linking house price rises to easing of liquidity constraints—may be a factor behind the recent empirical evidence on house prices and consumption.

The plan of the chapter is this. Section 6.2 develops a simple model of household decision-making with borrowing limits. The model will be used as our basis for empirical work so it is important to go beyond the models of earlier chapters where we assumed that agents were certain about future incomes and house prices. The impact of relaxing credit restrictions on saving and on the demand for housing is compared with the effects of reassessments of future earnings. Section 6.3 considers the empirical implications of that model and the problems in matching data to theory. Section 6.4 presents empirical results.

6.2   DEVELOPING A MODEL

6.2.1   SAVING AND HOUSING DEMAND WITH CREDIT LIMITS

As before we will assume that agents aim to maximize the expected value of a time-separable, lifetime utility function which depends upon consumption of housing services and of a composite consumption good. Agents earn income from their fixed supply of labour at employment terms which are exogenous; they receive (or pay) interest on net financial assets. Once again we assume that agents are only able to borrow against housing wealth. There is an initial *maximum* ratio of mortgage debt to house value of β. Credit conditions change as β varies. Households at the limit of their mortgage are unable to smooth consumption optimally; borrowing against future expected labour income is impossible once the mortgage limit has been reached. But until that limit is reached households are assumed to be able to costlessly vary the size of their mortgage. We assume that there is a single real interest rate (in terms of consumption goods) which is known and constant. Future labour incomes (y_{t+j}) and real house prices (p_{t+j}) are uncertain.

The household optimization problem at time $t = 0$ is the same as that analysed in Chapter 2. Using the same notation we write this

$$\max E_0(U_0) = \sum_{t=0}^{T} E_0[U(H_t, c_t)/(1 + \rho)^t] \qquad (6.1)$$

The period-to-period budget constraint is a simplified version of that introduced in Chapter 2. We shall not only assume that the mortgage rate equals the return on financial assets but also ignore maintenance charges on houses and taxes. The budget constraint becomes

$$c_t = y_t + (1 + r)S_{t-1} - S_t - (1 + r)M_{t-1} + M_t - p_t(H_t - (1 - \delta)H_{t-1}) \quad (6.2)$$

the constraints are

$$S_t \geq 0 \qquad \left.\right\} \qquad \text{for all } t \tag{6.3}$$
$$M_t \leq \beta(p_t H_t) \tag{6.4}$$
$$(0 \leq \beta \leq 1)$$

which imply

$$S_T + p_T H_T - M_T \geq 0 \tag{6.5}$$

Net worth at t, denoted W_t, is

$$W_t = S_t + p_t H_t - M_t \tag{6.6}$$

i.e. the sum of financial and physical assets net of mortgage debt.

As before, we assume that all purchases of goods, receipts of income and payments of interest are made at the beginning of each period.

$U(H_t, c_t)$ is the time-separable and time-invariant utility function describing preferences over consumption of housing services (which are assumed to be proportional to the house size H) and of consumption goods. We make the standard assumption that U is increasing, twice differentiable and concave in its arguments.

The first-order conditions are somewhat simpler than those derived in Chapter 2, largely because we assume a single interest rate. The conditions are

$$U'_c(c_t, H_t) = E_t[((1 + r)/(1 + \rho))U'_c(c_{t+1}, H_{t+1})] + \lambda_t \tag{6.7}$$

$$U'_H(c_t, H_t) = U'_c(c_t, H_t)p_t\{b(1 - \lambda_t/U'_c(c_t, H_t))$$
$$\times (1 - E_t(1 + \dot{p}_t)(1 - \delta)/(1 + r)) + (1 - b)$$
$$\times [1 - ((E_t(1 + \dot{p}_t)(1 - \delta)/(1 + r))(1 - \lambda_t/U'_c(c_t, H_t)))]$$
$$- \sigma_{u\dot{p}}(1 - \delta)/(1 + \rho)\} \tag{6.8}$$

where

$U'_c(c_t, H_t)$ is the marginal utility of (non-housing) consumption at t;

$U'_H(c_t, H_t)$ is the increment to utility from a marginal increase in housing in period t;

λ_t is the Lagrange multiplier associated with the (single) credit restriction;

b is the proportion of the value of an *increment* in house size financed on mortgage;

$\sigma_{u\dot{p}}$ is the risk premium defined in Chapter 2, a function of the conditional covariance between next-period marginal utility of consumption and the rate of change of house prices between t and $t + 1$.

The complementary slackness conditions are

$$\lambda_t S_t = 0 \tag{6.9}$$

$$\lambda_t(\beta p_t H_t - M_t) = 0 \tag{6.10}$$

We note that an implication of (6.10) is $\lambda_t(\beta - b) = 0$ so that, as in Chapter 2, a household which is credit-restricted would choose to finance as high a proportion of incremental housing expenditure as possible on mortgage.

Equation (6.7) is the standard Euler equation relating marginal utilities in successive periods. Condition (6.8) is the familiar one which equates the marginal utility of housing to the product of the marginal utility of consumption and the effective user cost of housing. It is helpful to rewrite (6.8) as

$$U'_H(c_t, H_t) = U'_c(c_t, H_t)p_t\{(1 - E_t(1 + \dot{p}_t)(1 - \delta)/(1 + r))$$
$$- \sigma_{u\dot{p}}(1 - \delta)/(1 + \rho) - \varphi_t(\beta - E_t(1 + \dot{p}_t)$$
$$\times (1 - \delta)/(1 + r))\} \qquad (6.8')$$

where $\varphi_t \equiv \lambda_t/U'_c(c_t, H_t) \geq 0$.

(6.8') shows that the user cost depends in the usual way on the expected rate of change of house prices between t and $t + 1$ (which we denote $E_t(\dot{p}_t)$), the depreciation rate (δ) and the interest rate (r). The non-standard feature of the user cost measure reflects the effects of credit restrictions; if they bind (in which case $\beta = b$ and $\lambda > 0$) then provided β is large the user cost is *lowered* because at the margin housing can be bought, largely, on credit. Since extra credit has a value to a restricted household the effective cost of housing is lowered relative to the cost of consumption which cannot be financed on credit. But if β is significantly lower than 1 the user cost will be *higher* for a credit-restricted household than for an unrestricted household; should the down-payment requirement be substantial the use of scarce funds to finance house purchase is so onerous to those who are credit-restricted as to make housing relatively unattractive. The condition under which the user cost of housing is higher for the credit restricted is $\beta < E_t(1 + \dot{p}_t)(1 - \delta)/(1 + r)$. If, for example, $r = 0.03$; $\delta = 0.05$ and $E(\dot{p}) = 0.02$, then if the maximum loan to value ratio is less than 0.94 housing is relatively more expensive for the credit restricted.

For a household which is not credit restricted $(\lambda = \varphi = 0)$ the user cost formula can be simplified substantially to a familiar form:

$$U'_H(c_t, H_t) = U'_c(c_t, H_t)p_t[r + \delta - E_t(\dot{p}_t) - \sigma_{u\dot{p}}(1 - \delta)/(1 + \rho)] \qquad (6.11)$$

where we have used the approximation that for small r, δ and $E_t(\dot{p}_t)$, $1 - E(1 + \dot{p})(1 - \delta)/(1 + r) \cong r + \delta - E(\dot{p})$. If, in addition, the covariance term is small, (6.11) implies that the usual approximation to the user cost of $p_t(r + \delta - E_t(\dot{p}))$ is a good one.

It is hard to use the first-order conditions to derive closed-form solutions for consumption and housing demand in terms of current wealth and expectations of future prices and earnings without making strong assumptions about the form of utility functions and the stochastic processes which govern exogenous variables. Even in a model with a single commodity and no credit restrictions, if utility functions do not imply certainty equivalence, as is plausible, it is often impossible to derive analytic solutions to the household optimization problem. (See Deaton (1992) for an excellent discussion of the problem). The presence of a durable commodity whose relative price varies through time, and which also depends on the credit status of the household and the lending criteria of financial intermediaries, makes the problem substantially harder. We can, however, gain significant insights from the first-order conditions if we assume that housing and (non-durable) consumption are, at least approximately, separable. (See Bernanke (1985) for US evidence consistent with the assumption of separability.)

Consider first households for whom credit restrictions are not binding[1]. If we assume that $U''_{cH}(c, H) \cong 0$ we can adapt some useful, recent results on optimal consumption plans without certainty equivalence. Skinner (1988) and Caballero (1990) derive the optimal consumption rule for agents with constant relative and absolute risk aversion. They show that for non-credit-restricted agents facing exogenous labour incomes subject to shocks which may persist, the consumption expansion path is steeper than if certainty equivalence held. The expected growth of consumption from period to period is greater the higher is the degree of convexity of the marginal utility of consumption and the greater is the variability in the rational forecast of the present discounted value of rest-of-life earnings. For agents with a limited horizon the extent to which expected consumption growth exceeds the certainty equivalence path will vary through time as the conditional variance of rest-of-life earnings is likely to depend on the time to (or since) retirement. With a further source of uncertainty, that stemming from the stochastic nature of real house prices, the optimal consumption path will be more complex. Even with separability between housing and other consumption, without certainty equivalence optimal consumption will depend on the variability and persistence of house-price shocks and on the covariance between those shocks and earnings. Once again it is likely that even if the relevant conditional moments are constant, the effect on the consumption growth path will vary over a household's life as housing tenure and employment status change.

We will assume that the overall impact of uncertainty on the consumption growth path can be captured, as in Skinner and Caballero, by the addition of a time-varying, precautionary factor to the certainty equivalence growth path. That factor will depend on household specific, time-varying factors (remaining working age, the stock of housing, and other, wealth) and on factors which we shall assume are constant across both time and agents (the conditional moments of house prices and of earnings and the degree of persistence of shocks). Thus we write an approximation to the optimal consumption rule for *credit-unconstrained* household i:

$$E_t(c_{it+1} - c_{it})/c_{it} = (r - \delta)/\Omega + \pi_{it} + \pi \qquad (6.12)$$

where $\Omega = -c(U''_{cc}/U'_c)$ (See Skinner (1988), equation (6.10), pp 243).
π_{it} and π are, respectively, the household specific and common parts of the precautionary element in planned consumption growth.

The first term on the right-hand side of (6.12) is a second-order Taylor approximation to the optimal consumption expansion rule consistent with the first-order condition (6.7) under certainty equivalence *and* assuming $U''_{ch} \cong 0$. We assume here that the utility function displays constant relative risk aversion which, with additive preferences, implies a constant intertemporal elasticity of substitution $(1/\Omega)$.

There are several implications of (6.12). First, the familiar result that anticipated changes to income will not affect consumption growth holds only provided that π_{it} is independent of y_{it}. Second, *anticipated* changes in house prices will only affect consumption growth if they affect the precautionary term in (6.12); this independence of the certainty equivalence consumption growth path to anticipated changes in house prices is dependent on the separability assumption. Third, the consumption growth path is uncoupled from the earnings growth path; this implies that net financial wealth $(S - M)$ has to fluctuate with earnings. Unconstrained householders for whom S is low will vary their mortgage so as to ensure the first-order condition (6.7) holds and that the expected growth in consumption satisfies (6.12). In this model, where we assume that unconstrained householders may vary M each period even if they do not move house, equity withdrawal (i.e. extra mortgage borrowing not matched by equivalent housing investment) will occur when dissaving is required to ensure (6.12) holds; equity withdrawal would be particularly high when current incomes are low relative to future expected incomes. Thus, equity withdrawal naturally occurs for unconstrained households and is in itself neither an indication of credit liberalization nor that consumption is driven by changes in housing wealth.

Finally we note that if (6.12) holds for a collection of n households who have the same preferences, but differ with respect to age and asset portfolios, their average expected growth in consumption at t is

$$(r - \delta)/\Omega + \pi + \sum_{i=1}^{n} \pi_{it}/n \qquad (6.13)$$

If the prime determinant of π_{it} is age, then for large n we could assume that $\sum_{i=1}^{n} \pi_{it}$ was approximately constant through time. We could then write the average growth in consumption for the credit-unconstrained:

$$(c_{t+1} - c_t)/c_t = k + (r - \delta)/\Omega + \varepsilon_{t+1} \qquad (6.14)$$

where k is a constant reflecting precautionary behaviour and ε_{t+1} is an unforecastable random variable with zero mean. Skinner (1988) shows that in a model with one consumer good ε_{t+1} is equal to the percentage change between t and $t+1$ in the expected value of discounted lifetime resources in period $t + 1$. In a model with uncertainty over house prices ε_{t+1} will also reflect news about current and future house prices. In Chapter 4 we described simulations which suggest that with separability in preferences between housing and consumption then for plausible values of risk aversion the induced change to optimal consumption from a shock to house prices is small for consumers *not* facing credit restrictions. That result suggests that ε will be dominated by news about current and future earnings.

For the currently credit constrained $\lambda_t > 0$, $S_t = 0$ and $M_t = \beta(p_t H_t)$. Assuming once again that $U''_{cH} \cong 0$, we can deduce the following from the first-order conditions. First, as is well known, anticipated changes in income will affect the path of consumption since they affect the degree to which the constraint bites; increases in income which are expected increase current consumption. Second, anticipated increases in house prices affect the path of non-housing consumption because they affect the borrowing limit. Given concavity and separability, an anticipated rise in house prices of $\dot{p}_a$, which increases current spending power by $\beta(H\dot{p}_a)$, will increase current consumption; unanticipated increases in house prices have the same impact because they increase borrowing potential to an equal extent. This is in contrast to the result noted above that anticipated changes in house prices only affect the consumption expansion path for unconstrained households to the extent that they affect the precautionary element in planned consumption growth. This difference between the effect of house-price changes on the credit-restricted and unrestricted is dependent on the way in which credit restrictions are modelled; equation (6.4) implies that households can top up their mortgage if their equity in housing rises. If that assumption were valid it would suggest that the impact of house prices on consumption is higher the more widespread are binding credit restrictions — a result which might appear at odds with the view that house-price changes are more important in the 1980s because of financial liberalization. But if borrowing backed by housing collateral, and available to finance non-housing consumption, only became available in the 1980s we should expect to see an enhanced impact of price changes (both unanticipated and anticipated) provided that a significant proportion of households remained credit-restricted. Assessing changes in the impact of house-price movements on consumption is one of the ways we aim to test alternative theories of the determinants of recent household saving.

Finally, equation (6.8') implies that if the maximum loan to value ratio (β) exceeds $E_t(1 + \dot{p}_t)(1 - \delta)/(1 + r)$ the user cost of housing is lower for the credit-restricted (since $b = \beta > 0$ and $\varphi > 0$). If this condition is satisfied the ratio of (non-housing) consumption to house value for the credit restricted will tend to be lower than for the unrestricted. But if $\beta < E_t(1 + \dot{p}_t)(1 - \delta)/(1 + r)$ the credit restricted will *under* consume housing relative to the unrestricted.

6.2.2   THE IMPACT OF INCOME SHOCKS AND CREDIT LIBERALIZATION

We consider the differences in the impact of income shocks and of changes in β on consumption. For the credit restricted a rise in β has the following impact:

(1)   Consumption immediately rises and the shadow price of the constraint falls; λ falls to zero if the rise in β is sufficiently large. There is a step increase in both consumption and the size of the mortgage.

(2)   The impact on the user cost of housing is ambiguous. (6.8′) shows that a rise in β, which for the credit restricted, means an equal rise in b, *reduces* the user cost; but easing restrictions will reduce φ which, in itself, would *increase* the user cost provided β exceeded $E_t(1 + \dot{p}_t)(1 - \delta)/(1 + r)$ before the relaxation of lending conditions. Under these conditions if the rise in β is large enough to remove restrictions the user cost rises since $\varphi \to 0$. In practice, the maximum loan-to-value ratio set by lenders was almost certainly below $E(1 + \dot{p})(1 - \delta)/(1 + r)$ *before* credit restrictions were first relaxed in the UK in the early 1980s; the down-payment requirement had been high enough that the effective cost of housing to credit-restricted households fell with financial liberalization. (See Bank of England (1985, 1989, 1991) and Goodhart (1986).)

(3)   At the macroeconomic level a rise in β will increase the proportion of households who do not face binding credit restrictions. Assuming that the impact of y_{it} on π_{it} is of second order it follows that the proportion of people who do *not* change consumption significantly in response to *anticipated* changes in income rises as β increases.

(4)   Holding constant the proportion of households who are credit restricted, a rise in β will increase the impact of a given change in house prices on consumption because the extra borrowing available from a given rise in house values is an increasing function of β. (Note the converse of this proposition: holding β constant, the aggregate effect of rises in house prices in boosting consumption, stemming from the enhanced value of collateral, will be lower the smaller the number of households for whom credit restrictions bind.)

(5)   For the credit unrestricted the only impact of changes in β comes from any general equilibrium effects — most obviously house price changes. As noted above, the impact of these changes on the slope of the optimal consumption path only depends on induced changes in the precautionary factor, π.

In contrast to the above, unanticipated shocks to earned income affect all agents. But as noted by Campbell and Deaton (1989) the effect of a positive shock on current consumption will be lower for the credit restricted than for the unrestricted *if* the persistence in the earnings process is high; if the revision to the present value of future earnings is large enough, the unconstrained optimal marginal propensity to consume (mpc) out of an unanticipated shock to current income exceeds unity and the response of the credit unrestricted exceeds that of the restricted, whose mpc cannot exceed one.

Indeed the sensitivity of expectations of future incomes to a shock to current income may be sufficient that an economy-wide positive shock to income may *increase* the proportion of households facing binding credit restrictions. Increases in β, however, have an unambiguously negative effect on the proportion of households facing restrictions. Thus if there is a high degree of persistence in the earnings

process we should not expect consumption to become less sensitive to anticipated income in the wake of large positive shocks; but after a large increase in β
consumption should become less sensitive to anticipated changes in income.

6.3   IMPLICATIONS AND PROBLEMS OF THE MODEL

6.3.1   SOME TESTS OF RIVAL HYPOTHESES ABOUT RECENT SAVINGS

We consider three sets of tests of the hypothesis that revisions to income expectations have been more significant than relaxation of credit restrictions in the late
1980s. These tests are based on the properties of the simple model of optimal
consumption outlined above and are therefore conditional on the way in which
credit restrictions were assumed to work and on the separability assumptions needed
to derive the approximation to the optimal consumption rule for unrestricted agents.

Test 1. If credit restrictions were eased substantially in the 1980s consumption
growth should have become less sensitive to anticipated changes in income; at
the same time the impact of unanticipated changes in income will have increased
if the degree of persistence in shocks is high. We test for these effects by estimating the income process and regressing consumption growth on anticipated and
unanticipated components of income changes for various periods.

Test 2. If credit restrictions bind, then increases in the value of collateral against
which borrowing is made boosts consumption. Since houses are the best collateral
most people have, increases in house values would be a major form of credit
relaxation *provided* financial firms are willing to increase lending when housing
equity rises. We aim to assess the importance of this mechanism by including
both the anticipated and unanticipated components of house-price changes in a
consumption equation. Our aim is to measure the relative contributions of credit
related factors to earnings shocks in driving changes in consumption.

Test 3. If significant, exogenous *changes* in credit conditions occur, the model
outlined above implies that equity withdrawal will change independently of the
path of earned income or of house prices. (In terms of the model of Section 6.2
an exogenous change in credit availability is a rise in β.) But if changes in credit
conditions are unimportant (constant β) equity withdrawal will be determined (for
the credit unrestricted) by current and expected future incomes and (for the credit
restricted) by changes in house prices. By estimating an equity withdrawal equation
we aim to assess whether credit flows in the mid- and late 1980s suggest a significant exogenous change in the availability of debt.

6.3.2   DATA ISSUES

Ideally, we would use time series of household-specific data on consumption,
income, housing and financial wealth to assess the relative impact of changing
credit conditions and income expectations. But no household panel data with the

relevant data exists. Most disaggregated studies of UK consumption use the Family Expenditure Survey (FES). There are two problems with using the FES, both of which will be addressed in the next chapter. First, and most serious, there is no way to follow households over time, which makes measurement of changes in income expectations and in credit availability difficult. Second, the data on housing in the FES is thin; there is no reliable measure of the value of the family home.

We use seasonally unadjusted, quarterly, aggregate data on the incomes, consumption and financial and physical asset holdings of the UK personal sector to implement tests 1–3. There are serious problems in finding measures of consumption, income and wealth which are appropriate to the model outlined above. Consumption should exclude housing consumption but include the flow of services of other durable goods; but no available series measures the services of durables adequately. A measure of y should include only earned income, but the aggregate numbers for the personal sector make it hard to disentangle some components of capital income from labour income. r should be a safe, real rate but uncertainty over consumer price inflation and the wedge between borrowing and lending rates makes construction of a suitable measure problematic. There are no easy answers to these problems. Our strategy has been to assess the robustness of our results to measurement error by trying different definitions of the key variables.

The data for consumption, income and house prices is the same as that used in Chapter 4. The equity withdrawal data was described in Chapter 2. Briefly, the data are

c: per capita, non-durable expenditure, deflated by the non-durable consumption price index (source: *Economic Trends*, various issues). Results using total consumption were little different from those reported below for non-durable consumption.

y: per capita personal sector disposable income minus capital income, plus an estimate of the tax paid on capital income. The measure of capital income is total non-wage income (which includes capital income *and* income from self-employment) scaled by one minus the ratio of wages and salaries to total income. This measure allocates a proportion of income from capital and self-employment to labour income. The capital income tax measure is simply the ratio of capital income to total income multiplied by total tax. National insurance contributions and income tax are deducted from pre-tax labour incomes as is the community charge; transfer payments (national insurance benefits and other current grants) are added. The resulting income series is deflated by the non-durable consumption price deflator (source: *Economic Trends*, various issues).

r: the nominal rate used to construct r is the quarterly average of the building society mortgage rate (*Financial Statistics*, various issues).

Equity withdrawal: total mortgage lending to the UK personal sector net of all mortgage repayments and minus total investment in residential property. Total investment includes estimates of home improvements and repairs plus private fixed residential investment. The series is expressed in per capita terms and deflated by the appropriate consumer price index. (Sources: *Economic Trends*; *Financial Statistics*; *Housing Statistics*, various issues).

House prices: are the Department of Environment mix adjusted series. (See Holmans (1990); source: *Housing Finance*, various issues).

Housing wealth: is the value of residential property owned by the personal sector as reported in the Balance Sheets of the Personal Sector. (*Financial Statistics*, various issues). The series is measured per capita and relative to the non-durable consumption price deflator.

6.4 ECONOMETRIC ISSUES AND RESULTS

6.4.1 TESTS 1 AND 2: THE REACTION OF CONSUMPTION TO INCOMES AND HOUSE PRICES

The first tests involve regressing the change in log consumption on anticipated and unanticipated components of the growth of labour incomes and of real house prices. We follow the same strategy as in Chapter 4 of constructing these expected and surprise components with auxiliary regressions on our quarterly data and then using the fitted values and residuals in a structural equation for consumption. As is well known this procedure poses several econometric problems. First, the use of quarterly averages for consumption and income will generate a moving-average error process if the period over which individuals adjust expenditure is finer than one quarter. If, for example, all households were to be unconstrained and followed a consumption strategy in continuous time, equation (6.14) implies that quarterly average consumption is the time average of a random walk. Woking (1960) shows that an estimated consumption function would then have first-order serial correlation. This time aggregation problem implies that if unbiased estimates of the impact of anticipated and unanticipated events are to be derived, measures of expectations should be based on information lagged by at least two periods. Furthermore, standard errors will need to be adjusted for the MA error process.

Second, the use of generated regressors also causes a bias to the standard errors computed from an OLS regression. (See Pagan (1984,1986), McAleer and McKenzie (1991) and Oxley and McAleer (1993)). In Chapter 4 we addressed this issue by estimating the consumption, income and house-price equations as a system; but that technique proved infeasible over all but the longest data periods. Given the importance of assessing *changes* in the impact of income shocks and house-price changes the inability to use systems estimates for short sub-periods is serious. So here we follow a different strategy and compute adjusted standard errors using the variances and covariances of the residuals from all the auxiliary regressions. This procedure adjusts for the error in measuring expectations and surprises, the source of the bias to OLS estimates. (The procedure used to adjust the standard errors, and the conditions under which parameter estimates are unbiased, are described in an Appendix.)

Third, in measuring the impact of shocks on the change in consumption we need to allow for variations in the anticipated one period ahead real interest rate. Fortunately, equation (6.14) generalizes straightforwardly to the case of variable (expected) real interest rates. Our strategy here is to assume that agents base their expectations of the real interest rate on the same information set used to construct forecasts of house prices and incomes. We include the fitted value from this third auxiliary regression in the consumption equation; were there to be no credit restrictions the associated parameter is an estimate of the inverse of the elasticity of substitution. This procedure will result in the same parameter estimate as that generated by the inclusion of the ex-post real interest rate in a regression where the instrument set are the variables used in the auxiliary regressions; our two-step procedure will allow us to make correct inferences because the adjusted standard errors allow for the error in measuring expectations.

The variables used to generate anticipations of labour income, house prices and real interest rates include the second, third and fourth lags of growth in labour income, house-price changes, nominal interest rates, consumer price inflation and (real, per capita) equity withdrawal. The fourth lag of the log *levels* of real labour income and of real house prices, as well as the ratio of housing wealth to income, were also included. A constant, seasonal dummies and a time trend were included in each auxiliary regression. We also include the second to fourth lags of the ratio of savings to labour income. Campbell and Deaton (1989) note that if consumption smoothing is possible for at least some households savings should help predict changes in future labour income. We find that the savings ratio does indeed have predictive power over future labour income growth; the higher is the savings rate the lower is subsequent growth of income.

Table 6.1 shows the (non-durable) consumption growth equation for the whole period. The second column shows uncorrected, OLS estimates of parameter standard errors with no allowance made for either serial correlation in residuals nor for the bias due to the presence of generated regressors. The third column shows standard errors allowing for the presence of generated regressors. The adjustment is very small. (Appendix 1 shows why the adjustment can be small even if the fit of the auxiliary regressions is poor.) The final column shows the standard errors once allowance is made for residual serial correlation and for heteroscedasticity. (These are the Newey and West (1987) heteroscedasticity and autocorrelation consistent estimates based on a truncation in the serial correlation process at lag 4). Given the clear evidence of serial correlation it is not surprising that this correction is substantial.

Table 6.2 shows the consumption regressions for three sub-periods: 1964.2–1969.4; 1970.1–1979.4; 1980.1–1992.1. In the light of the relative sizes of the two sources of bias to OLS estimates of standard errors revealed in Table 6.1, in Table 6.2 we report only the errors adjusted for serial correlation and heteroscedasticity.

Table 6.1   Accounting for the change in non-durable consumption

		Dependent variable DCN		
		OLS standard errors	corrected two step errors	Newey–West errors
Const.	−0.0955	0.003472	0.003473	0.002827
Q2	0.1321	0.005441	0.005443	0.005592
Q3	0.1181	0.004314	0.004315	0.003221
Q4	0.1429	0.005319	0.005321	0.004666
UY	0.4198	0.068478	0.068478	0.091965
AY	0.3254	0.097456	0.098112	0.089425
UP	0.0182	0.060641	0.060641	0.055589
AP	0.1096	0.050660	0.050837	0.041037
ARR	0.1536	0.106320	0.107101	0.070760

Mean of dependent variable	0.00669
R^2	0.96855
$\bar{R}^2$	0.96611
Std error	0.012029
L4	31.384
Norm	0.4069
Hetero	0.0217

DCN is the change is log per capita real non-durable consumption. UY and UP are the residuals from the auxiliary equations for income changes and for house prices respectively. AY, AP and ARR are the fitted values from the income, house price and real interest rate regressions. A common set of explanatory variables is used in those regressions (see text for a full list). $Q2$, $Q3$, $Q4$, are seasonal dummies. $L4$ is a Lagrange Multiplier statistic for testing for up to fourth-order serial correlation; distributed; χ^2_4 under the null. Norm is the test statistic suggested by Bera and Jarque (1981) for testing the normality of errors assumption; distributed χ^2_2 under the null. Hetero is a test for the independence of squared residuals from squared values and cross products of the explanatory variables; distributed χ^2_1 under the null of homoscedastic disturbances.

The whole sample results reveal several things. First, anticipated changes in income have a significant impact on changes in consumption. Indeed, their impact is only slightly less than the effect of shocks to income. Furthermore, and in the light of the unit root in the labour income process, the effect of a shock to income on consumption growth looks low. These results strongly suggest that, at least *on average* over the last thirty years, credit restrictions have prevented consumption smoothing. The full sample results also suggest that anticipated changes in house prices have a small positive impact on the growth of consumption; unanticipated price changes appear to have no significant effect. The result that house price effects are quite small accords with the findings of Chapter 4 where we used a simpler technique to measure the impact of house price changes.

The difference in the impact of anticipated and unanticipated house price changes suggests that the mechanism whereby price changes have influenced consumption over the past three decades has not consistently been via easing of credit

Table 6.2 Sub-period consumption functions

	Dependent variable: change in log of per capita, real non-durable consumption		
	64.2–69.4	70.1–79.4	80.1–92.1
Const.	−0.0834	−0.1077	−0.0934
	(0.0206)	(0.0058)	(0.0043)
Q2	0.1301	0.1594	0.1204
	(0.0353)	(0.0103)	(0.0052)
Q3	0.1101	0.1309	0.1227
	(0.0123)	(0.0068)	(0.0036)
Q4	0.1325	0.1682	0.1435
	(0.0260)	(0.0073)	(0.0042)
UY	0.5340	0.3459	0.4355
	(0.2044)	(0.1109)	(0.0938)
AY	0.4980	0.0557	0.1660
	(0.6120)	(0.1173)	(0.1710)
UP	−0.0548	−0.0078	0.1504
	(0.2701)	(0.0633)	(0.0646)
AP	0.1094	0.0633	0.1413
	(0.4931)	(0.0742)	(0.0598)
ARR	−1.002	0.4569	0.1404
	(0.9687)	(0.2456)	(0.1575)
$\bar{R}^2$	0.9648	0.9758	0.9867
SE	0.01195	0.01148	0.00689
L4	11.84	8.26	2.55
DW	2.8	2.3	2.2
Mean	0.0098	0.0067	0.0053
Norm	0.99	0.26	2.03
Hetero.	0.028	1.96	0.33
Chow1	26.11 (.002)	43.70 (0.0)	

Figures in parentheses under coefficients are Newey–West (serial correlation and heteroscedasticity-consistent) standard errors. Chow1 is a test of parameter stability based on the change in coefficients when the model is estimated on the remaining observations (Chow's first test). Rejection implies that the parameter values from a model estimated on future decades are significantly different. The test statistic is distributed χ_k^2 under the null of stability in the model parameters, where k is the number of coefficients estimated (χ_9^2 at 95% is 16.9). Figures in parentheses after the test statistic show the significance level. Other notes as above.

restrictions due to enhanced collateral — if that mechanism had operated over the whole period the coefficient on unanticipated price changes would be significant and positive.

The full sample estimate of the coefficient on the expected real interest rate is small but significant; in the presence of clear evidence of credit restrictions it cannot, however, be taken as an unbiased estimate of the average degree of substitutability in household consumption across time.

The sub-sample regressions shown in Table 6.2 reveal important changes in the effects of anticipated and unanticipated events over time. The hypothesis of structural stability across the three sub-periods can be overwhelmingly rejected. Relative to their size in the first sub-period, and also relative to the full sample estimates, the coefficient on expected income changes is lower in the most recent period. In the regressions based on data from the 1980s and 1990s the coefficient on anticipated income is insignificant. Furthermore for the most recent period the impact of house-price shocks is now almost exactly equal to that of anticipated changes. These results are consistent with the hypothesis that credit restrictions have been substantially loosened; the fact that house-price rises now seem to have a stronger impact upon consumption than in the past is consistent with the idea that greater availability of funds to borrow against housing wealth is one mechanism whereby credit restrictions have been eased. But to be clearer on the links between borrowing against housing collateral and consumption we need to study the equity withdrawal process more closely — a subject to which we turn in describing the third of our tests in the next section.

The estimated impact of income shocks and of changes in house prices shown in Table 6.2 can be used, in conjunction with our estimates of expected and unexpected changes in income and house prices from the auxiliary regressions, to assess the causes of the boom in consumer spending in 1986–88. Between 1986.1 and 1988.4 the average *quarterly* increase in per capita, real non-durable consumer spending was 1.75%. The equation estimated over the most recent period tracks this boom in consumption closely; over 90% of the rise in consumption over 1986–88 is predicted. Over that period anticipated real income growth is estimated to have contributed, on average, 0.2% a quarter; unanticipated income growth accounts for only 0.13% a quarter. House price rises are estimated to explain around 0.6% growth per quarter — accounting for one third of the overall growth in consumption. The real interest rate is estimated to add 0.35% to growth (per quarter) over the period whilst the effect of seasonal factors and of the constant is to add another 0.35% to growth.

In short changes in income — either anticipated or unexpected — account for only around one fifth of the rise in consumption over the boom period while house price rises account for around one third of the rise in consumption.

6.4.2 TEST 3: THE DETERMINANTS OF EQUITY WITHDRAWAL

If agents are not credit restricted equity withdrawal is simply a means of smoothing consumption which has no causal role in aggregate expenditure; it reflects a discrepancy between current and expected future incomes. For the unrestricted, shocks which cause future incomes to be revised up will tend to increase equity withdrawal. If some agents are credit restricted, and the rules used by financial firms to allocate credit are as modelled above (i.e. maximum loan to value ratios) and *do not change*, some element of equity withdrawal will also be determined by changes in house prices.

In contrast, if there is an *exogenous* increase in the availability of housing finance in a world where restrictions had been binding the model of Section 6.2 predicts an increase in equity withdrawal independent of changes in house prices and incomes. We aim to test for exogenous changes in credit availability by estimating regressions which, in the absence of regime changes, should track equity withdrawal.

As noted, current and predicted labour incomes, house-price changes, and the levels of housing and other wealth will determine equity withdrawal in the absence of a major shift in credit availability. But it is very hard to use the model outlined above to derive any tight specification of how these factors interact. We follow

Table 6.3   Equity withdrawal equations

Period	Dependent variable: per capita, real equity withdrawal relative to labour income					
	1964.2–1992.1		1964.2–1981.4		1964.2–1985.4	
const.	−0.066	(0.033)	−0.106	(0.037)	−0.117	(0.037)
UY	0.115	(0.054)	0.116	(0.044)	0.101	(0.045)
AY	0.135	(0.119)	0.179	(0.106)	0.113	(0.104)
AP	−0.084	(0.081)	−0.158	(0.073)	−0.144	(0.070)
DPH_i	−0.055	(0.046)	0.014	(0.039)	−0.002	(0.040)
$DLYL_1$	0.088	(0.052)	0.073	(0.044)	0.042	(0.045)
$DLYL_2$	−0.024	(0.054)	−0.091	(0.047)	−0.082	(0.046)
$DLYL_3$	−0.005	(0.062)	−0.028	(0.053)	−0.019	(0.054)
EW_1	0.868	(0.108)	0.518	(0.138)	0.726	(0.125)
EW_2	−0.002	(0.144)	0.210	(0.160)	0.080	(0.156)
EW_3	−0.054	(0.135)	0.074	(0.160)	−0.002	(0.156)
EW_4	0.249	(0.121)	0.065	(0.149)	0.112	(0.140)
LY_1	0.049	(0.022)	0.071	(0.021)	0.069	(0.022)
sr_1	−0.011	(0.052)	−0.066	(0.045)	−0.051	(0.045)
HW_1	−0.005	(0.002)	−0.006	(0.002)	−0.004	(0.002)
S_1	0.0014	(0.0008)	0.0018	(0.0012)	0.003	(0.001)
$\bar{R}_2$		0.877		0.703		0.836
SE		0.0088		0.0061		0.0067
L_4		7.83		4.44		8.29
DW		2.06		1.95		2.00
Mean		0.0163		0.00074		0.0067
Norm		11.23		2.58		4.49
Hetero		26.92		0.12		9.74
Predictive failure 1				137.8		90.57
Parameter stability				49.4		57.10

$DLYL_i$ is the ith lag of the change in log labour income. DPH_i is the ith lag of the change in log house prices. EW_i is the ith lag of the dependent variable. S_1 is the lag of per capita, real financial wealth relative to income. HW_1 is the first lag of per capita real housing wealth relative to income. sr_1 is the lag value of the savings rate. Seasonal dummies were included but are not reported. Predictive Failure 1 is Chow's (1960) second test of predictive adequacy over the period 1982.1–1992.1 (for column two) or for 1986.1–1992.1 (column 3); under the null this test statistic is distributed χ^2_{41} (95% critical value = 55.9) or χ^2_{25} (95% critical value 37.6) respectively. Parameter stability is Chow's first test of equality of equation coefficients (Chow 1960); under the null it is distributed χ^2_{16} (95% level 26.3). Other notes as in Tables 6.1 and 6.2.

the strategy of including the determinants of equity withdrawal noted above in an admittedly *ad hoc* specification. We then analyse the extent to which big outliers occur in the mid- and late 1980s — the existence of big positive residuals is indirect evidence of an exogenous relaxation in credit conditions.

Table 6.3 shows the equity withdrawal specification estimated over the whole sample, and for two sub-periods. Lags of labour income growth, the anticipated and unanticipated components of current labour income growth and a lag level are all included. Current anticipated, and lagged actual, changes in real house prices are also included. The lagged stock of housing and financial wealth are also allowed to affect the scale of equity withdrawal. Four lags of the dependent variable are included.

The table shows the full sample regression; but to avoid problems from estimating over periods when credit liberalization may have occurred we prefer to calculate residuals constructed from regressions estimated over earlier periods. Figure 6.1 shows the dynamic residuals for the 1980s from an equity withdrawal equation estimated over the 1960s and 1970s. The dependent variable in the regression is equity withdrawal relative to (lagged) labour income; a residual of 0.01 represents an unexplained increase in housing finance which was *not* used to finance housing related expenditure equal to 1% of labour income. The chart shows that equity withdrawal was substantially higher in the 1980s than could have been predicted from past data. The peak of 'unexplained' lending occurs in the period 1987–88.

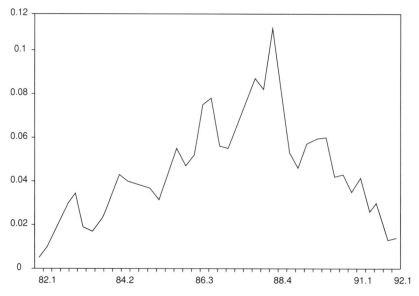

Figure 6.1   Forecast residuals from equity withdrawal equation (Sample for estimation 64.2–81.4)

Tests of parameter stability and predictive adequacy reported in Table 6.3 confirm the view that for the 1980s as a whole, and also for the shorter period from the end of 1985, the determinants of equity withdrawal changed. All tests of equation stability overwhelmingly reject the hypothesis that the process generating leakage of funds from the housing finance market remained unchanged. The results provide some support for the view that unexpectedly large equity withdrawal came in two waves: one in the early 1980s, particularly 1982, and a later and bigger wave in 1986–88. Furthermore the scale of unexpected equity withdrawal in 1986–88 was substantial and more than sufficient to account for the decline in the savings ratio. If we interpret *all* of the residuals for 1986–88 as being due to credit liberalization which added directly to consumer expenditure that would account for a boost to consumption of around 8.0% *each year*.

6.5   CONCLUSIONS

In this chapter three bits of evidence have been presented. First, standard Euler equation tests for the effect of anticipated changes in income on consumption revealed clear signs of excess sensitivity over the past three decades as a whole. But over the period since the early 1980s anticipated changes in income no longer seem to have a significant impact on consumption. Consumption does, however, consistently and significantly respond to unanticipated changes in income. Further more, labour income grew rapidly in the mid 1980s, though a large part of this rise may have been anticipated. But the contribution of changes in incomes, either anticipated or not, to the consumption boom of 1986–88, while significant, is not the dominant factor. Second, the influence of a given house-price change on consumption seems to have become more powerful over the last decade. Our evidence is that changes in prices contributed substantially more to the boom in consumption in the mid 1980s — and price falls contributed more to the subsequent rise in the savings rate — than did changes in labour incomes. Third, the explosion of borrowing backed by housing collateral in the 1986–88 period is not well explained by a model which makes anticipated and unexpected changes in incomes and house prices the key determinants of credit flows. There appears to have been a clear change in the process generating leakage of funds from the mortgage market.

These pieces of evidence are consistent with the hypothesis that credit liberalization was more significant in accounting for the decline in the savings rate in the UK than changes in income. But the use of aggregate data to test for the impact of relaxing restrictions which are likely to have affected different people in different ways remains problematic. Essentially we have had to make a representative agent assumption and this sits uneasily with the idea that credit restrictions are likely to affect people differently at various stages of the life cycle. A more satisfactory way of testing for the impact of credit restrictions and of income shocks, and also for addressing the links between housing wealth and consumption, is to use household data. The use of such data poses its own problems. In the next chapter we consider the issues and present results derived from household survey data.

REFERENCES

Attanasio, O. and Weber, G. (1992) The UK Consumption Boom of the Late 1980s: Aggregate Implications of Microeconomic Evidence. Paper presented at a CEPR meeting on Financial Markets and Real Economic Behaviour, Madrid, December.

Bank of England (1985) The housing finance market: recent growth in perspective, *Bank of England Quarterly Bulletin*, March, 80–91.

Bank of England (1989) The housing market, *Bank of England Quarterly Bulletin*, February, 66–77.

Bank of England (1991) Housing finance — an International Perspective, *Bank of England Quarterly Bulletin*, February, 56–66.

Bera, A. and Jarque, C. (1981) An Efficient Large Sample Test for Normality of Observations and Regression Residuals. Australian National University Working Papers in Econometrics, No 40, Canberra.

Bernanke, B. (1985) Adjustment costs, durables and aggregate consumption, *Journal of Monetary Economics*, **15**, 41–68.

Bosworth, B., Burtles, G. and Sabelhaus, J. (1991) The decline in saving: some microeconomic evidence, *Brookings Papers on Economic Activity*, **3**, 183–256.

Caballero, R. (1990) Consumption puzzles and precautionary savings, *Journal of Monetary Economics*, **25**, 113–36.

Campbell, J. (1987) Does saving anticipate declining labour income? An alternative test of the permanent income hypothesis, *Econometrica*, **55**, 1249–73.

Campbell, J. and Deaton, A. (1989) Why is consumption so smooth?, *Review of Economic Studies*, **56**, 357–74.

Campbell, J. and Mankiw, G. (1990) Permanent income, current income and consumption, *Journal of Business and Economic Statistics*, **8**, 265–79.

Chow, G. (1960) Tests of equality between sets of coefficients in two linear regressions, *Econometrica*, **28**, 591–605.

Deaton, A. (1991) Saving and liquidity constraints, *Econometrica*, **59**, 1221–48.

Deaton, A. (1992) *Understanding Consumption*, Clarendon Press, Oxford.

Goodhart, C. (1986) Financial innovation and monetary control, *Oxford Review of Economic Policy*, **2**(4), 79–99.

Hayashi, F. (1985) The effects of liquidity constraints on consumption: A cross sectional analysis, *Quarterly Journal of Economics*, **100**, 183–206.

Holmans, J. (1990) House Prices: Changes Through Time at National and Sub-national Level. Government Economic Service Working Paper no. 110.

Jappelli, T. and Pagano, M. (1989) Consumption and capital market imperfections, *American Economic Review*, **79**, 1088–1105.

King, M. (1990) Discussion of 'Is the UK balance of payments sustainable?', Muellbauer and Murphy, *Economic Policy*, **11**, 383–7.

McAleer, M. and McKenzie, M. (1991) Keynesian and new classical models of unemployment revisited, *Economic Journal*, **101**, 359–81.

MacKinnon, J. (1990) Critical values for cointegration tests. UC San Diego Discussion Paper, 90–4.

Miles, D. (1992) Housing markets, consumption and financial liberalization in the major economies, *European Economic Review*, **36**, 1093–1136.

Miles, D. (1993) House prices, personal sector wealth and consumption: some conceptual and empirical issues, *The Manchester School*, **61**, 35–69.

Muellbauer, J. and Murphy, A. (1990) Is the UK balance of payments sustainable? *Economic Policy*, **11**, 345–83.

Oxley, L. and McAleer, M. (1993) Econometric issues in macroeconomic models with generated regressors, *Journal of Economic Surveys*, **7**, 1–40.

Pagan, A. (1984) Econometric issues in the analysis of regressions with generated regressors, *International Economic Review*, **25**(1), 221–47.

Pagan, A. (1986) Two stage and related estimators and their applications, *Review of Economic Studies*, **53**, 517–38.

Pagano, M. (1990) Discussion of Muellbauer and Murphy (1990), *Economic Policy*, **11**, 387–90.

Skinner, J. (1988) Risky income, life cycle consumption, and precautionary savings, *Journal of Monetary Economics*, **22**, 237–55.

Skinner, J. (1993) Is Housing Wealth a Sideshow?, NBER Discussion Paper No. 4552.

Stiglitz, J. and Weiss, A. (1981) Credit rationing in markets with imperfect information, *American Economic Review*, **71**, 393–440.

Woking, H. (1960) Note on the correlation of first differences of averages in a random chain, *Econometrica*, **28**, 916–18.

Zeldes, S. (1989) Consumption and liquidity constraints: an empirical investigation, *Journal of Political Economy*, **97**, 305–46.

NOTE

1. For such a household $S > 0$ and/or $M < \beta(pH)$. If such a household has mortgage debt it is indifferent between having higher M and S or lower M and S; equality of the return on savings and debt means that only *net* financial assets $(S - M)$ matters. We shall assume that in these circumstances households aim to reduce their mortgage so $S > 0$ only if $M = 0$. (If the return on savings were slightly lower than the cost of mortgage debt this would be optimal.)

APPENDIX: CORRECTIONS TO OLS STANDARD ERRORS WITH GENERATED REGRESSORS

The consumption function estimated in the paper aims to assess the contribution of anticipated and unanticipated events to changes in expenditure; it uses the fitted values and residuals from auxiliary equations for labour income and house prices, and the fitted values from a real interest rate regression, as proxies for expectations and shocks. The way in which unbiased estimates of coefficient standard errors were constructed is described in this appendix.]

The consumption function can be written

$$c = \gamma_0 + \varepsilon_y \gamma_1 + y^e \gamma_2 + \varepsilon_p \gamma_3 + p^e \gamma_4 + r^e \gamma_5 + \varepsilon_c \tag{A6.1}$$

where
c is a $T \times 1$ vector of the change in consumption
ε_y is the unanticipated element of income growth
y^e is the anticipated element of income growth
p^e is the anticipated element of house price changes
ε_p is the shock in house price growth
r^e is the expected real interest rate
ε_c is the divergence in actual from planned consumption
$\gamma_0, \gamma_1, \ldots, \gamma_5$ are parameters to be estimated.
Assume that agents use a linear rule to predict future variables from a vector of relevant, observed variables X. That is,

$$y^e = X\beta_1 \tag{A6.2}$$

$$p^e = X\beta_2 \tag{A6.3}$$

$$r^e = X\beta_3 \tag{A6.4}$$

where X is a $T \times k$ matrix and β_i is a $k \times 1$ vector of coefficients. Clearly

$$y = X\beta_1 + \varepsilon_y \tag{A6.5}$$

$$p = X\beta_2 + \varepsilon_p \tag{A6.6}$$

$$r = X\beta_3 + \varepsilon_r \tag{A6.7}$$

We assume that agents are efficient in their use of information, which implies that ε_y, ε_p and ε_r are serially uncorrelated; they are, however, likely to be contemporaneously correlated. We will also assume that ε_c is a zero mean, constant variance, serially uncorrelated process which is independent of ε_y, ε_p and ε_r.

Let the OLS estimate of β_i be written $\hat{\beta}_i$. Thus

$$y = X\hat{\beta}_1 + \hat{u}_y \equiv \hat{y} + \hat{u}_y \tag{A6.8}$$

$$p = X\hat{\beta}_2 + \hat{u}_p \equiv \hat{p} + \hat{u}_p \tag{A6.9}$$

$$r = X\hat{\beta}_3 + \hat{u}_r \equiv \hat{r} + \hat{u}_r \tag{A6.10}$$

Combining (A6.1)–(A6.10) yields

$$c = \gamma_0 + \hat{u}_y \gamma_1 + \hat{y}\gamma_2 + \hat{u}_p \gamma_3 + \hat{p}\gamma_4 + \hat{r}\gamma_5 + (\varepsilon_y - \hat{u}_y)\gamma_1$$
$$+ (y^e - \hat{y})\gamma_2 + (\varepsilon_p - \hat{u}_p)\gamma_3 + (p^e - \hat{p})\gamma_4 + (r^e - \hat{r})\gamma_5 + \varepsilon_c \tag{A6.11}$$

We write (A6.11):

$$c = Q \oplus +\varepsilon \tag{A6.12}$$

where
Q is a $T \times 6$ matrix of ones and OLS residuals and fitted values $(1, \hat{u}_y, \hat{y}, \hat{u}_p, \hat{p}, \hat{r})$;
$\oplus$ is a 6×1 coefficient matrix $(\gamma_0, \gamma_1, \ldots, \gamma_5)$
and

$$\varepsilon = (\varepsilon_y - \hat{u}_y)\gamma_1 + (y^e - \hat{y})\gamma_2 + (\varepsilon_p - \hat{u}_p)\gamma_3 + (p^e - \hat{p})\gamma_4 + (r^e - \hat{r})\gamma_5 + \varepsilon_c \tag{A6.13}$$

OLS estimation of (A6.12) will produce consistent estimates of the parameter vector $\oplus$ provided the assumption we make about the independence of ε_c from the other shocks is valid.
From (A6.12) the variance covariance matrix of the parameters of interest is

$$V_{\oplus} = E[(Q'Q)^{-1}(Q'\varepsilon\varepsilon'Q)(Q'Q)^{-1}] \tag{A6.14}$$

we may rewrite (A6.13)

$$\varepsilon = (\varepsilon_y - \hat{u}_y)\gamma_1 + X(\beta_1 - \hat{\beta}_1)\gamma_2 + (\varepsilon_p - \hat{u}_p)\gamma_3 + X(\beta_2 - \hat{\beta}_2)\gamma_4 + X(\beta_3 - \hat{\beta}_3)\gamma_5 + \varepsilon_c \tag{A6.15}$$

using

$$\varepsilon_y - \hat{u}_y = X(X'X)^{-1}X'\varepsilon_y$$

$$X(\beta_1 - \hat{\beta}_1) = -X(X'X)^{-1}X'\varepsilon_y, \quad \text{etc.}$$

we may now write

$$E(\varepsilon\varepsilon') = \sigma_{\varepsilon c}^2 I + X(X'X)^{-1}X'\{\sigma_{\varepsilon y}^2(\gamma_1 - \gamma_2)^2 + \sigma_{\varepsilon p}^2(\gamma_3 - \gamma_4)^2 + \sigma_{\varepsilon r}^2(\gamma_5)^2$$
$$+ 2\sigma_{yp}^2(\gamma_1 - \gamma_2)(\gamma_3 - \gamma_4) + 2\sigma_{yr}^2(\gamma_1 - \gamma_2)(\gamma_5)$$
$$+ 2\sigma_{pr}^2(\gamma_3 - \gamma_4)(\gamma_5)\} \tag{A6.16}$$

where $\sigma_{\varepsilon c}^2 I$ is $E(\varepsilon_c \varepsilon_c')$ and I is a $T \times T$ identity matrix, and

$$\sigma_{\varepsilon y}^2 I = E(\varepsilon_y \varepsilon_y') \quad \text{etc.,} \qquad \sigma_{yp}^2 I = E(\varepsilon_y \varepsilon_p') = E(\varepsilon_p \varepsilon_y') \quad \text{etc.}$$

Let the term in $\{\ldots\}$ in (A6.16) be denoted Ψ. From (A6.14) the correct estimate of $V_{\oplus}$ is then

$$\sigma_{\varepsilon c}^2 (Q'Q)^{-1} + (Q'Q)^{-1}Q'X(X'X)^{-1}X'Q(Q'Q)^{-1}\Psi \tag{A6.17}$$

The standard OLS estimate of $V_{\oplus}$ omits the second term in this expression. Our corrected estimate of $V_{\oplus}$ is based on (A6.17) where we use the OLS estimates of $\sigma_{\varepsilon y}^2$, $\sigma_{\varepsilon p}^2$ and $\sigma_{\varepsilon r}^2$ from the auxiliary equations and use the OLS residuals from those regressions to generate sample covariances as estimates of σ_{yp}^2, σ_{yr}^2 and σ_{pr}^2. These values are used to construct an estimate of Ψ. Note that since these covariances can be negative, and $(\gamma_1 - \gamma_2)$, $(\gamma_3 - \gamma_4)$ and γ_5 are of unknown sign, the corrected standard errors may differ little from the OLS estimates and may be either larger *or smaller*. If there were only one generated regressor the OLS standard errors are unambiguously smaller than the corrected errors.

CHAPTER 7

Consumption, human capital and housing wealth; evidence from household data

7.1 INTRODUCTION

The models we have used to analyse the housing and consumption decisions of the personal sector are based on specifications of the behaviour of individual households. In previous chapters we have used aggregate data to measure the user cost of housing and to assess the impact of changes in credit conditions and of asset values. The link between the models and that empirical work is looser than one would wish; the jump from theories about individual agents to data on economy-wide averages is worryingly long. The natural way to test and calibrate models of individual behaviour is using micro-data; theories of household behaviour are best assessed with household data. It is not surprising that the most convincing empirical work on the impact of credit conditions, on the portfolio allocation of agents, on consumption decisions over time and on the demand for housing should have used disaggregated, household data. (See, for example, King (1980), King and Dicks-Mireaux (1982), Hayashi (1985), Zeldes (1989a), Attanasio and Weber (1989) and Guiso, Jappelli and Terlizzese (1992).)

Despite the clear advantages of using household data there have been few disaggregated studies of the links between the housing market, credit conditions and household decisions on consumption and saving; those that exist (e.g. Zeldes, 1989a; Skinner, 1989) use US data. One of the major reasons is that although there exist for many countries data sets with information on household consumption and incomes, it is hard to find reliable measures of the values of financial and tangible assets; and often those data sets which do contain information on household wealth do not allow one to follow households through time. In this chapter we consider the problems of using household data where information on assets is incomplete. We investigate the roles of housing wealth and of human capital in consumer spending and measure the impact of house-price changes, and of income shocks, on saving. We look at cross-section data on the consumption of households at various periods during the past thirty years.

This chapter focuses on the determinants of consumption because it is through their impact on household expenditure that shocks to the housing market are likely to have their most significant macroeconomic impact. (See Blanchard (1993), Hall (1993), Perry and Schultze (1993) and King (1993) on the importance of changes in consumption in the recession of the early 1990s).

We will use household-level data to address three issues about consumption. First, we aim to analyse the determinants of human capital — the present value of lifetime earnings — and to assess the ways in which the lifetime pattern of incomes vary across households. We estimate how the demographic make-up of households, and the education and occupations of the members of the household, contribute to human wealth; we also estimate how human capital affects consumption. We use a technique which allows us to identify age–earnings profiles for different occupational groups and to separate the impact on human wealth of age from that of cohort effects. It is essential to control for the determinants of human capital if we are to assess the impact of events in the housing market on household behaviour; shocks to human capital are likely to influence consumption, saving and housing decisions so failure to allow for the separate influences of the driving forces behind human wealth will contaminate any measure of the importance of housing market conditions.

Second, in this chapter we try to measure income uncertainty and then estimate its effect on saving and spending. Again, accounting for uncertainty is likely to be important and household attitudes to risk may have a major impact on the way in which housing conditions affect household behaviour. For example, if certainty equivalence were to hold, then an expectation that house prices were to rise faster than the sum of the tax-adjusted cost of funds (plus depreciation and maintenance charges) would generate an infinite demand for housing and could, therefore, not be sustainable (Chapter 2). But if higher moments of the conditional distribution of house prices matter this is no longer the case because precautionary behaviour implies a finite demand for housing even when the point estimate of the user cost is negative. We aim to shed light on the recent debate as to whether precautionary behaviour can account for the apparent discrepancies between consumer spending patterns and the path of expenditure consistent with optimization of a lifetime utility function where capital markets are perfect. At issue here is whether dropping the assumption of certainty equivalence can help account for the excess smoothness of consumption (with respect to unanticipated changes in income) and excess sensitivity (with respect to anticipated changes in income) better than the hypothesis that binding credit restrictions are alone responsible. (On this issue see Skinner (1988), Zeldes (1989b), Caballero (1990) and Guiso, Jappelli and Terlizzese (1992); Deaton (1992) offers an excellent overview of the issues.) King (1993) has argued that precautionary behaviour is what underlies an important propagation mechanism for economic shocks in an economy where the stock of outstanding debt is large and unevenly distributed. He presents evidence consistent with Irving Fisher's debt deflation hypothesis and argues that declines in the relative value of assets held by the personal sector and which back nominal liabilities — most obviously housing wealth — have significant macroeconomic effects. This argument depends on the importance of precautionary behaviour; behaviour which is different from risk aversion. The important aspects of precautionary behaviour are a function of the third and fourth derivatives of utility with respect to wealth, the magnitude of which are hard to estimate from existing empirical evidence or even from introspection.

Whether or not precautionary behaviour is significant is relevant to one of the central issues we address in this book — the transmission mechanism from house price shocks to consumption and saving; whether shocks to house prices have aggregate, rather than purely distributional, effects is dependent on variability across households in the marginal propensities to spend out of wealth. King (1993) presents a model where, as an implication of precautionary behaviour, those propensities differ systematically across agents. In estimating the impact of earnings uncertainty on spending we assess whether precautionary behaviour is, in fact, important; we analyse whether cross-section variation in saving is more closely linked to life-cycle effects (consumption smoothing) or to variability across households in income risk. We take care to correct for the fact that households' perceptions of risk are likely to differ from the econometrician's estimate of the variability of the unforecastable element of income because agents have better information about their own earnings prospects than is revealed by survey data. Guiso, Jappelli and Terlizzesse (1992) argue that this is particularly important when using micro-data to estimate the impact of uncertainty.

Our third goal in this chapter is to see what effects changes in the market value of certain types of assets have upon household consumption. More specifically, we use household-level data to estimate how home owners react to capital gains, or losses, on housing. Our aim is to assess whether such gains are treated in the same way as other sources of income. We have noted several times that since house price rises simultaneously increase the market value of the assets of home owners *and* the opportunity cost of consuming current and future housing services, it is in theory unclear whether we should expect a positive wealth effect on consumption. (See Chapter 4 and also Skinner (1989).) Given the importance of housing wealth in the portfolios of the household sectors of most developed countries, whether or not there is an impact of changes in house values on consumption is a key policy issue. House prices, like the values of other durable assets, are likely to be sensitive to expectations of future interest rates; so if consumption does respond significantly to changes in house prices one important element of the transmission mechanism of monetary policy would be via the impact of interest rate changes on house values. But there is little empirical evidence on the scale of the effects of housing wealth on consumption; and what evidence does exists is open to several different interpretations. Muellbauer and Murphy (1990), for example, have found a strong link between rising UK house values and consumers' expenditure. King (1990) and Pagano (1990) are sceptical that the relation reflects a causal link from changes in house values to consumption, a scepticism reinforced by the simulation results reported in Chapter 4.

But in Chapter 6 we found evidence that house-price effects on spending had become more significant in the 1980s and argued that this was consistent with a collateral enhancement interpretation of how price increases work, but was harder to see as a pure wealth effect. Those results were based on aggregate data where controlling for variable, household-specific factors was impossible. Our aim here is to see if those results are consistent with evidence from household data where we can drop the representative agent assumption.

Our strategy is to use household-specific data on consumption, income, housing wealth and other household characteristics to address the three issues outlined above. A major advantage in using micro-data is that we are likely to be able to measure the determinants of variability in human capital and in earnings uncertainty better than with aggregate data. The point has particular force for the measurement of uncertainty; aggregate data cannot be used to measure household-specific risks and these may be far more important to agents than the effects of economy-wide shocks. Furthermore, at the micro-level changes in house values are likely to be exogenous to individual home owners; with such data we are better able to avoid the problem that changes in house values are likely to reflect changing expectations of home owners' future incomes — something which makes the investigation of housing wealth effects using aggregate data particularly difficult.

Our data source is the Family Expenditure Survey (FES) which provides a sample of over 5000 UK households in each of the five survey years we use (1968, 1977, 1983, 1986, 1990). For each year we have a cross-section of households which constitutes a representative sample. Because we have data from four decades we are able to assess whether the processes driving incomes and consumption have changed over time.

The plan of this chapter is this. Section 7.2 considers some theoretical issues. In Section 7.3 issues in the measurement and estimation of human capital, consumption and housing wealth are addressed. Section 7.4 describes the results of estimating models of household income and consumption. Conclusions are presented in Section 7.5. The data set and variable definitions used are described in an appendix.

7.2   THEORY

As usual we assume that agents aim to maximize the expected value of lifetime utility. Lifetime utility is assumed to be the sum of current period utility and discounted values of future utilities. We use the standard assumptions of additivity and time separability of preferences and assume that utility depends only upon consumption. For householder i at time t the maximand is

$$E_t \left[\sum_{j=0}^{T-age_{it}} (1+\rho)^{-j} U(c_{i,t+j}) \right] \qquad (7.1)$$

where $E_t(.)$ is the householder's conditional expectation of some variable at time t, T is the length of life of the householder (assumed known and constant across householders), and age_{it} is the 'age' of the householder *at time t*. (In our empirical work we will assume that for single adult householders 'age' is simply that adult's age; for couples 'age' will be the average of their ages). ρ is the discount rate. c_t is consumption in period t and $U(c_t)$ is the instantaneous utility function. (For simplicity we aggregate all forms of consumption; c_t is a measure of total consumption including spending on goods and services and the flow of benefits from home ownership.)

The budget constraint is very simple:

$$c_{i,t+j} = Y_{i,t+j} + (1+r_{t+j})A_{i,t+j-1} - A_{i,t+j} \qquad (7.2)$$

where $Y_{i,t+j}$ is post-tax labour income in period $t+j$
$A_{i,t+j}$ is the stock of wealth
r_{t+j} is the real return on wealth.

Caballero (1990) and Skinner (1988) derive approximations to closed-form solutions to the consumption function implied by the solution to this maximization problem. The form of those solutions are dependent on assumptions about the stochastic processes for income and for rates of return as well as on the form of utility functions. Their results reveal that consumption can be approximated by the certainty equivalence level of consumption adjusted by a precautionary element which is a known function of parameters of the stochastic processes generating household incomes and of the structure of preferences. Caballero, for example, considers the case where the instantaneous utility function is exponential (so preferences imply constant absolute risk aversion (CARA)), where the real interest rate is constant and equal to ρ, and where the only source of uncertainty is shocks to labour income. The optimal consumption rule he derives for an infinite horizon problem (p. 119) implies that, for our finite horizon case,

$$c_{i,t} = \kappa_1(PY_{i,t}) + \kappa_2(A_{i,t}) + \psi_{it} \qquad (7.3)$$

where

$$PY_{i,t} = E_t[\sum_{j=0}^{T-age_{it}} Y_{i,t+j}/(1+r)^j]/(T+1-age_{it}) \qquad (7.4)$$

and

$$\kappa_1 = \{T+1-age_{it}\}[r/(1+r)]\{1-(1/(1+r))^{T+1-age_{it}}\}^{-1}$$

$$\kappa_2 = [r/(1+r)]\{1-(1/(1+r))^{T+1-age_{it}}\}^{-1}$$

For small r, $\kappa_1 \simeq 1$; $\kappa_2 \simeq 1/(T + 1 - age_{it})$, so that the propensity to consume human capital (PY) is independent of age and close to unity while the propensity to consume wealth is a positive function of age.

The final term in (7.3) is the difference between optimal consumption and the certainty equivalence level of consumption. Certainty equivalence consumption is a function of human capital (i.e. PY, the present discounted value of future lifetime earnings) and the level of non-human wealth. The precautionary element, ψ_{it}, depends upon the degree of prudence (a function of the third derivative of utility) and on the variance and persistence of income shocks. (The solution (7.2) is consistent with a quite general process for the persistence of income shocks, including a random-walk model of income.) Caballero shows that ψ is negative, implying that optimal consumption is lower than the certainty equivalence level and by an amount which is a positive function of the conditional volatility of rest-of-life income.

Skinner derives an equation analogous to (7.3) for the case of a constant relative risk aversion utility function. (In that case the optimal consumption rule is to consume a proportion of the sum of the present discounted value of future earnings plus current wealth; the proportion is a negative function of the coefficient of risk aversion and of the volatility of rest-of-life earnings.)

These results are crucially dependent upon the assumption that households are able to borrow against future labour income to finance current consumption. If that is not possible consumption will be more heavily dependent upon cash in hand — the sum of current labour income and gross financial assets — and less upon the present value of future earnings (see Deaton (1992) for a discussion of the issues and references to the huge literature on credit restrictions). Our aim here is not to test directly for credit restrictions, but the likelihood of their presence (at least in the 1960s and 1970s) will have an important impact on the interpretation of our results below. In particular, the greater ease with which households may have been able to borrow against housing wealth to finance non-housing consumption in recent years means that any impact of house-price changes may have as much to do with increasing the scope for borrowing, thereby easing credit restrictions, as with pure wealth effects. The distinction between wealth effects of house-price changes and what we call collateral enhancement effects was noted in Chapters 4 and 6; we shall return to it below.

We will take (7.3) as our basic specification and use it to consider several issues. One of these is whether the gains on housing are treated in the same ways as other components of income. If $A_{i,t}$ is a comprehensive measure of wealth it should include the value of tangible wealth and r_t should reflect the returns on those tangible assets. Equation (7.3) implies that an increase in the value of $A_{i,t}$ — due, say, to unforeseen capital gains on some assets — should increase consumption. We test to see whether it is appropriate to think of housing wealth as being on a par with other components of wealth (bank and building society deposits, equities, etc.) by testing whether capital gains on owner-occupied housing do increase consumption;

equation (7.3) would imply that such gains should boost spending *provided* housing wealth is treated in the same way as other wealth.

A second issue we address is whether there appear to be significant precautionary elements to household expenditure. We aim to assess the scale of ψ_{it} by including a measure of (labour) income uncertainty in our empirical version of equation (7.3).

A third set of issues arises out of the measurement of human capital — the discounted value of future labour incomes. In estimating (7.3) we require a measure of household human capital; in constructing such a measure we are able to assess the contribution of household characteristics to income inequality and to see how the determinants of household income have changed over time. The first issue we address in modelling household consumption in Section 7.3 is the measurement of human capital.

7.3   ESTIMATING THE IMPACT OF INCOMES AND HOUSING GAINS ON CONSUMPTION

7.3.1   MEASURING HUMAN CAPITAL

We have defined a householder's human capital (PY_i) as the expected present discounted value of future labour incomes, expressed as a per period rate (equation (7.4)).

We assume that for all t household i's labour income, $Y_{i,t}$, is a function of a vector Z_i of household characteristics (number of people in the household working, region of the country in which the household lives, sex of head of house, marital status and education of head of house, occupation of head of house, etc.) and the age of the household at t.

We assume that the influence of particular household characteristics upon labour income is the same across households and is linear in the elements of Z; we also assume that, conditional on Z, household income, Y_i, is a quadratic function of age. That is,

$$Y_{i,t} = Z_i \beta + \alpha_1 (age_{it}) + \alpha_2 (age_{it})^2 + \varepsilon_{it} \qquad (7.5)$$

where β is a vector of parameters and α_1 and α_2 are scalar parameters. ε_{it} is the unexpected element of income. For the moment we assume that ε is purely transitory, though when we come to estimate permanent income we will allow for the more general case where the current shock to income affects estimates of future income. Because it is likely that the earnings profile over a working life has a very different shape across occupations, in estimating (7.5) we will also let α_1 and α_2 differ across occupational groups, but for the moment we ignore this point. We will estimate (7.5) in a series of cross-section regressions with no restriction that the values of α_1, α_2 and the equation constant be the same across years; in this way we allow the systematic component of the income of someone who is 25 years of age in 1990 to differ from the 1968 income of an otherwise identical individual born 22 years earlier. The advantage of estimating the income process on a series of cross-sections is that we thereby allow for cohort effects. In comparison, in other empirical models of household income it is hard to separately identify the age–earnings profile and the cohort effect. King and Dicks-Mireaux (1982), for example, need to use information from outside their sample of households to allow for the separate influences of age and cohort.

We assume that a household's income changes through time not only as a result of its progressing through the life cycle (as reflected in α_1 and α_2) but also due to exogenous productivity growth. We assume that productivity growth is expected to be at a constant rate n. Thus

$$E_t[Y_{i,t+j}] = \{Z_i\beta + \alpha_1(age_{it+j}) + \alpha_2(age_{it+j})^2\}(1+n)^j \qquad (7.6)$$

In (7.6) we make the assumption that in assessing its future earnings j periods ahead a household considers its current household charactersistics (Z_i), its age at period $t+j$ and the effect of general real wage rises $((1+n)^j)$. If we assume that $r \simeq n$ we can now write

$$PY_{i,t} \simeq Z_i\beta + \{1/(T+1-age_{it})\} \sum_{j=0}^{T-age_i} [\alpha_1(age_{it+j}) + \alpha_2(age_{it+j})^2] \qquad (7.7)$$

Using the fact that $\sum_{j=0}^{T} j^2 = T(T+1)(2T+1)/6$ we can, after some manipulation, write (7.7) as

$$PY_{i,t} \simeq Z_i\beta + (\alpha_1/2 - \alpha_2/6 + T\alpha_2/3)age_{it} + (\alpha_2/3)age_{it}^2 + (\alpha_1/2 + \alpha_2/6)T$$
$$+ (\alpha_2/3)T^2 \qquad (7.8)$$

Since T is assumed to be the same for all households we can write (7.8) as

$$PY_{i,t} \simeq \gamma_0 + Z_i\beta + \gamma_1(age_{it}) + \gamma_2(age_{it})^2 \qquad (7.9)$$

where γ_0 is a constant which depends upon α_1, α_2 and T; γ_1 is also a function of T, α_1 and α_2; γ_2 is a function only of α_2. Specifically,

$$\gamma_0 = (\alpha_1/2 + \alpha_2/6)T + (\alpha_2/3)T^2 \qquad (7.9a)$$

$$\gamma_1 = \alpha_1/2 - \alpha_2/6 + T\alpha_2/3 \qquad (7.9b)$$

$$\gamma_2 = \alpha_2/3 \qquad (7.9c)$$

We can use (7.5), along with FES data on age and other household characteristics, to run cross-section regressions to estimate parameters β, α_1 and α_2. But in practice, our FES data on household characteristics will be an imperfect measure of Z_i; characteristics which are likely to be important determinants of earnings and which individuals will have more information on than is reported in the FES are ability, motivation and health. An implication of this is that the residual from estimation of (7.5) will reflect both ε_{it} (the truly random component of earnings) and a part of income systematically linked to household characteristics *not* measured by the econometrician. Defining the fitted values from cross-section estimation of (7.5) by $\hat{Y}_i$:

$$\hat{Y}_i = Z_i\hat{\beta} + \hat{\alpha}_1(age_{it}) + \hat{\alpha}_2(age_{it})^2 \qquad (7.10)$$

we decompose the residual from this regression into a systematic component ω_i, and the random element ε_i:

$$Y_i - \hat{Y}_i \equiv u_i = \omega_i + \varepsilon_i \qquad (7.11)$$

So ω_i is, by definition, that part of the deviation of current income from its expected value, conditional on the econometrician's information, which is accounted for by household-specific characteristics which are not public information but are known to the household. ω_i is independent of ε_i. A key point to note is that the impact of ω_i on consumption is likely to be greater than the impact of ε_i since it reflects attributes of the household rather than random, and possibly transitory, shocks. In fact the coefficient on ω_i in a consumption function should be the same as the estimated impact of that part of income which is systematically related to the subset of Z_i measured by the econometrician, i.e. $\hat{Y}_i$. The coefficient on ε_i, however, will be equal to κ_2 (a number close to $1/(T - age_i)$) if the unexpected part of current income is purely transitory. Only if the current shock to income is permanent, so that (adjusting for age) Y_i follows a random walk, will the effect of ε_i be the same as that of ω_i. With cross-section data there is no way we can untangle the estimated residuals (the $\hat{u}_i$) into random shocks and systematic components; we can however include $\hat{u}_i$ as a determinant of consumption, the coefficient on which will reflect the relative variability in ω and ε across households and the degree of persistence in ε.

Using (7.9) and (7.10), noting that the *household's* estimate of the systematic component of income is $\hat{Y}_i + \omega_i$, and using the decomposition of $\hat{u}_i$ given by (7.11), we can write (omitting time subscripts):

$$PY_i \simeq \gamma_0 + \hat{Y}_i + Z_i(\beta - \hat{\beta}) + (\gamma_1 - \hat{\alpha}_1)age_i + (\gamma_2 - \hat{\alpha}_2)age_i^2 + \hat{u}_i - \varepsilon_i \quad (7.12)$$

Using (7.9b) and (7.9c) this can be written

$$PY_i \simeq \gamma_0 + \hat{Y}_i + (\alpha_2 T/3 - \alpha_2/6 - \alpha_1/2)age_i - (2\alpha_2/3)age_i^2 + v_i + \hat{u}_i - \varepsilon_i \quad (7.13)$$

where v_i is the composite error term $Z_i(\beta - \hat{\beta}) + (\alpha_1 - \hat{\alpha}_1)age_i + (\alpha_2 - \hat{\alpha}_2)age_i^2$ and, as before, γ_0 is a function of α_1, α_2 and T and is constant across households.

(7.13) shows that human capital (PY_i) can be written as the sum of a constant, the fitted value from a cross-section income regression ($\hat{Y}_i$), terms in age_i and age_i^2, and a composite error term. That error term will not generally have zero mean in cross section because for any particular period the truly random components of incomes (ε_i) are likely to be correlated across households; the effect of these systematic, or macroeconomic, shocks will be picked up in the constant.

7.3.2   MEASURING WEALTH AND INCOME RISK

Equation (7.3) shows that to model consumption we need to measure wealth as well as human capital. We split wealth into financial assets and housing wealth (for most households other forms of tangible wealth besides the family home are of secondary importance). The FES provides measures of the income from these assets but not direct measures of their market value. We can, however, use the income series to derive measures of wealth. Denoting the (instantaneous) income from financial wealth by YW and the stock of financial wealth by FA we can write

$$FA_{i,t} = YW_{i,t}/r_t \tag{7.14}$$

where r_t is the (instantaneous) return at t on financial assets.

We consider two ways of measuring housing wealth. First, we can decompose the income from housing wealth to home owners into two components: the imputed rent from owner-occupation (IMP) and the capital gain on housing wealth ($\dot{P}H$). The analogue to (7.14) for housing wealth, denoted HW, is

$$HW_{i,t} = (IMP_{i,t} + \dot{P}H_{i,t})/r_t \tag{7.15}$$

We have assumed in (7.15) that the return on housing at time t is the same as the return on financial assets; in theory there are strong reasons why they should not be the same and in practice neither rate of return is observable. This does not pose a problem econometrically because we use cross-section data and estimate separate regressions for each year. In our consumption function the coefficients we estimate on the flows of income from wealth differ across the two types of asset and across years; the coefficients reflect the (unobserved) rates of returns as well as the propensity to consume out of wealth. Because we will allow the coefficients on different sorts of capital income to vary we will have allowed for differences in the returns on the components of wealth. We also experiment with an alternative method of measuring housing wealth. Here we use the value of house prices in the region in which an owner-occupier has a house at the time that household reports its income and consumption. We construct an index of the value of the house by multiplying the local, average house price with a measure of the size of the house; we use the rateable value — a function of the number of rooms in the house and floor size — as the indicator of house size.

If we use the first method of measuring housing wealth we can combine (7.3) with (7.14) and (7.15). Dropping time subscripts, and using the identity

$$A_{i,t} = FA_{i,t} + HW_{i,t}$$

we can now write

$$c_i = \lambda_0 + \lambda_1(PY_i) + \lambda_2 YW_i + \lambda_3 IMP_i + \lambda_4 \dot{P}H_i + \psi_i + e_i \tag{7.16}$$

where

c_i is total household consumption expenditure (excluding housing);

λ_1 is the propensity to consume out of human capital;

λ_2 is the propensity to consume out of financial wealth divided by the return on financial wealth;

λ_3 is the propensity to consume out of housing wealth divided by the return from the services provided by housing;

λ_4 is the propensity to consume out of housing wealth divided by the required return on housing;

e_i is the divergence between planned and actual consumption, which we will assume is independent of PY_i, YW_i, IMP_i, ψ_i and $\dot{P}H_i$.

If we use the second strategy to measure housing wealth we replace the terms in IMP and $\dot{P}H$ with a direct measure of the value of the home.

Caballero (1990) shows that in a model with no uncertainty over capital income, ψ_i is a function of the conditional variability of rest of life earned income and the degree of prudence (defined as the ratio of the third to the second derivative of utility with respect to consumption). Caballero's approximation to the closed-form solution for optimal consumption (our equation (7.2)) is derived under quite general conditions for the degree of persistence in the impact of income shocks, but it depends upon shocks to income being i.i.d. He shows that ψ_i is a function of the variance of the i.i.d shocks and the persistence of the income process. This implies that ψ_i should be an increasing function of the variance of the random component of a household's current income. What we should like to measure is the variability of the random component of earnings (ε_i), but as noted, we cannot disentangle this component of the regression residual $\hat{u}_i$ from the systematic (at least to the household) element ω. Assuming that ψ_i is proportional to the square of the random component of earnings we can, however, write

$$\psi_i = \lambda_5(\varepsilon_i)^2 \qquad (7.17)$$

where Caballero's results imply that the absolute value of λ_5 is an increasing function of the persistence of income shocks and that λ_5 should be negative if the utility function implies prudent behaviour.

Using (7.11) in (7.17), we have

$$\psi_i = \lambda_5(\hat{u}_i)^2 - \lambda_5(\omega_i)^2 - \lambda_5(2\omega_i\varepsilon_i) \qquad (7.18)$$

Using (7.13) and (7.18) in (7.16) we now have

$$c_i \simeq \lambda_0 + \lambda_1\{\gamma_0 + \hat{Y}_i + (\alpha_2 T/3 - \alpha_2/6 - \alpha_1/2)age_i - (2\alpha_2/3)age_i^2 + v_i + \hat{u}_i - \varepsilon_i\}$$
$$+ \lambda_2 YW_i + \lambda_3 IMP + \lambda_4 \dot{P}H_i + \lambda_5(\hat{u}_i)^2 + e_i - \lambda_5(\omega_i)^2 - \lambda_5(2\omega_i\varepsilon_i) \qquad (7.19)$$

Finally, we write this:

$$c_i \simeq \pi_0 + \lambda_1(\hat{Y}_i) + \pi_1(age_i) + \pi_2(age_i)^2$$
$$+ \lambda_2 YW_i + \lambda_3 IMP + \lambda_4 \dot{P}H_i + \lambda_5(\hat{u}_i)^2 + \lambda_1(\hat{u}_i) + \xi_i \qquad (7.20)$$

where

$$\pi_0 = \lambda_0 + \lambda_1\gamma_0 \qquad (7.20a)$$

$$\pi_1 = \lambda_1(\alpha_2 T/3 - \alpha_2/6 - \alpha_1/2) \tag{7.20b}$$

$$\pi_2 = -\lambda_1(2\alpha_2/3) \tag{7.20c}$$

ξ_i is a composite error equal to $\lambda_1(v_i - \varepsilon_i) + e_i - \lambda_5(\omega_i)^2 - \lambda_5(2\omega_i\varepsilon_i)$ which is independent of all right-hand side variables *except* $\hat{u}$ and $\hat{u}_i^2$. But from (7.11), the decomposition of $\hat{u}_i$, we know that provided the distributions of ω and of ε across households are symmetric (in which $E(\omega_i^3) = E(\varepsilon_i^3) = 0$), and so long as ω_i and ε_i are independent of each other and of v_i and e_i, then

$$E(\xi_i \hat{u}_i^2) = -\lambda_5(\sigma_\omega^4 + 5\sigma_\varepsilon^2 \sigma_\omega^2)$$

$$E(\xi_i \hat{u}_i) = -\lambda_1 \sigma_\varepsilon^2$$

where $\sigma_\varepsilon^2 = E(\varepsilon_i^2)$; $\sigma_\varepsilon^2 = E(\omega_i^2)$; $\sigma_\varepsilon^4 = E(\omega_i^4)$.

Provided $\hat{u}_i$ and $(\hat{u}_i)^2$ are independent of the other explanatory variables in (7.20), and conditional on the independence and symmetry of ε and ω, we can write the bias in the OLS estimates of the coefficients on $\hat{u}_i$ and $(\hat{u}_i)^2$, respectively, as

$$-\lambda_1\sigma_\varepsilon^2/(\sigma_\varepsilon^2 + \sigma_\omega^2) \tag{7.21}$$

$$-\lambda_5(\sigma_\omega^4 + 5\sigma_\varepsilon^2\sigma_\omega^2)/(\sigma_\omega^4 + \sigma_\varepsilon^4 + 6\sigma_\varepsilon^2\sigma_\omega^2) \tag{7.22}$$

From (7.21) the coefficient on $(\hat{u}_i)$ is downwards biased from λ_1 to an extent dependent on the relative contributions of cross-section variations in ε and ω in contributing to variation in $\hat{u}$. Using this result we can infer the relative variances of ε and ω, across households, by the shortfall in the coefficient on $\hat{u}$ from the coefficient on $\hat{Y}$. We are able to avoid making assumptions about the relative variances of random and privately observed components of earnings; nor do we need rely on estimates of these variances from other studies based on different samples, a problem faced by other authors (King and Dicks-Mireaux, 1982).

From (7.11) $\sum_{i=1}^n \hat{u}_i^2/(n-k)$ is an unbiased estimate of $\sigma_\omega^2 + \sigma_\varepsilon^2$ (where n is the sample size and k the number of coefficients to be estimated in the income regressions). Using this, and our estimate of the ratio of σ_ε^2 to σ_ω^2, we can identify σ_ε^2 and σ_ω^2 separately. We then use these estimates to adjust the OLS coefficient on $(\hat{u}_i^2)$ using (7.22). This requires an auxiliary assumption about the link between $E(\varepsilon_i^4)$ and $E(\varepsilon_i^2)$ and between $E(\omega_i^4)$ and $E(\omega_i^2)$. Assuming ε_i and ω_i are normally distributed $E(\varepsilon_i^4) = 3(E(\varepsilon_i^2))^2$ and $E(\omega_i^4) = 3(E(\omega_i^2))^2$. This normality assumption allows us to use (7.23) to generate a corrected estimate of λ_5.

We will test the cross-equation restrictions implicit in (7.20) by seeing whether the freely estimated, occupation-specific, coefficients on age and age^2 satisfy (7.20b) and (7.20c). One reason why these restrictions may not hold is if age affects the ability of agents to extract utility from consumption; if age alters the form of the utility function there will be an impact of age upon consumption independent of the effect of age upon income.

7.4   DATA AND RESULTS

7.4.1   DATA

We use FES data on labour incomes and household characteristics to estimate (7.10) and then use the fitted values and residuals from this regression, along with measures of other incomes, to estimate (7.20).

All flow variables are measured in weekly equivalents and are at 1990 prices. Household human (or labour) income (Y_i) is the 'normal' level of receipts of net of tax earnings of the household. (Households are asked to adjust their most recent incomes for unusual or exceptional receipts.) Y_i includes income from paid employment, income from self-employment and receipts of benefits. (For those who have been unemployed for less than thirteen weeks at the time of the survey income is based upon usual working earnings and not upon current receipts of unemployment benefit.) The variables used to explain human income (Z_i) include: age, marital status of head of house, sex of the head of household, number of working people in the household, number of adults in the household, number of children, occupation/employment status of head of house (eleven categories including unemployed, retired, professional, unskilled, clerical, skilled manual, etc). Age and age squared were interacted with the employment status variable to allow the life-cycle profile of earnings to vary across occupations. Regional dummies were included in the regressions. The age at which the head of household left full-time education was included as an (imperfect) measure of qualifications (unfortunately this variable was not available in 1968 and 1977). We also included the level of income from financial assets in the labour income equation to pick up wealth effects on the supply of labour.

7.4.2   INCOME REGRESSIONS

Table 7.1 shows the OLS income regressions for each of our survey years. We estimate a different income model for each of the five surveys. This allows us to account for cohort effects but also allows for changes over time in the ways in which incomes depend upon household characteristics. For example, because average real earnings rise over time the impact upon household income of an extra worker (the first coefficient in the table) should be higher in later years than in early years; Table 7.1 reveals that this is indeed the case.

In all cases there were clear signs of heteroscedasticity, which is unsurprising in a specification using the levels of household income. Although parameter estimates from the levels specifications are consistent, and the (Whites') standard errors are robust to heteroscedasticity, there is a danger (even with a sample size in excess of 5000 for each year) that the results will be heavily influenced by a few outliers. As a check on this we used the estimated residuals from the levels specifications reported in the tables in a two-step procedure. In the second-round regression we ran an OLS regression on the weighted observations with the weight on observation i the

Table 7.1   Explaining cross-section variations in household incomes: effects of selected variables

	1968	1977	1983	1986	1990
No. workers in house	40.28	53.31	56.83	61.86	90.42
	(2.98)	(3.31)	(4.07)	(6.45)	(6.08)
No. people in house	30.66	33.71	51.69	54.47	−0.02
	(3.28)	(3.80)	(4.45)	(5.98)	(0.03)
No. children	−24.16	−27.29	−46.62	−55.77	4.41
	(3.60)	(4.23)	(5.45)	(7.85)	(2.77)
Sex head of house	17.76	14.43	0.72	20.30	54.03
(1=male; 0=female)	(3.37)	(3.57)	(3.94)	(5.25)	(4.00)
Age left school	—	—	−2.65	−1.41	0.313
			(1.72)	(1.56)	(2.06)
(Age left school)^2	—	—	0.26	0.27	0.21
			(0.08)	(0.07)	(0.09)
Investment income (YW)	0.81	1.22	0.94	0.81	1.51
	(0.10)	(0.20)	(0.09)	(0.08)	(0.23)
Regions*					
North	−32.4	−16.4	−23.2	−30.5	−45.5
	(4.84)	(6.25)	(7.41)	(8.86)	(11.34)
Yorks and Humberside	−35.2	−12.1	−30.2	−32.9	−65.4
	(4.61)	(5.84)	(6.27)	(6.67)	(11.50)
North-west	−25.3	−15.9	−19.7	−20.4	−43.9
	(4.48)	(4.61)	(6.00)	(9.02)	(11.27)
East Midlands	−16.6	−26.6	−28.7	−17.2	−51.6
	(6.89)	(4.88)	(6.40)	(10.91)	(11.68)
West Midlands	−17.6	−15.6	−30.7	−32.1	−51.9
	(4.92)	(5.14)	(6.06)	(6.70)	(11.32)
East Anglia	−32.3	−22.3	−17.1	−37.0	−57.8
	(7.30)	(5.66)	(10.69)	(7.49)	(12.69)
South-east (except GL)	−14.74	−5.1	−6.9	−5.0	−24.1
	(4.92)	(4.80)	(6.44)	(6.57)	(12.36)
South-west	−28.0	−25.3	−27.2	−14.1	−54.4
	(6.41)	(5.95)	(6.72)	(19.23)	(12.23)
Wales	−33.6	−11.4	−28.9	−40.9	−46.4
	(5.30)	(6.82)	(7.41)	(6.72)	(11.64)
Scotland	−28.3	−13.6	−27.6	−26.2	−43.9
	(4.66)	(5.44)	(5.80)	(7.67)	(12.30)
N. Ireland	−49.9	−22.4	−45.4	−40.96	−69.4
	(6.62)	(7.08)	(8.00)	(11.25)	(13.42)
No. observations	5178	5538	5372	5089	5614
Mean Y (1990 prices)	162.1	177.8	196.5	216.3	239.4
Standard error	72.38	83.05	102.5	159.2	151.3
R^2	0.52	0.53	0.48	0.34	0.60
Breusch–Pagan test for heteroscedasticity (χ^2 48 under null)	15 656	14 217	5198	23 119	25 318

*Effects of regions are measured relative to a household in Greater London.
Heteroscedasticity-consistent standard errors in parentheses. Other variables included in the regressions but not reported were a constant, dummies for occupation/labour market status, age and age squared interacted with the employment status dummies. Table 7.2 summarizes the effect of the age variables by occupation.

reciprocal of the squared error from the levels regression. Although the distribution of the resulting estimates is unclear they provide a check on the robustness of the least squares estimator. The parameter estimates from this two-step procedure were always very close to the levels results and are not reported. As a further check on the reliability of the estimated parameters from the levels specification we also re-estimated the model a second time using an alternative form of weighted least squares; here we use as weights the inverse of the squared fitted values from the first-round regression. Once again the parameter estimates were little different from those reported in Table 7.1.

The results reveal a powerful impact of the demographic make-up of the household upon income. Not surprisingly, household income is strongly influenced by the number of people in the household and, more significantly, by the number of adults employed. Conditional on the numbers of people and workers in the household, income is a diminishing function of the number of children; kids reduce earnings. Region has a strong influence upon household income in all years. Relative to a household in the Greater London area households with similar characteristics in the North of England, in Wales and in Northern Ireland consistently have significantly lower incomes. By 1990 households in Northern Ireland had, on average, 29% lower earnings after adjusting for differences in education and family composition; in the North of England incomes were around 20% less than in the London area.

Age effects are powerful and vary considerably across occupations. Table 7.2 shows the implied age at which earnings peak for households whose head works in different occupations. (The table lists the average of the implied peak earning years from the coefficients estimated for each of the five years.)

The coefficient estimates imply that peak earnings come in the mid-forties for managerial, professional and technical workers; in the mid-thirties for manual workers; and in the early forties for clerical workers. Peak earnings for those in the armed services appear to come shortly before retirement. This result may reflect survivorship bias; in the armed forces most of those who do not reach the top of the profession are encouraged (often forced) to retire long before they reach 60. For the retired, earnings peak at around five years after usual (male) retirement age (65). Earnings peak earliest for unskilled manual workers (at age 33).

Table 7.2   Age at which earnings peak

Professional/technical	44.4
Managerial	45.8
Teachers	45.5
Clerical	41.0
Shop assistants	45.5
Skilled manual	35.4
Semi-skilled manual	38.4
Unskilled manual	33.3
HM forces	57.6
Retired	69.9

Education (as measured by the age at which full-time education finished) has a powerful and non-linear impact on income. Leaving school at eighteen rather than at sixteen is estimated to increase incomes by between 6% and 7% for all future ages. Staying in full-time education for a further three years from age eighteen is estimated to add between 10% and 12% *more* to earnings. These are, however, somewhat artificial results since we hold occupation constant while changing education; this almost certainly biases down the estimated returns to education since occupation is strongly correlated with education and earnings vary significantly across occupations.

Households with a male 'head of house' consistently show up as having higher earnings. Surprisingly this effect is at its strongest at the end of the period; in 1990 a household headed by a male had earnings around 20% higher than an otherwise identical (in terms of occupation, region, education, etc.) household headed by a woman. This effect had been around half that size in 1968 and 1977 and had been even lower in the early 1980s.

Investment income shows up strongly with a significant positive effect on labour incomes in all years. This is somewhat surprising if we interpret the effect as saying something about the impact of wealth on the supply of labour. But a more plausible interpretation is that wealth is correlated with household abilities and that the latter are not perfectly proxied by education, age, occupation and the other measured household characteristics.

7.4.3   CONSUMPTION REGRESSIONS

The fitted values from the income regressions are used to estimate cross-section consumption functions (equation (7.20)). We use a wide definition of consumption including expenditure on durable and non-durable goods and on services. Including durables is problematic because of the infrequency of large purchases and the mismatch between the timing of expenditure and the flow of services from the ownership of the goods. But excluding durables is not an attractive option since the propensity to consume durables out of gains in wealth may be both significant and larger than the propensity to consume other goods and services. We decided to include expenditure on all durable goods except on cars, where the scale and infrequency of purchases is particularly problematic.

We measure YW by taking the reported income earned on all types of financial assets. As equation (7.3) shows, when households have finite lives the propensity to consume wealth depends on age; households with less time to live are likely to consume financial wealth at a higher rate. We allow for this by including an age-adjusted flow of financial asset income as well as the unadjusted flow. The adjusted flow is $YW_i(1/(1 - (1/(1 + r))^{T-age_i}))$. We set $r = 0.03$. Because households do not know how long they will survive, and are likely to be risk-averse, it would be inappropriate to take a value of T based on the average life expectancy of men and women. We make an *ad hoc* adjustment for uncertainty by assuming that households use an horizon significantly greater than the average life expectancy of the longest lived adult. We set T equal to 90.

Imputed income from home ownership, *IMP*, is based on rateable values of the family house adjusted for the number of habitable rooms. Measuring $\dot{P}H$ poses more serious problems. Home owners report neither the market value of their home nor the capital gain (or loss) made on their house. We try two measures for capital gains. First, for each household we compute the percentage change in the regional index of real (in terms of consumer goods) house prices over the four quarters prior to the quarter in which the household answers the survey questions. This is multiplied by a 0,1 home ownership dummy to give the simpler measure of capital gains *($\dot{P}H1$)*. With this measure no attempt is made to take account of the value of the home; home owners in the same region reporting at the same time will have the same measure of capital gains regardless of the relative values of their homes. The second measure of capital gains *($\dot{P}H2$)* tries to account for this; it is the first measure multiplied by the imputed income from home ownership — a variable likely to be significantly correlated (at least in cross-section) with house value. We discovered that our alternative measure of owner-occupier's housing wealth — the local, average house price multiplied by the household-specific indicator of house size (rateable value) was insignificant in all regressions.

Equation (7.20) shows that the same age variables must be included in the consumption equation as in the income regressions; i.e. age and age squared, each interacted with the occupation/employment dummies.

Evidence from other studies using micro-data strongly suggest that, conditional on incomes and wealth, household consumption is influenced by the employment status of the adults and by the composition of the household (Barten, 1964; Muellbauer, 1974; Browning and Meghir, 1991; Deaton, Ruiz-Castillo and Thomas, 1989; Blundell, Browning and Meghir, 1989). To allow for this we also include the raw occupation dummies in the consumption function as well as the number of working adults. The demographic structure of the household is also likely to influence consumption; we include the number of persons in the household using a weight of one half for children.

Tables 7.3 and 7.4 show the results of estimating the consumption functions for our two measures of housing capital gains for each of the survey years. Here we have not imposed the cross-equation restrictions (7.20a)–(7.20c). As with the income specifications, there is obvious heteroscedasticity in these levels regressions, though again the parameter estimates are unbiased. OLS standard errors are unreliable both because of the heteroscedasticity and, in the case of the coefficient on $\hat{Y}$, because of the use of generated regressors. White's heteroscedasticity standard errors are reported in the tables. We make no further adjustment to the standard errors, so the estimated standard error for the coefficient on $\hat{Y}$ is downwards biased (see Pagan, 1984, 1986), but it seems most implausible that a correction would render the parameter estimate insignificant. Once again we checked for the influence of outliers by following a two-step procedure where the first-round OLS residuals are used to construct weights (equal to the inverse of the squared residual) for the second-step regression. As with the income regressions the coefficient estimates

Table 7.3 Explaining cross-section variations in household consumption: effects of selected variables

	Results using $\dot{P}HI$				
	1968	*1977*	*1983*	*1986*	*1990*
$\hat{Y}$	0.84	0.99	0.65	0.69	0.48
	(0.09)	(0.11)	(0.08)	(0.08)	(0.16)
$\hat{u}$	0.55	0.41	0.41	0.41	0.31
	(0.05)	(0.04)	(0.03)	(0.08)	(0.03)
$\hat{u}^2/1000$	−0.236	−0.20	−0.40	−0.06	−0.08
(income uncertainty)	(0.08)	(0.08)	(0.07)	(0.01)	(0.02)
No. people in house	10.88	−0.12	14.45	16.71	26.70
	(2.80)	(4.04)	(3.05)	(4.40)	(4.21)
No. workers in house	−9.24	−18.91	1.01	−8.24	−2.02
	(5.15)	(7.68)	(6.38)	(7.67)	(15.20)
Investment Income	1.15	−0.41	0.51	−0.41	−0.29
(YW)	(0.48)	(0.23)	(0.42)	(0.35)	(0.27)
Imputed Housing Income	1.38	2.27	2.05	2.24	1.83
(IMP)	(0.28)	(0.40)	(0.16)	(0.24)	(0.17)
Capital gains on	−1.37	1.20	−0.47	−0.43	0.36
Housing ($\dot{P}HI$)	(0.36)	(0.41)	(0.20)	(0.34)	(0.24)
No. observations	5178	5538	5372	5089	5614
Mean of Consumption					
(1990 prices)	165.0	175.8	192.1	213.7	208.3
Standard Error	88.40	94.02	99.62	139.7	126.2
R^2	0.44	0.45	0.48	0.40	0.46
Breusch–Pagan Test					
for heteroscedasticity					
(χ^2 38 under null)	12 603	19 724	6 402	18 133	3 884

Heteroscedasticity-consistent standard errors in parentheses. Other variables included in the regressions but not reported were a constant, dummies for occupation/labour market status, age and age squared interacted with the employment status dummies.

from the two-step procedure were almost identical to the levels estimates and are not reported. We found similar results when the second-round regressions used the inverse of the squared fitted values from the first-round regressions, rather than the residuals, as weights.

As expected $\hat{Y}$ is a prime determinant of spending; λ_1 (the propensity to consume out of human capital) is estimated to be between 0.5 and 1.0; the average for the five years is 0.75. The coefficient is generally significantly less than unity, and therefore lower than is implied by (7.3). But Caballero (1990) has shown that if the variance of lifetime incomes is stochastic it is no longer the case that the marginal propensity to consume out of income with a CARA utility function equals that of a certainty equivalence model. If labour incomes and the variance of innovations are positively correlated the marginal propensity to consume with CARA utility is lower than that of a certainty equivalence model. Our results are consistent with this interpretation because our measure of income risk ($\hat{u}_i^2$) is highly variable across

Table 7.4 Explaining cross-section variations in household consumption: effects of selected variables

	Results using $\dot{P}H2$				
	1968	*1977*	*1983*	*1986*	*1990*
$\hat{Y}$	0.85	1.03	0.65	0.67	0.48
	(0.09)	(0.12)	(0.08)	(0.08)	(0.16)
$\hat{u}$	0.56	0.42	0.41	0.42	0.31
	(0.05)	(0.04)	(0.03)	(0.08)	(0.03)
$\hat{u}^2/1000$	−0.246	−0.20	−0.40	−0.06	−0.08
(income uncertainty)	(0.08)	(0.08)	(0.07)	(0.01)	(0.02)
No. people in house	10.96	−1.25	14.48	17.41	26.58
	(2.80)	(4.41)	(3.05)	(4.56)	(4.23)
No. workers in house	−9.57	−22.07	0.97	−6.73	−2.63
	(5.17)	(8.54)	(6.36)	(8.06)	(15.18)
Investment income	1.17	−0.47	0.52	−0.40	−0.29
(YW)	(0.48)	(0.24)	(0.42)	(0.35)	(0.27)
Imputed housing income	1.53	1.78	2.02	2.07	1.83
(IMP)	(0.29)	(0.20)	(0.17)	(0.23)	(0.17)
Capital gains on	−0.10	−0.02	−0.008	0.004	0.019
Housing ($\dot{P}H2$)	(0.03)	(0.04)	(0.01)	(0.01)	(0.01)
No. observations	5 178	5 538	5 372	5 089	5 614
Mean of consumption					
(1990 prices)	165.0	175.8	192.1	213.7	208.3
Standard Error	88.40	94.16	99.66	139.7	126.1
R^2	0.44	0.45	0.48	0.40	0.46
Breusch–Pagan Test					
for heteroscedasticity	12 617	22 449	6 423	18 152	3 895
(χ^2 38 under null)					

Heteroscedasticity-consistent standard errors in parentheses. Other variables included in the regressions but not reported were a constant, dummies for occupation/labour market status, age and age squared interacted with the employment status dummies.

households and is positively correlated with $\hat{Y}_i$. In the case of CRRA preferences, Skinner (1988) shows that the average propensity to consume human capital is lower than its certainty equivalence value (of unity) by an amount which is larger the more important is precautionary behaviour.

We tested restrictions (7.20b) and (7.20c) by constructing the variable

$$\hat{Y}_i + (\hat{\alpha}_2 T/3 - \hat{\alpha}_2/6 - \hat{\alpha}_1/2)age_i - (2\hat{\alpha}_2/3)age_i^2$$

and including this in place of $\hat{Y}_i$, age_i and age_i^2 separately. The resulting reduction in the number of parameters to be estimated is 22, rather than 2, because the coefficients on age and age^2 are occupation-specific (there are 11 occupational groups). Imposing the 22 restrictions led to a small decline in the goodness of fit of the model and could be rejected for every year using a standard F test. But with sample sizes in excess of 5000 such tests can be misleading; in the limit as the sample size becomes large enough almost any null hypothesis can be rejected. An alternative criterion suggests that the restrictions are not seriously violated. We calculated Schwarz's Posterior Odds Criterion, where restricted and unrestricted models are judged against each other by the relative values of log likelihood minus half the product of log sample size and the number of parameters to be estimated. (See Schwarz (1978) and Klein and Brown (1988), who argue that the criterion is particularly useful when the sample size is very large.) In four of the five years the restricted model is preferred.

The coefficient on the deviation of current income from the econometrician's estimate of permanent labour income ($\hat{u}_i$) is lower than on $\hat{Y}_i$, as expected, and is around 60% of the size. This result implies that, on average, just over one half of the deviation of $\hat{Y}_i$ from Y_i is due to the systematic, non-transitory influence of household characteristics which we do not observe but which households know. Because the coefficient on $\hat{u}_i$ is significantly less than the coefficient on $\hat{Y}_i$ we can easily reject the hypothesis that true shocks to income are permanent.

The effect of earnings uncertainty — proxied by $(\hat{u}_i)^2$ — on consumption is negative, a result consistent with the existence of precautionary saving. The effect is quantitatively important. The table below shows the impact of risk in different years. In constructing this table we adjust the OLS estimate of the coefficient on $\hat{u}_i^2$ (shown in Tables 7.3 and 7.4) using an estimate for the ratio of σ_ε^2 to σ_ω^2 of $\frac{2}{3}$ — the value implied by a ratio of the OLS coefficient on $\hat{u}_i$ to that on $\hat{Y}_i$ of 0.6. Assuming that ε and ω are normal we find, using (7.22), that a corrected estimate of λ_5 is just over four times larger than the coefficient on $\hat{u}_i^2$, reflecting the fact that $\hat{u}_i^2$ is a substantial overestimate of true income uncertainty to households which seriously biases down the OLS estimate. We then use (7.18) to construct a measure of average income risk equal to

$$\left(\sum_{i=1}^{n} \hat{u}_i^2 / (n - k) \right) / \left(1 + \tfrac{3}{2} \right)$$

where we use the fact that $E(\varepsilon_i \omega_i) = 0$ and again take $\sigma_\varepsilon^2 = \left(\tfrac{2}{3} \right) \sigma_\omega^2$.

The first column of the table shows that a household with a level of income uncertainty twice the mean consumes, on average, around 1.8% less than an averagely risky household. Furthermore, the spread of risks between households is great;

Table 7.5 The impact of uncertainty on consumption

	Effect of twice average risk (%)	Risk measure 1 standard deviation above average (%)
1968	−1.24	−16.8
1977	−1.36	−8.23
1983	−3.70	−23.5
1986	−1.19	−35.4
1990	−1.44	−17.5

across the five years the average coefficient of variation of estimated risk (the ratio of the standard deviation of $\hat{u}_i^2$ to its mean) is 13. The second column shows how much lower consumption is for a household with risk one standard deviation above the mean for that year. In most years a household with risk one standard deviation above average consumes more than 15% less. These estimates suggest that precautionary saving, as opposed to consumption smoothing or life-cycle saving, may account for a large proportion of total saving. This finding confirms those of Zeldes (1989b) and Caballero (1990) who argue that precautionary saving is quantitatively important, but it is in contrast to other US studies (e.g. Skinner, 1988) which cast doubt on the ability of the precautionary saving hypothesis to account for some of the puzzling features of consumption.

Age and age squared are significant and vary considerably across occupations — a finding which mirrors the variability in age effects revealed in the income regressions. As earlier studies have found, the demographic and work status of the household influence consumption. Households with more people, which in our sample invariably means more children, consume more. A child adds about 5% to consumption.

Income from financial assets did not appear to have a well-defined impact on consumption, but imputed income from home ownership seems to have a powerful and consistent effect — those who owned their own home appeared to consume more than non home owners by an amount equal to about twice their imputed income. One way to interpret this result is to see the estimate of imputed income as around one half the rent which home owners would otherwise have to pay to buy the level of housing services; all else being equal, an owner-occupier would then be better off (in flow terms) than a renter by twice the imputed income. In fact, since the propensity to consume this higher income is likely to be less than unity, to account for the coefficients reported in the tables the value of home ownership (in terms of saved rental payments) would need to be slightly greater than twice measured imputed income.

One of our main interests is in measuring the impact of capital gains on housing. We found that it was hard to judge which was the better measure of housing capital gains — in two of the five years the fit was marginally better using $\dot{P}H2$, in the other years $\dot{P}H1$ gave slightly better results. In either case there were changes in the sign of coefficients across the five years. In the earlier years real housing capital gains appear to *reduce* household consumption; but the coefficients on both capital gains measures become less negative between 1977 and 1968 and for our second measure continue to rise between 1983 and 1977. In 1990 the impact of housing capital gains is positive for both measures, though not very precisely estimated and at the borders of significance at conventional levels (heteroscedasticity-consistent t statistics of 1.5 and 1.9 for $\dot{P}H1$ and $\dot{P}H2$ respectively). The scale of the effects is dependent upon which measure of capital gains is used. For the most recent year (1990) the percentage change in consumption induced by a 1% change in house prices over the previous year is either 0.17 (based on $\dot{P}H1$) or 0.13 (based on $\dot{P}H2$).

7.5   CONCLUSIONS

The results reported in this chapter suggest that the effect of house price rises upon consumption has changed over time. There is little evidence that capital gains on housing boosted consumption before the late 1980s; indeed there is more evidence that increases in house prices then reduced consumption. But there is evidence that the impact of house price rises upon consumption does appear to be positive for the most recent period, although the scale of the effect is hard to estimate with much confidence. Income volatility, however, consistently shows up as a significant determinant of consumption, suggesting that precautionary motives are important factors behind savings decisions. As regards human capital, we find that expectations of future labour incomes is the key determinant of consumption and that age, occupation, sex, education and regional location are the main factors influencing the level and shape of earnings over the life cycle.

What are we to make of our results on housing wealth? First, the results from this analysis of UK household data are consistent with the picture which emerged in chapters 4 and 6 where we used aggregate data: house price rises seem to have had a limited impact upon consumption prior to the 1980s; if anything the evidence suggests that price rises reduced spending in the 1960s and 1970s. But in the most recent period there is evidence that price rises boost consumption and that falling prices increase saving. The variability over time in the size, and even the sign, of the impact of house price changes on consumption seems hard to reconcile with a simple wealth effects story; if capital gains on housing were treated as a source of income comparable to the returns on financial assets we would expect a consistently positive coefficient. If we are to explain changes over time in the impact of housing capital gains it is more fruitful to think about how the ability to borrow against housing wealth may itself have changed. If an important constraint on home buyers in the 1960s and 1970s was the need to save a deposit to finance house purchase, whilst existing home-owners could not easily borrow against accumulated housing wealth, then price rises would have then reduced spending. If borrowing against housing collateral subsequently became easier — as it surely did over the course of the 1980s — then changes in house value will now boost the spending power of credit-constrained home owners. The results of this chapter are more evidence that it is this mechanism that underlies the enhanced effect of house price rises upon spending rather than a simple wealth effect.

REFERENCES

Attanasio, O. and Weber, G. (1989) Intertemporal substitution, risk aversion and the Euler equation for consumption, *The Economic Journal*, **99**, 59–73.

Barten, A. (1964) Family composition, prices and expenditure patterns. *In Econometric Analysis for National Economic Planning* edited by P. Hart, G. Mills and J. Whitaker, Butterworth, London.

Blanchard, O. (1993) Consumption and the recession of 1990–91, *American Economic Review Papers and Proceedings*, **83**, 270–4.

Blundell, R., Browning, M. and Meghir, C. (1989) A Microeconometric Model of Intertemporal Substitution and Consumer Demand. Micro to Macro Paper No. 4, Institute for Fiscal Studies, London.

Browning, M. and Meghir, C. (1991) The effects of male and female labor supply on commodity demands, *Econometrica*, **59**, 925–52.

Caballero, R. (1990) Consumption puzzles and precautionary savings, *Journal of Monetary Economics*, **25**, 113–36.

Deaton, A. (1992) *Understanding Consumption*, Clarendon Press, Oxford.

Deaton, A., Ruiz-Castillo, J. and Thomas, D. (1989) The influence of household composition on household expenditure: theory and Spanish evidence, *Journal of Political Economy*, **97**, 179–200.

Guiso, L., Jappelli, T. and Terlizzesse, D. (1992) Earnings uncertainty and precautionary saving, *Journal of Monetary Economics*, **30**, 307–37.

Hall, R. (1993) Macro theory and the recession of 1990–91, *American Economic Review Papers and Proceedings*, **83**, 275–279.

Hayashi, F. (1985) The effects of liquidity constraints on consumption: a cross-sectional analysis, *Quarterly Journal of Economics*, **100**, 183–206.

King, M. (1980) An econometric model of tenure choice and demand for housing as a joint decision, *Journal of Public Economics*, **14**, 137–59.

King, M. A. (1990) Discussion of Muellbauer and Murphy (1990), *Economic Policy*, **11**, 383–7.

King, M. (1993) Debt deflation: theory and evidence, Presidential Lecture to the European Economic Association, Helsinki. *European Economic Review* (Papers and Proceedings).

King, M. and Dicks-Mireaux, L. (1982) Asset holdings and the life-cycle, *The Economic Journal*, **92**, 247–67.

Klein, R. and Brown, S. (1988) Model selection when there is 'Minimal' prior information, *Econometrica*, **52**, 1291–1312.

Muellbauer, J. (1974) Household composition, Engel curves and welfare comparisons between households: a duality approach, *European Economic Review*, **5**, 103–22.

Muellbauer, J. and Murphy, A. (1990) Is the UK Balance of Payments Sustainable? *Economic Policy*, **11**, 345–83.

Pagan, A. (1984) Econometric issues in the analysis of regressions with generated regressors, *International Economic Review*, **25**, 221–47.

Pagan, A. (1986) Two-stage and related estimators and their applications, *Review of Economic Studies*, **53**, 527–38.

Pagano, M. (1990) Discussion by Muellbauer and Murphy (1990), *Economic Policy*, **11**, 387–90.

Perry, G. and Schultze, C. (1993) Was this recession different? Are they all different?, *Brookings Papers on Economic Activity*, **1**, 145–211.

Schwarz, G. (1978) Estimating the dimension of a model, *Annals of Statistics*, **6**, 461–4.

Skinner, J. (1988) Risky income, life cycle consumption, and precautionary savings, *Journal of Monetary Economics*, **22**, 237–55.

Skinner, J. (1989) Housing wealth and aggregate saving, *Regional Science and Urban Economics*, **19**, 305–24.

Zeldes, S. (1989a) Consumption and liquidity constraints: an empirical investigation, *Journal of Political Economy*, **97**, 305–46.

Zeldes, S. (1989b) Optimal consumption with stochastic income, *Quarterly Journal of Economics*, **104**, 275–98.

APPENDIX

The data used in this study are drawn from various UK Family Expenditure Surveys (FES). Each annual survey comprises information on incomes, expenditures and demographic characteristics of around 7000 households. The source for expenditure information are diary entries made over a two-week period by members of the household. Data from the surveys undertaken in 1968, 1977, 1983, 1986 and 1990 are used. In this appendix definitions of the key variables are given and the way in which the sample of households was selected is described.

7A.1 DATA DEFINITIONS

All flows of income and expenditure are measured in weekly equivalents which we have converted to 1990 values using the consumer price deflator.

Consumption (C_i): This is a comprehensive measure of household expenditure. It is the sum of household expenditure on fuel, light, power, food, alcohol, tobacco, clothing and footwear, durable goods (excluding cars), transport, rates, rent, water charges, home repairs and services. Consumption includes an assessment of the value of imputed services from home ownership.

Household labour income (Y_i): The income measure is based upon householders' assessment of their normal earnings. It includes income from employment, from self-employment, from pensions and from state benefits. The measure excludes the imputed income from owner occupation.

Imputed income from home ownership (IMP_i): The measure is based upon the rateable value of the property with an adjustment for the number of habitable rooms. For renters the measure is zero.

Income from financial assets (YW_i): The sum of interest income on bank and building society accounts, dividends from share ownership, rent from property and other unearned income.

Capital gains on housing:

(a) $\dot{P}H1$: For home owners this is the percentage increase in real, regional house prices over the four quarters up to the quarter in which the questionnaire was completed. For renters the measure is set to zero. The regions are the twelve standard UK regions; the house price data is from *Housing Statistics* (various editions).

(b) $\dot{P}H2$: this is $\dot{P}H1$ multiplied by IMP_i.

7A.2   SAMPLE SELECTION

We exclude all multiple family households, i.e. we include only households where there is a single adult or a couple (married or unmarried). Households for whom reported income was zero or negative were excluded. Households were also excluded if the ratio of consumption to income exceeded 10.

CHAPTER 8

Financial liberalization and the design of mortgage contracts

8.1 INTRODUCTION

Mortgage debt has been more easily available in the US, UK and, more recently, in Scandinavia than in most other countries; home owners there are more heavily indebted than their counterparts in the rest of Europe and in Japan. These facts suggest, though do not prove, that higher debt levels — and perhaps also higher rates of owner-occupation — are a reflection of more liberal credit conditions and not just the result of an aversion by households on the Continent of Europe and in Japan to highly geared house purchase. The recent removal of most of the remaining barriers to free trade in financial services within the European Community, and the plans to further co-ordinate the regulation of financial institutions, may result in convergence in the range of debt contracts available to finance house purchase. But the recent and dramatic rise in the level of debt-repayment problems encountered in the UK, which have caused repossessions by lenders on an unprecedented scale and have generated substantial losses on bad debts, makes it less likely that contracts that became common during the 1980s in the UK will be widely available throughout Europe. Indeed it is possible that 100% mortgages and mortgages equal to three or four times the annual salary of home owners — which were readily available in the late 1980s — are a thing of the past even within the UK. How tenure choices made by households will be affected by changes in the type of financial contracts on offer can have a dramatic impact upon the demand for owner-occupied housing. In this chapter we will consider the issues in the European context.

First, we consider the evidence on current lending conditions within Europe. We then consider the changes brought about by the establishment of a single market in financial services. The characteristics of various types of financial contracts — on the risk of debt-servicing problems and on the scope for house purchase — are considered in Section 8.4. In Section 8.5 we bring the strands together and analyse how financing and home ownership patterns might evolve within Europe.

8.2   HOUSING FINANCE WITHIN EUROPE

Table 8.1, reproduced from the *Bank of England Quarterly Bulletin* (1991), shows the nature of loan contracts available in various countries at the end of the 1980s. The table shows that the amount of housing finance available to *individual* households has been greater in the US and UK than in other countries. In France and Germany it has been rare for institutions to lend more than 80% of the value of a home; in Italy loans have rarely covered more than 50% of the value of a home. In the UK loan-to-value ratios have been higher and have been rising. Table 8.2 shows that the average advance from UK building societies to home buyers rose from under 60% of the average purchase price in 1980 to over 70% by the end of 1992. For first-time buyers the ratios are significantly higher; the *average* percentage advance was around 83% at the end of 1992. The relatively low requirement for a deposit within the UK has made house purchase feasible for young people. Table 8.3 shows home ownership rates for various age groups in various countries at the start of the 1980s. Over 50% of adults in the age range 25–29 were owner-occupiers in the UK — in Germany only 15% of people in this age range owned their own home. Furthermore, the average age at which a first home is purchased in the UK fell significantly in the 1980s. By the first quarter of 1993 almost a quarter of first-time buyers in the UK were less than 25 years of age *(Housing Finance*, August 1993, Table 8.9a).

Not only have loan-to-value and loan-to-income ratios been greater in the UK than in other countries but the proportion of lending which is at variable rates of interest has also been higher. Table 8.4 describes the way in which mortgage payments are determined in the major countries; only in the UK have variable-rate loans been common. The combination of predominantly variable rate loan contracts with volatile and unpredictable nominal rates of interest has made the risks of mass default higher in the UK than in the other European economies. While defaults on mortgage loans are rare in France, Italy and Germany the levels of serious arrears in mortgage repayments and the rate of repossessions of homes by lenders rose dramatically in the UK in the early 1990s. Table 8.5 tells the story. In the first half of the 1980s annual repossessions had been rising slowly but were never more than 0.2% of the outstanding stock of mortgages. In 1991 repossessions were in excess of 75 000 — over 0.75% of all mortgages. The number of households in serious arrears with mortgage payments was about ten times higher in 1992 than in the early 1980s. The great majority of those who fell seriously behind with payments had taken out mortgages in the late 1980s and early 1990s when prices reached a peak and when financial firms had been prepared to lend up to 100% of the value of homes (Bank of England, 1992). The decline in nominal house prices in the

Table 8.1[†]   Credit availability in housing finance markets

	United Kingdom	Japan	United States	Germany	Spain	France	Italy
Extent of credit rationing	Slight	To a limited extent	Slight	To a limited extent	To a limited extent	To a limited extent	To a limited extent
Rationing chosen by lender or due to regulation?	Chosen	Chosen	Chosen	Chosen and regulatory	Chosen and regulatory; credit controls exist.	Chosen and regulatory	Chosen and regulatory
Loan-to-value ratio	Up to 100% though > 95% is rare	Typically around 60%	To circulate on secondary markets must meet certain criteria. 95% possible.	Contract savings loans do not normally cover more than 25–30% (linked to accumulated savings)* Mortgage bond funded loans cannot exceed 60%.	Savings banks offer loans up to 80%	Free sector loans up to 80% available	Normal limit is 50%
Maturity (typical)	25 years	25–30 years	28 years	Vary considerably. Bausparkassen up to 12 years. Mortgage bond funded loans up to 30 years.	10–15 years	15 years	10–25 years

(Continued overleaf)

Table 8.1 *(Continued)*

	United Kingdom	Japan	United States	Germany	Spain	France	Italy
Loan to income ratios	Typically 3 1/2 is the limit	Varies according to loan maturity 3.7 possible	The standard loan/income ratio is 3:1	Bausparkassen loans are linked to accumulated savings	—	Loan limits often set so that interest payments are usually no more than 35% of net cash flow	—
Queuing	No	—	No	No	No	No	There are 6 month waits for some SCI loans
Deposits with lender required to get a loan?	No	No	No	For loans obtained from Bausparkassen	For savings home loan accounts	Required for 'comptes d'epargne logement' and 'plans d'epargne logement' loans	No

*It is common in Germany for a package of loans from several lenders to be assembled for the borrower by one of the lenders.
†Reproduced from Bank of England (1991).

Table 8.2   Building societies average loans relative to average house prices %

	All buyers	First-time buyers	Average advance/ average income first-time buyers
1975	62.6	76.4	1.94
1976	65.8	79.3	1.88
1977	65.1	78.4	1.77
1978	65.5	79.9	1.82
1979	58.6	75.7	1.79
1980	56.7	73.8	1.67
1981	61.9	79.1	1.74
1982	67.9	85.1	1.76
1983	67.5	85.1	1.87
1984	68.6	84.7	1.93
1985	69.2	85.3	1.94
1986	69.5	86.1	2.03
1987	67.2	84.7	2.05
1988	66.1	84.8	2.15
1989	65.8	82.9	2.16
1990	67.0	82.5	2.19
1991	68.9	82.7	2.21
1992	70.4	83.3	2.16
1993 (H1)	71.4	82.0	2.11

Reproduced from *Housing Finance* (various issues) by permission of the Council for Mortgage Lenders

Table 8.3   Owner-occupation by age — international comparisons

Age	Great Britain	Canada	USA	Italy	W. Germany	France	Nethlnds
< 25	30	17	19	41	4	7	16
25–29	54	44	38	—	15	42	35
30–44	67	68	—	53	—	—	53
45–59	50	78	74	—	—	61	45
60–64	50	75	—	—	49	—	—
65+	45	61	71	67	63	58	31

Figures refer to 1982 or 1983; blanks indicate raw data not available.
Reproduced from Boleat (1989) by permission of the Council for Mortgage Lenders

early 1990s left millions of households with negative equity — mortgage debt in excess of the value of the home.

   This recent experience prompted the Governor of the Bank of England in 1993 to speculate on the welfare implications of the structure of housing markets in the UK relative to conditions in other countries. He was sceptical whether the current system of housing finance and of housing taxation was compatible with the efficient allocation of investment expenditure:

Table 8.4 Mortgage contracts in the major economies

United Kingdom	The overwhelming majority of existing mortgages (around 90%) is at variable rate.
France	Loans are predominantly at fixed rate, usually for between 15 and 20 years. Some variable rate mortgages are used, often with caps on the increase in interest rates possible.
Sweden	Only between 8% and 10% of mortgage lending is at variable rate. Fixed-rate loans are mainly financed by issues of securities by lenders.
Germany	Most loans are at rates fixed for 5 to 10 years and are funded by long-term, fixed-rate savings or by the issue of fixed-rate bonds.
Canada	The most common mortgage instrument has a fixed interest rate for a term of between one and five years.
United States	74% of mortgages are at fixed rates; rates are often fixed for the life of the mortgage.
Australia	The overwhelming majority of existing mortgages are at variable rate. However, changes in interest rates frequently lead to a change in the term to maturity of existing loans, rather than a change in payments. Fixed-rate mortgages (up to 5 years) were introduced in 1989.
Denmark	Most loans are at fixed rate for an original maturity of between 20 and 30 years.
The Netherlands	Nearly all household sector borrowing is in the form of long-term loans with fixed rates.
Japan	Most lending is at reviewable rates, but these are related to the long-term prime rate. The housing loan corporation, which accounts for about 40% of loans, reviews rates twice a year and has a cap on rates (which at end 1993 was 5.5%).
Italy	Italian households make comparatively little use of mortgage debt to finance house purchase; around half of mortgages are at variable rates.

Reproduced from Miles (1994), Table G, by kind permission of the Bank of England.

The pent-up demand of the Second World War and the years after it when building materials were scarce, created the conditions for a boom which was accentuated by tax incentives. Home ownership was seen as a laudable social goal, especially as post-war purchasers saw the value of the investment in their property rise. The building societies which helped purchasers achieve this goal also helped savers by offering them good rates of return yet apparently minimal risk, since their money was ultimately secured against property whose nominal value scarcely ever fell. The effect of growing demand was to drive prices upward more rapidly than inflation: this added the final twist... which... stimulated demand as purchasers extended themselves financially in order to participate as much as possible in a game in which it then seemed no one could lose. We know only too well what trouble this game could bring, especially to purchasers who now find themselves owing more than their property is worth at a time when many families face hardship through reduced earnings and unemployment.... The encouragement towards home purchase in the United Kingdom

Table 8.5 Mortgage arrears and repossessions

	Number of mortgages at year end	Repossessions during the year
1980	6,210,000	3,480
1981	6,336,000	4,870
1982	6,518,000	6,860
1983	6,846,000	8,420
1984	7,313,000	12,400
1985	7,717,000	19,300
1986	8,138,000	24,090
1987	8,283,000	26,390
1988	8,564,000	18,510
1989	9,125,000	15,810
1990	9,415,000	43,890
1991	9,815,000	75,540
1992	9,922,000	68,540

Properties taken into possession include those voluntarily surrendered.
Reproduced from *Housing Finance*, Table 11, No. 18, May 1993, by permission of the Council for Mortgage Lenders.

has been made greater in the post-war period by the bias against renting which was supported by legislation and the tax system.... . Moreover low deposit requirements and high earnings multiples for lending for house purchase have meant that savings have been channelled into bricks and mortar, rather than commercial enterprise. But it is no use casting envious eyes on other economies like Germany's with healthy rented sectors unless we establish the same conditions here which make this possible .... .

(Bank of England Quarterly Bulletin, February 1993).

We shall consider the role of tax reform and of changes in the treatment of the rental sector in the next chapter. Our concern in this chapter is with changes in the type of financial contract to finance house purchase. There are two questions: first, whether-in the light of widespread financial distress in the early 1990s-the type of loan contract available in the UK will change. We analyse this issue in Section 8.4 by considering the characteristics of various alternatives to the standard, variable-rate, fixed-period mortgage that has until very recently been the dominant debt contract in the UK mortgage market. Second, we consider whether the establishment of a single European market in financial services will increase the range of contracts available on the Continent. In the next section we consider how barriers which may have prevented financial firms offering credit contracts throughout the European Community are being removed. We then look at the risk characteristics of various types of credit contracts and consider how they affect tenure patterns. Future trends in lending for house purchase are analysed in Section 8.6.

8.3   THE ESTABLISHMENT OF THE SINGLE EUROPEAN MARKET[1]

In the period from the late 1970s, and then throughout the 1980s, European financial markets underwent significant changes which saw numerous forms of regulation on the activities of financial institutions abolished. This process of deregulation continued in the 1990s as a part of the establishment of a single European market in goods and services.

Several causal factors can be identified behind the process of deregulation. Technological progress has so reduced the cost of marketing and trading financial claims that new products have been created at a rapid rate. The Cross report (Bank for International Settlements, 1986) notes that... 'Some observers have contended... that the costs of processing and transmitting information have declined by as much as 98% over the past twenty years' (p. 195).

That report describes a range of new financial instruments (currency and interest rate swaps, interest rate options, new forward and futures contracts) which have extended the choices facing households and companies in raising funds and accumulating wealth. What these new possibilities have meant is that in the 1980s existing regulations designed to control a particular activity — lending to finance consumption or investment, or to take advantage of yield differentials in different European financial centres — have become easier to avoid. The exposures from borrowing in a foreign currency, for example to avoid restrictions on domestic lending, can be more cheaply handled if technology allows hedging transactions to be undertaken at small cost. The increasing ability of financial and non-financial firms to fund activities in new ways — one instance of which is the process of securitization and the rise of off-balance sheet finance — presented monetary authorities throughout Europe with a dilemma. Either new and more wide-ranging forms of regulation would be needed to prevent existing controls (for example on bank lending) being side-stepped, thus rendering their impact merely cosmetic, or the strategy of using administrative restrictions as a tool of macroeconomic policy had to be abandoned.

One factor has been central in explaining why European countries followed the second route — namely the increasing political support for the establishment of a single European market. The feasibility of national authorities preserving a regime of administrative controls aimed at enhancing their control over particular financial aggregates, most commonly measures of the money supply and credit aggregates, was simply not consistent with the goal of a free market in financial services. The experience of the UK government in the wake of the abolition of exchange controls in 1979 is instructive here. The freedom of UK financial and non-financial corporations to raise funds abroad — which is essential to the establishment of the single market — made limits on the rate of expansion of UK banks' liabilities largely ineffective as a means to control the rate of growth of domestic lending. The abolition of the Corset, which had been designed to penalize banks for increasing domestic liabilities beyond stated limits, followed soon after the liberalization in exchange controls (Goodhart, 1987, 1989b). More generally it is clear that once one part of the edifice of regulations is removed this can have dramatic implications on the effectiveness of remaining restrictions — one card in the pack being removed can bring the rest tumbling down.

Yet the extent to which controls were abandoned in the 1980s varied greatly across countries. In part this reflects significant variation in the degree to which countries had relied upon restrictions in their domestic financial markets. Germany, for example, had not relied upon exchange restrictions nor quantitative limits on lending in the post-war period; the process of deregulation there has consequently been less marked than in France, the UK and the Nordic countries. Summarizing the process of deregulation in the 1980s is difficult precisely because European countries started from such different positions. It is still instructive to briefly describe some of the major measures which have been taken. Deregulation in five distinct areas can be identified. In each case I list below some of the major changes in the 1980s, though in no way is the list comprehensive. I then describe the rules governing the access of firms located in one country to the markets of other member states and then focus on changes specific to housing markets.

Exchange and capital controls. The UK abolished foreign exchange controls in 1979. Denmark effectively abolished controls in 1983. In the first half of 1990 both France and Italy dismantled their longstanding capital controls, some months before the deadline set in the Directive of the European Communities of June 1988. In that Directive a deadline was also set for the abolition of restrictions on movements of capital in Greece, Ireland, Portugal and Spain. The Directive also required the abolition of dual exchange rate systems operated in Luxembourg and Belgium (Grilli, 1989a, b).

Interest rate ceilings. In Sweden ceilings on bank deposit rates were abolished in 1978; restrictions on bank loan rates were dismantled in 1985 (Englund, 1990). Liberalization of interest rate setting in Spain, already established for maturities over one year by 1977, was completed in 1987 (Vives, 1990). In 1980 Switzerland abolished punitive restrictions on non-resident Swiss franc deposits. In France there was, as recently as 1983, a 'wide range of cartelized and administered interest rates' (Melitz, 1990, p. 394). By 1990 the only interest rates which were administered were on bank deposits (Baltensperger and Dermine, 1987).

Lending restrictions. In the UK the 'Corset', a system of sliding penalties on banks designed to control the growth of their balance sheets, was abolished in 1980. In France the 'encadrement du credit', a credit ceiling arrangement which impinged on banks, was abolished on New Year's Day 1985. In 1985 Sweden abolished ceilings on loans from banks and finance companies.

Securities market reforms. Minimum commission rules and membership restrictions on the London Stock Exchange were abolished with the advent of the Big Bang in 1986 (Bank of England, 1985a, 1987). The Banking Act of 1984 in France abolished old divisions between commercial and investment banks. A bond futures market (the MATIF) was established in Paris in 1986 and companies were allowed to float commercial paper.

Ownership rules and foreign activity in domestic markets. Several of those European countries which had restrictions on overseas' institutions ability to operate in domestic markets eased them in the 1980s: Sweden allowed foreign bank subsidiaries to operate in 1986; Spain has allowed (restricted) entry of foreign banks since 1978; Portugal repealed its prohibition against foreign banks establishing subsidiaries or branches in 1983; in 1985 Norway permitted subsidiaries of overseas banks to be established; Finland allowed foreign banks to establish branches in 1991.

The single European passport. Under the 1992 programme financial institutions which are authorized to trade in any EC country will be able to offer services throughout the community. (See, in particular, the European Commission's Second Banking Directive and the directive on 'Investment in the Securities Field' — 1988 and 1989 respectively). The Second Banking Directive came into force on 1 January 1993. It is the establishment of the EC 'passport' which will allow financial firms with the experience of financing highly geared house purchases in partic- ular countries to offer these contracts throughout the European community. It is this process — the creation of the passport — which is the significant change in the 1990s in financial services within Europe; we have seen that many of the other barriers to a single market — most obviously capital controls — had already been abolished by the end of the 1980s. The implications of the EC rules governing the removal of regulatory barriers to firms operating outside their country of origin were spelled out clearly by the Bank of England in 1993:

> Under the passport, an EC firm authorized in one member state (its 'home state') and wishing to operate in other Member States ('host states') will generally be able to choose whether to supply services through branches (i.e. to establish a physical presence of the same legal entity) or to supply services on a cross-border basis without having a permanent physical presence in the host state. It will, of course, still be free to apply to set up subsidiaries in other Member States. These subsidiaries will remain subject to local authorisation requirements, on a non-discriminatory basis.
>
> An EC passport helps to increase competition by opening markets to a wider range of participants and by allowing firms to choose the most cost-effective means of supplying services to a particular market. It will, for example, generally allow a firm to operate throughout Europe on a single unified capital base. This removes the need to establish subsidiaries with separate capital (which might not be very easily transferable and therefore might be underutilized if business shifted temporarily from one country to another), or to maintain capital in branches. It will give firms greater flexibility in organising their management structure and internal systems. It will also enable them to deal with fewer sets of regulations and regulators.
>
> (Bank of England, 1993, p. 92).

In the next section we analyse the nature of various types of loan contract before considering the supply and demand for these contracts within a single European market in Section 8.5.

8.4   THE STRUCTURE OF FINANCIAL CONTRACTS

8.4.1   VARIABLE-RATE MORTGAGES

At the household level the types of mortgage contracts available affect the timing
and size of house purchase and also influence the risk of default. At the aggregate
level the rate of owner-occupation, the level of house prices and also the transmission mechanism of monetary policy — itself a function of the size, distribution and
servicing cost of debt — are likely to be influenced by the terms of loan contracts.
Those terms are not exogenous but the result of decisions by financial institutions
made in the light of their perceptions of risks and the costs of funds, and made
subject to legal regulations and financial supervision. We saw in the last section that
the legal and regulatory environment within Europe is changing; the evidence on
the scale of mortgage defaults in the UK reviewed in Section 8.2 makes it likely
that perceptions of risk by lenders in that country have also changed. Here we
consider how these factors could interact and how new types of financial contract
could appear within Europe.

There are several characteristics of a loan contract: maturity, or repayment
period; rate of interest; the size of loan relative to the value of collateral; the size
of loan relative to household income; and the degree of flexibility in the repayment
profile, and in the maturity, of the loan. The ability to service debt — to make
regular repayments — is a function of each of these characteristics. If we assume
that there is no other source of debt available to a household, so that repayments
must be made out of disposable income, then the probability of a household being
unable to avoid arrears is the probability of its repayments exceeding the maximum
proportion of disposable income that it can allocate to debt servicing. We can
develop a simple expression for the servicing burden of mortgage repayments in
terms of the loan characteristics described above. Let us denote the outstanding
mortgage t periods into its life by M_t and the size of the original mortgage, which
we assume is made when a house was purchased, by M_0. Let y_t denote the current
value of disposable income. Denote the current value of the house by p_{ht}, and its
value at the time of purchase by p_{h0}. The nominal interest rate is r_t and we let the
consumer price index be p_{ct}.

A standard, variable-rate, repayment loan, which has been the dominant credit
contract for house purchase in the UK, is one where if nominal interest rates were to
remain unchanged nominal mortgage payments would be constant and the present
value of future repayments discounted at the current mortgage rate would equal
the size of the loan. If we denote the period t repayment by m_t this implies that,
for a variable-rate mortgage,

$$m_t = (r_t/(1 + r_t))M_t/(1 - (1/(1 + r_t)^{T+1-t})) \tag{8.1}$$

where T is the original (at $t = 0$) term to maturity of the mortgage.

We can write the ratio of mortgage repayments to household income:

$$m_t/y_t = (r_t/(1 + r_t))(M_t/p_{ht})(p_{ht}/y_t)/(1 - (1/(1 + r_t)^{T+1-t})) \tag{8.2}$$

Now define the following rates of increase in prices and incomes. Denote the per-period consumer price inflation rate between time 0 and time t by π_{ct}; let per-period, real (in terms of consumer goods) income growth over the same period be g_{yt} and real (again in terms of consumer prices) house price inflation be π_{ht}. By definition,

$$(1 + \pi_{ct})^t \equiv p_{ct}/p_{c0} \tag{8.3}$$

$$(1 + g_{yt})^t \equiv (y_t/y_0)(p_{c0}/p_{ct}) \tag{8.4}$$

$$(1 + \pi_{ht})^t \equiv (p_{ht}/p_{h0})(p_{c0}/p_{ct}) \tag{8.5}$$

Using (8.4) and (8.5) in (8.2) we can now write

$$m_t/y_t = (r_t/(1+r_t))(M_t/p_{ht})(p_{h0}/y_0)[(1+\pi_{ht})/(1+g_{yt})]^t/(1-(1/(1+r_t)^{T+1-t})) \tag{8.6}$$

If interest rates between 0 and t have not changed we can write the outstanding mortgage at t as a simple function of M_0, t, T and r_t. Using (8.1), and noting that, if interest rates are unchanged between 0 and t, $m_0 = m_s$ for all $s (0 < s \leq t)$, we can deduce

$$M_t = M_0\{[1 - (1/(1 + r_t))^{T+1-t}]/[1 - (1/(1 + r_t))^{T+1}]\} \tag{8.7}$$

(8.7) implies that as we approach the end of period T (i.e. as we approach period $T + 1$, so $t \to T + 1$), $M_t \to 0$ and the mortgage is repaid. Using (8.7) in (8.6) and nothing that $p_{ht} = p_{h0}(1 + \pi_{ht})^t(1 + \pi_{ct})^t$ gives

$$m_t/y_t = (r_t/(1+r_t))(M_0/p_{h0})(p_{h0}/y_0)[(1+\pi_{ct})(1+g_{yt})]^{-t}/[1 - (1/(1+r_t)^{T+1})] \tag{8.8}$$

(8.8) expresses the debt service burden at time t as a function of the original loan-to-value ratio (M_0/p_{h0}), the house-price–income ratio at the time of the house purchase (p_{h0}/y_0), the rates of increase of real incomes (g_{yt}) and of consumer goods prices (π_{ct}) over the period since the mortgage was granted, the term to maturity of the loan (T), the time since the loan was taken out (t) and the nominal interest rate (r_t).

We use (8.8) to show how a variable-rate mortgage makes the fraction of income devoted to servicing debt heavily dependent upon the rate of inflation — a phenomenon known as front-end loading. Figure 8.1 shows the time series of the servicing ratio (m_t/y_t) for various steady state rates of inflation (π_c). We assume here that real interest rates are constant so that the nominal interest rate is equal to the real rate (which we take to be 2.5%) plus an inflation adjustment $(r = (1.025)(1 + \pi_c) - 1)$. We take the real income growth rate to be equal to the real interest rate at 2.5%. We use a house price to income ratio of 2.5, a loan to value ratio of 0.9 and a loan maturity of 25 years — figures which are typical for a young, first-time buyer in the UK. These figures imply that the loan-to-income ratio at the time of house purchase is 2.25 (which was the ratio of average advance

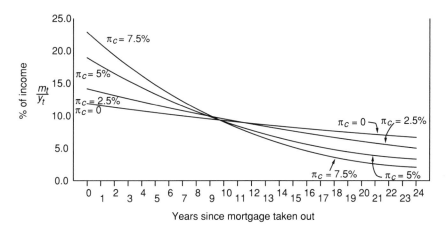

Figure 8.1   Debt servicing burden

to average house price for first-time buyers at the end of 1991). The figure shows that at zero inflation the proportion of income taken by mortgage payments is initially around 12%; this falls to 10% by year six as a result of the growth in real income. When inflation is low, but non-zero, the impact on the servicing ratio is still significant; with prices rising at a steady 2% a year the initial repayments are now over 14.5% of income and only fall to 10% by year nine. At 5% inflation the initial burden of servicing debt is 19% but by year ten the combination of inflation and real income growth generates a servicing ratio half that size. At high consumer price inflation of 7.5% mortgage payments take almost 23% of initial income; the front-end loading of payments is now severe and by year eight payments are down to around 10% of income and by year fifteen payments only account for 5% of income.

Figures 8.2(a) and 8.2(b) show the impact of a change in the *real* interest rate for home-owners who had bought homes at various points in the past. We assume that inflation has been running at 2% and that the house-price–income and loan-to-value ratios are as before. The charts show the impact of an increase in the real rate from 2.5% to 4.5% upon home-owners who bought their home at various times (this increase means nominal rates have to rise from 4.55% to 6.6%). Figure 8.2 (a) shows the effect of a rise in rates in the fifth year after house purchase; Figure 8.2 (b) shows what happens to the servicing burden if the increase in the real rate of interest comes one year after the mortgage is taken out. If a household has had a chance to let inflation and income growth erode the mortgage burden over five years before interest rates rise the impact is moderate — the servicing ratio would have been 11.6% at unchanged interest rates but jumps to 13.6%. Notice from the figure that as time passes the servicing burdens approach each other since as $t \rightarrow T$ the interest element in repayments falls to zero. The increase in the debt service burden is somewhat more severe if it comes

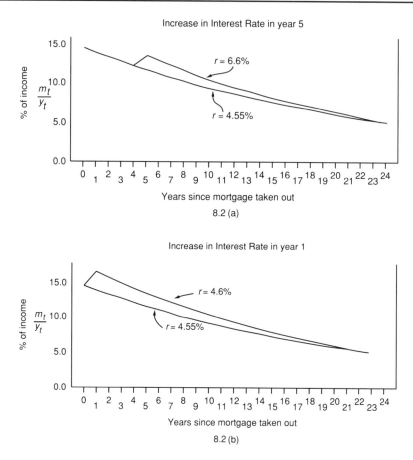

Figure 8.2   Increase in interest rate in (a) year 5; (b) year 1

soon after house purchase (Figure 8.2 (b)); after one year mortgage repayments jump from 14% of income to almost 17% when interest rates go up 2%.

Increases in inflation clearly exacerbate the front-end loading problem. But it is important to note that the effect of a jump in inflation from, say, 0% to 5%, and a rise in nominal interest rates sufficient to keep real rates constant, cannot be inferred from Figure 8.1, which shows the steady-state paths of the ratios. Figures 8.3(a) and 8.3(b) show what happens to the servicing ratios when we move from one inflation regime to another. Figure 8.3 (a) shows the path taken by the servicing ratio in the wake of a rise in inflation and in nominal interest rates for a household which has had a mortgage for five years when inflation increases; Figure 8.3 (b) shows what happens to a household who has only had a mortgage for one year when higher inflation arrives. If the increase in inflation from zero to 5% comes after five years the debt repayments jump in that year from 10% of income to

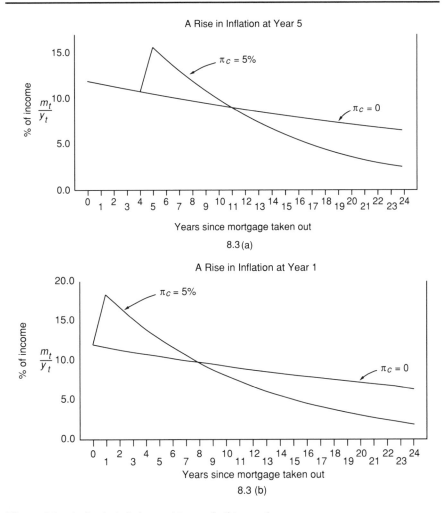

Figure 8.3   A rise in inflation at (a) year 5; (b) year 1

15.5%; but five years later the debt burden along the higher inflation path is lower than on the stable price path. Figure 8.3 (b) shows how serious the impact is on a recent home owner; with no inflation the debt repayment would have been 11.5% of income after one year. If inflation and nominal interest rates jump at that point the burden rises to over 18%. Eight years later the burden along the high inflation path is lower than it would have been with constant prices.

With variable-rate debt contracts the most crippling combination of events for recent buyers is an increase in inflation—which makes the front-end loading problem serious—which prompts the monetary authorities to raise *real* interest rates to counter the inflationary pressure. Figure 8.4 shows what happens to the

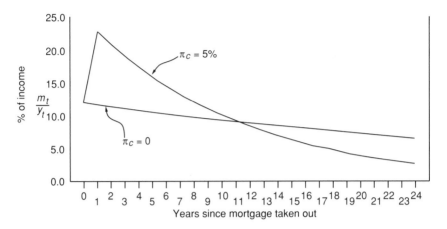

Figure 8.4   Rising inflation and real rates

servicing ratio of a household one year into home ownership when a jump in the rate of inflation from 0 to 5% causes the authorities to increase the nominal rate of interest by an amount sufficient to raise the real rate to 4.5%. In the figure we are assuming that the increase in the real interest rate is slow to affect actual inflation, which remains at 5%; in fact the impact effect on the debt burden will be as shown so long as inflation does not respond immediately to the tightening of monetary policy. The figure show how dramatic that initial impact is; the servicing ratio doubles from 11.5% to around 23%. This simulation shows clearly the problems for a government which aims to use the interest rate as its counter-inflationary policy instrument in an economy where house purchases for new owner-occupiers are financed largely on credit whose servicing costs vary with nominal rates of interest. If increases in real interest rates have a greater short-run impact upon house prices than upon consumer prices — and in the light of the asset market approach to house prices developed in Chapter 2 that is likely — then the debt-servicing problems of recent home owners will be combined with a rise in capital gearing, i.e. an increase in the ratio of outstanding debt to current house value. So a rise in interest rates to combat inflationary pressures is likely to significantly increase problems amongst recent home buyers in making mortgage repayments and also increase the number of households with negative equity.

Events in the UK between the late 1980s and the early 1990s illustrate the problem (Table 8.6). Between 1986 and 1987 consumer prices rose, on average, at an annual rate of slightly under 3.7% and short-term, nominal interest rates fell to 7.5% by the middle of 1988. In 1988 consumer prices rose by over 5% and in 1989 by over 6%. As it became clearer that inflation was rising the Government increased nominal interest rates, and by much more than the rise in inflation, so as to bring downwards pressure on prices. Base lending rates — which are tied to the short-term money market rates most closely controlled by the Bank of

Table 8.6   Inflation and interest rates in the UK

	Consumer price inflation (%)	Interest rates (%)	Change in house prices (%)
1984	4.1	9.6	8.5
1985	5.1	11.5	8.6
1986	3.4	11.0	13.4
1987	3.9	8.5	15.4
1988	5.1	13.0	34.2
1989	6.1	15.0	4.9
1990	9.3	14.0	0.3
1991	5.6	10.5	−2.5
1992	3.7	7.0	−8.0

Inflation is the percentage change in the retail price index excluding mortgage interest payments (quarter 4 on quarter 4); the interest rate is the base rate of selected retail banks at the year end; house-price inflation is the change in the Halifax House price index (quarter 4 on quarter 4).
Reproduced from Miles (1994) by permission of the Bank of England

England—rose from 7.5% in May of 1988 to 15% by October of 1989. Mortgage rates followed. Consumer price inflation was slow to respond; indeed inflation increased to more than 9% in 1990. But the *level* of *nominal* house prices was flat in 1990 and fell in 1991 by 2.5%; in 1992 average house prices fell by 8.0%. House-price falls were most dramatic in those regions—the South East and East Anglia—where the level of prices had been highest and where first-time buyers had needed to borrow most to enter owner-occupation.

Looking at the expression for the servicing ratio—equation (8.8)—suggests that there are two ways in which variable-rate mortgage contracts could come to pose fewer problems of debt-servicing and which would make the cost of using monetary policy to counter inflation fall less heavily upon recent home buyers. First, the maturity of mortgages could be increased beyond the usual 25 years. Second, the ratio of initial home loan to initial income—the product of the house-price–income ratio at the time of purchase and the loan-to-value ratio—could be reduced. We consider each of these in turn before analysing alternatives to the variable—rate mortgage.

Increasing the Repayment Period

Table 8.7 shows the result of varying the term to maturity on the initial debt service ratio at various rates of inflation. As before we use a loan-to-value ratio of 0.9 and a house-price–income ratio at the time of house purchase of 2.5. While increasing the loan maturity obviously reduces the debt service burden at all inflation rates it is apparent that the reduction is less significant the higher is the rate of inflation; with inflation at 7.5% increasing the term of the loan substantially from 25 to 35 years only reduces the servicing burden from 22.8% to 21.5%. Indeed the longer is the

Table 8.7   The impact of loan maturity on the debt-servicing burden

T	$\pi_c = 0$ (%)	$\pi_c = 2$ (%)	$\pi_c = 5$ (%)	$\pi_c = 7.5$ (%)
25	11.9	14.6	19.0	22.8
30	9.5	13.3	17.9	22.0
35	8.7	12.4	17.3	21.5

term to maturity the greater is the *change* in the servicing ratio from unexpected increases in inflation. With a 25-year mortgage an increase in inflation from zero to 5% means an extra 7% of income needs to be devoted to debt repayments. With a 35-year mortgage an extra 8.6% of income is taken up by repayments. It is clear from the table that lengthening the repayment period is not a very effective means of solving the front-end loading problem for variable-rate mortgages.

Lower Home Loan–Income Ratio

Lenders could reduce the maximum multiple of income that home buyers can borrow. The figures and tables above are based on a house-price–income ratio of 2.5 and a loan-to-value ratio of 0.9, implying a ratio of loan-to-income at the time of purchase of 2.25. Equation (8.8) shows that, for any inflation rate and for any loan maturity and interest rate, the debt-servicing burden is proportional to the loan-to-income ratio, so a substantial reduction in either M_0/p_{h0} or in p_{h0}/y_0 would reduce the debt servicing burden significantly. Lenders certainly do appear to vary the loan-to-value ratios and loan-to-income multiples (Table 8.2); but the short-term implications of a substantial change in the lending criteria of banks and building societies upon the demand for, and price of, housing in the short term can be significant. The impact upon the longer-term pattern of home ownership can also be dramatic. A simple example helps make the point.

Consider a stylized economy with characteristics similar to the UK. We assume that the population is constant; people become adults at eighteen when they leave home and people die at 72. Everyone prefers to live in their own home but they have to save for a deposit before their first purchase. We assume that in an initial equilibrium the maximum loan-to-value ratio for first-time buyers is 0.9 and that the ratio of house prices to incomes is 3.0. Suppose that young people are able to save for a deposit only once they reach their mid-20s, from when they are able to devote 10% of income to a house-buying fund. If the return on savings is relatively small people will then be able to buy their first home just before they are 28. We assume that until they buy adults rent. Once they buy, people stay in the owner-occupied sector until death. We assume owner-occupiers move, on average, every seven years, but move more frequently when they are younger. (These assumptions are consistent with moves by home owners in the UK). Specifically, assume that the first house move comes five years after the initial purchase; the next move is six

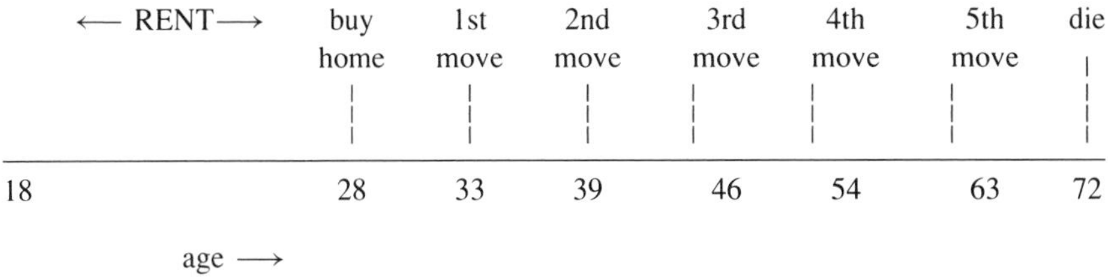

← RENT→	buy home	1st move	2nd move	3rd move	4th move	5th move	die
18	28	33	39	46	54	63	72

age →

Figure 8.5

years later and the one after that comes in seven years etc. The resulting lifetime tenure pattern in our simple model is shown in Figure 8.5.

With a constant population, this lifetime pattern of housing tenure implies that the rate of owner-occupation — the number of adults living in their own house as a proportion of all adults — is

$$(72 - 28)/(72 - 18) = 81\%$$

a figure substantially higher than owner-occupation in the UK, where a large proportion of the elderly move out of owner-occupation and back into the rented sector for the last years of their lives. (For the sake of simplicity we ignore this re-entry into the rented sector in old age.) In any one year in our simple economy the number of last-time sellers (the dead) equals the number of first-time buyers. As well as these transactions there are sales and purchases by those aged 33, 39, 46, 54 and 64. The stylized model implies that the total number of houses traded in any year, relative to the total stock of owner-occupied homes, is about 11%; it is the number of people aged 33, 39, 46, 54, 64 and 72 at any one time relative to the number of people aged over 18. (With a constant population the ratio of these numbers is 6/53.) This turnover figure is very close to the average for the UK in the 1980s. Notice that in the stylized model 1 in 6 of the transactions in the housing market involve first-time buyers.

Suppose now that lenders decide to reduce the maximum loan-to-value ratio to 0.8. At unchanged house prices the new batch of first-time buyers cannot enter the market (more accurately they cannot buy the house they had intended). If they continue to save 10% of income a year they have to postpone purchase for a further three years. Under this extreme assumption — that house prices are unchanged and that first-time buyers are inflexible over the type of house they want to buy — transactions involving first-time buyers dry up *completely* for three years. The demand for rented accommodation goes up as the proportion of adults in the rented sector rises, but the number of people looking to buy homes for owner-occupation falls 17% and stays depressed. The implications for house prices depends crucially on whether the extra demand for rented accommodation makes up for the absence of first-time buyers; so long as landlords buy the homes which first-time buyers are prevented from buying, and convert them to rented property, house prices need not change. In practice houses which are suitable for owner-occupiers are not perfect substitutes for letting accommodation; so at least in the short run there is likely to be a rise in rents and a fall in the price of owner-occupied homes. (The fall in house prices itself goes some way towards relieving the burden of saving a deposit worth 20% of a home.)

The simple example shows that the impact, at least over the short to medium term, on the demand for housing of even a relatively modest change in the maximum loan-to-value ratio set by lenders can be great. In our example the reduction in the maximum loan-to-value ratio would, at unchanged house prices and interest rates, only reduce the debt-servicing burden by about 12% (so at 5% inflation and a 2.5% real rate of interest the initial burden would only fall from 22.8% of income to 20.2% of income). But that change would increase the age at which first-time buyers could enter the market from 28 to 31 and reduce the steady-state rate of owner-occupation from 81% to 74%. These effects would be different if house prices were to be reduced, and as we saw in Chapter 2 it is plausible that prices should fall if credit become less easily available. Reductions in house values relative to incomes clearly reduces the debt-servicing burden of new buyers; but as a means of reducing the servicing problems with variable-rate mortgages, reducing house prices is a two-edged sword; those who are *not* helped are those who bought just before the fall in prices, for whom the resultant rise in the gearing ratio on their home could cause insolvency.

In an economy where highly geared house purchase at variable rates of interest has been possible, neither of the two means for reducing debt-servicing problems — increasing the maturity of loans or reducing the loan-to-value ratio — looks attractive. Rather than changing the parameters of variable-rate mortgage contracts it may be more fruitful to consider alternative means of financing house purchase. In the next section we consider three such alternatives.

8.4.2   ALTERNATIVES TO VARIABLE-RATE MORTGAGES

Fixed Nominal Rate Mortgages

Fixing the nominal interest rate over the life of the loan reduces some of the front-end loading problems analysed in the previous section; but it creates other sorts of risks. The advantage of the fixed nominal rate mortgage is that *unanticipated* increases in inflation and in short-term nominal rates of interest leave unchanged the profile of nominal repayments. But at alternative *steady-state* rates of inflation, with different levels of short-term interest rates, the front-end loading problem revealed in Figure 1 is no different with a fixed nominal rate contract. However, so long as periods of high inflation are not expected to persist long-term, nominal interest rates will be less responsive to inflation than are short-term interest rates. Under the expectations theory of the term structure of interest rates, for example, longer rates are simply the average of expected short-term rates over the relevant horizon; more generally the long rate will be a function of expected future short rates plus a term-specific risk premium (Goodhart, 1989; Elton and Gruber, 1991). In either case long rates will be less responsive to changes in short-term nominal interest rates provided those rates display mean reversion. (Mean reversion in short rates would arise if the authorities successfully used the short rate as its policy instrument to control inflation.) The availability of fixed-rate loans is therefore likely to mean that new buyers who enter the market at times when inflation is unusually high will face lower debt servicing burdens than with variable-rate loans.

But fixed-rate loans generate other risks to borrowers. For while nominal interest-rate changes cannot alter the debt-servicing burden of fixed-rate debt, unanticipated changes in inflation will. The danger with fixed-rate debt is that inflation will turn out lower than expected. Figure 8.6 shows the servicing burden on fixed-rate debt when inflation has been running at 5%, and has been expected to continue at that rate, but falls to 0% one year into the loan contract. The nominal interest rate on fixed-rate debt is assumed to be high enough to generate an annual real rate of 2.5% over the life of the loan, assuming constant 5% a year inflation. When inflation falls to zero there is no immediate increase in the real burden of debt repayments, but the burden rises as time passes. Nine years into the loan, the servicing cost would have been 10% of income at steady 5% inflation; at zero inflation interest payments would constitute 15% of income. Figure 8.3(b) and Figure 8.6 reveal the important and distinct risks of variable and fixed-rate contracts. Figure 8.3(b) shows how, with variable-rate debt, a sharp *rise* in inflation and nominal rates causes a step jump in the real burden of repayments; but real debt payments later in the life of the contract become lower. Although there is no change in the overall real value of debt-servicing, there is a significant shift forward in the time profile of payments. Figure 8.6 shows that an analogous risk for a fixed-rate borrower — a 5% unanticipated *fall* in inflation — changes the overall real burden of debt repayments but has no immediate impact on the real servicing cost. By contrast, unexpected

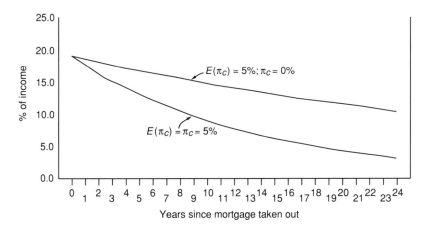

Figure 8.6   Falling inflation with fixed rates

changes in short-term interest rates at unchanged inflation raise the overall burden of payments on variable-rate debt (Figures 8.2(a) and 8.2(b)) but leave real payments for existing, fixed-rate borrowers unchanged.

While fixed nominal interest rate contracts avoid some front-end loading problems and protect mortgagees from unanticipated increases in the debt-servicing burden, they pose risk problems for lenders which, ultimately, are likely to be passed on to borrowers in a higher average cost of funds. The problem stems from the interest-rate risk that is passed to lenders when the debt contract they offer is long-term (20 to 30 years) and the interest rate is fixed in nominal terms. If lenders use funds raised at short-term rates of interest — as is currently overwhelmingly the case for banks and building societies in the UK — then the maturity mismatch between assets and liabilities creates interest rate risks to lenders. It was this maturity mismatch that led to substantial losses for US Savings and Loans in the 1980s; as short-term nominal interest rates increased the cost of funds, a large proportion of which were raised on short-term deposits, increased whilst the return on assets — primarily fixed-rate, long-term mortgage debt — was unchanged. (About 80% of home mortgage loans in the US are at fixed rates.)

The interest-rate risk problem can be avoided if lenders issue liabilities with the same duration as their assets. (Duration measures the sensitivity of asset prices to changes in short-term interest rates; it is a function of the term to maturity of an asset and of the repayment profile of the debt; see Elton and Gruber (1992)). This would imply that lenders would either issue long-term, fixed-rate instruments to finance fixed-rate mortgages or else continue to raise retail funds paying variable rates of interest and swap the fixed interest on their assets into variable-rate income. (Swapping the variable-rate obligations on their deposits into a commitment to pay at a fixed rate also removes interest-rate mismatch). The feasibility and cost of swap arrangements clearly depends upon the level of demand for a corresponding reverse swap from counter-parties.

In the UK a significant move away from funding mortgages by issuing floating-rate liabilities would mean a fundamental change in the nature of the balance sheets of banks and building societies. In the past they have relied for the majority of their funds on retail deposits, most of which payed interest at a variable rate that moved closely with the mortgage rate; a high proportion of the wholesale funds raised by these institutions have also been at short-term, money market rates. The counterpart to the variable-rate liabilities issued by deposit-takers to finance loans are liquid, variable-rate assets held, in the main part, directly by the personal sector. In the UK, at the beginning of 1993, around a quarter of the financial assets of the personal sector were deposits with banks and building societies. If a large proportion of those funds were to become long-term and fixed-rate, the portfolio of the personal sector would look very different; essentially either direct or indirect holdings of long-term bonds, which would be comparable to government bonds (gilts), would have to rise dramatically. Whether or not the cost of funds to lenders — and therefore the cost of mortgages — would have to rise depends upon two factors: (1) how willing the personal sector might be to switch a substantial proportion of its wealth to less liquid, fixed-interest assets; (2) whether alternatives to raising fixed-rate funds from the domestic personal sector are easily available to banks and building societies. As regards the second factor, the abolition of most capital controls within Europe makes tapping overseas capital easier; but the remaining substantial variability in exchange rates within Europe (at least at the time of writing) limits substitutability between assets denominated in different currencies.

Even if the maturity of each side of the balance sheet is balanced there remain risks to lenders who make fixed-rate loans that borrowers will repay mortgages early if short-term interest rates fall unexpectedly and new fixed-rate loans are available at lower rates than is being paid on existing debt. In those countries where prepayment is not prohibitive, either the suppliers of funds to lenders who finance fixed-rate mortgages, or the lending institution itself, bear risk. In the US — where many state laws prohibit lenders making penalty charges for early payment of mortgages — many of those who hold fixed-income, mortgage-backed bonds bear the risk that their securities will be called if mortgages are prepaid. The risk is that, as rates fall, securities will be redeemed and the proceeds can only be re-invested at lower rates. This risk is reflected in the yield on the securities and, ultimately, on the fixed rates charged on loans. (In the US between the middle of 1990 and the middle of 1993 the rate of interest on 80% loan-to-value, long-term, fixed-rate loans fell from around 10.5% to below 7%; over that period the level of applications for refinancing mortgages more than tripled (*Financial Times*, 17 September 1993).)

Whichever way the prepayment risks are handled — through explicit charges (as is the case for many fixed-rate loans currently issued in the UK) or indirectly via mortgage rates being high enough to compensate the providers of loans for their risk — the cost will be reflected in the terms of debt contracts.

Indexed Loans

Making it more costly for borrowers to repay mortgages is one answer to the problem of unanticipated repayments for institutions issuing long-term, fixed-rate debt. An alternative strategy is for lenders to offer mortgages where the interest rate continues to be linked to short-term nominal rates of interest but where the payment profile is designed to avoid the most serious problems of front-end loading. If nominal payments are indexed to the current price level, front-end loading is avoided. Suppose that the (steady-state) rate of increase in prices is π_c and that a contract is designed to repay the loan over T periods. With an indexed scheme, at unchanged inflation and real interest rates, payments will be constant in real, rather than nominal, terms. The repayment scheme must satisfy

$$m_t = m_0(1 + \pi_c)^t \qquad (8.9)$$

$$M_0 = \sum_{t=0}^{T} m_t/(1 + r)^t \qquad (8.10)$$

which imply

$$m_0 = M_0((r - \pi_c)/(1 + r))[1/(1 - ((1 + \pi)/(1 + r))^{T+1})] \qquad (8.11)$$

Plugging (8.9) and (8.11) into our formula for the debt-servicing burden gives

$$m_t/y_t = ((r - \pi_c)/(1+r))(M_0/p_{h0})(p_{h0}/y_0)[1 + g_{yt}]^{-t}/(1 - (1/(1+r)^{T+1})) \qquad (8.12)$$

Comparing (8.12) with (8.8) we see that the rate of inflation term drops out and that it is the adjusted real rate of interest, $(r - \pi_c)/(1 + r)$, rather than the adjusted nominal rate, $(r/(1 + r))$, that premultiplies the loan-to-value and price-to-income ratios on the right-hand side. Indexing could be taken one step further so that nominal repayments rise by the growth in nominal incomes $((1 + g_y)(1 + \pi_c) - 1)$ rather than by the growth in prices; in this case the real income growth term in (8.12) drops out and the right-hand side is independent of t, so the debt-servicing ratio is flat.

By changing only the profile of payments — while preserving the dependence of the level of payments upon the current level of interest rates — this simple indexing scheme allows lenders to continue financing loans at variable rates of interest. It is because this sort of scheme does not mean that lenders need change the financing pattern of debt that lenders in the UK were quick to offer something close to it for first-time buyers in the wake of the rise in arrears and repossessions in the early 1990s. Low-start mortgages — where initial nominal repayments are lower than future payments (assuming interest rates do not change) — are a rough form of indexing and one which has recently proved popular with first-time buyers.

Debt–Equity Contracts

The most radical alternative to the high loan-to-value, variable-rate repayment mortgage as a means to finance house purchase are contracts where the lender takes an equity stake in the house. A part-equity contract has the advantage of allowing a lower gearing ratio than a typical variable-rate mortgage while not requiring that the remainder of the funds should come from the buyer (which can put home ownership out of the reach of younger people unable to tap other sources of funds, like parents). Such schemes have two advantages to home buyers: first, so long as the payment to the lender for the right to live in that part of the house financed by the lender's equity is not dependent on changes in interest rates, the servicing costs of home ownership become less sensitive to shifts in the real or nominal cost of debt. Second, because the lender takes an equity stake in the house the net worth of the occupier becomes less sensitive to fluctuations in house prices. Lenders, or those to whom they sell on equity rights, acquire portfolios of partial shares in a stock of residential property. The risk characteristics of a portfolio of this sort to a nationwide company depends on whether shocks to house values are largely specific to particular regions or are largely systematic, or macroeconomic. The experience of the US and the UK over the 1980s — where nominal house prices rose substantially in some regions and then fell sharply (Holmans, 1990) — suggests that a high proportion of short-run variability is region specific. If there is longer-term mean reversion in regional house prices then the medium-term benefits of risk sharing are less than the short-term benefits. Even so, house-specific price risk is never zero at any time horizon and the proportion of the assets held by home-owners in their homes is generally high for many years after house purchase; consequently the risk reduction potential from part equity contracts is substantial. We shall see in the next chapter that the feasibility of such schemes in the UK may depend upon changes in the regulations of bank and, especially, building society balance sheets. In the next section we consider the issue of contract design in the European context.

8.5   MORTGAGE CONTRACTS WITHIN
THE SINGLE MARKET

In his encyclopaedic study of housing finance systems Boleat (1985) argued that while it was neither essential, nor desirable, for each country to have a shipbuilding capacity or to have car companies it was, at least in market economies, necessary to have a system of housing finance. But while in the past it has been true that finance for residential house purchase has invariably been provided by domestic institutions, with varying degrees of government control, the establishment of the single European market opens the possibility of housing finance within one country being provided largely by overseas firms.

The diversity in housing finance systems that currently exists within Europe is great. Tables 8.1 and 8.5 show that the type of financial contracts offered to borrowers, and the ways in which loans are financed by financial intermediaries, differ significantly. Some stylized facts emerge from the data presented in the tables; loans are available for longer in the US and UK than in the other European countries and in Japan; loan-to-value and loan-to-income ratios tend to be higher in the English-speaking countries; variable-rate finance has been the dominant form of lending within the UK; in the US and on the Continent fixed-rate loans have been more common and have generally been backed by the issue of long-term fixed-rate bonds. In this section we consider whether there will be convergence in the type of contracts used to finance house purchase within Europe. We are looking into the future here and as a result the ratio of speculation to tested hypothesis in this section is high.

There are at least four reasons to doubt whether we will see substantially less variability in housing-finance methods within Europe over the next few decades. First, the removal of capital restrictions and convergence in the system of financial supervision and regulation leaves huge differences in the systems of property law within Europe. So wide are the differences between the Napoleonic Code, Roman Law and British Law — sets of principles upon which national practices are based — that mortgage contracts that are suited to one country may be quite inappropriate in others. Within the Italian system, for example, repossession of property by lenders in the wake of defaults is problematic; the delay between default and foreclosure can be up to four years (*Housing Finance International*, 1988). The problem is similar in France where there is a minimum period of 30 months from initial 'delinquency' to final disposal of the collateral. Lenders who are prepared to offer 90% or 95% loans to home buyers in a country where repossession is relatively easy (at least in a legal sense) are unlikely to be willing to finance highly geared purchases in Italy and France.

Second, rental markets within Europe differ substantially. In part this is because of differences across countries in the tax treatment of owner-occupied and rental property and also because of differences in the control of rental agreements. Within Germany, for example, the tax system has not discriminated in favour of owner-occupation while rent controls have not prevented landlords earning an economic return on property (in the next chapter we shall contrast this record with that of the UK). An implication of this relatively favourable treatment of the rental sector is that the quantity and quality of rental property available within Germany is far greater than in the UK and households are willing to remain in the rental sector longer. As a result there is likely to be lower demand there for mortgages which allow people to buy houses without waiting to accumulate a 20% or 30% deposit.

Third, so long as there are distinct currencies within Europe there is the possibility — and for most of the 1990s the near certainty — of currency fluctuations; associated with these are fluctuations between countries in nominal, and real, rates of interest. This has two implications. The obvious one is that any financial institution based in one country which aims to lend in another is either going to have to take some currency risk — if it funds the loans by issuing liabilities in its domestic currency — or else will have to issue liabilities in the currency of the target country. The second option would not put the foreign-based firm at a disadvantage relative to domestic firms provided it could tap domestic currency funds at the same cost. But the existence of a branch network to directly tap domestic retail savings — a substantial element of the cost of which is sunk — may give encumbents an advantage over foreign lenders for many years.

The second implication of continuing variability in currency values and in interest rates is that the risk characteristics of a particular type of loan contract will vary across countries. Fixed nominal rate mortgage loans funded at short-term market rates of interest would have caused far greater risks to UK financial firms over the past twenty years than loans funded in that way in Germany, because unpredictable variability in nominal rates of interest in the UK has been much higher. To take another example, the relatively low variability in nominal rates of interest in Switzerland should make the incentives of financial firms there to offer fixed-rate mortgages less than in the UK, where unpredictable changes in nominal rates have been much greater.

Table 8.8   The take-up of fixed-rate mortgages in the UK
(Percentage of all mortgages granted)

	Variable rate	Rate fixed for up to 1 year	Rate fixed for > 1 year
Q2 1992	79	5	17
Q3 1992	77	4	19
Q4 1992	70	7	23
Q1 1993	65	6	29
Q2 1993	54	6	40
Q3 1993	40	10	50

Reproduced from *Housing Finance*, August 1993, by permission of the Council for Mortgage Lenders.

The final factor which suggests that convergence to a common type of financial contract within Europe will be slow is an implication of the simulation results reported in Chapter 5. We saw there that the demand for loan contracts which allow equity withdrawal may well be lower on the Continent of Europe than within the UK, US and Japan.

8.6 CONCLUSIONS

The factors outlined in the final section of this chapter mean that the argument implicit in the Cecchini Report — that mortgage lenders in the UK would have a great competitive advantage within a single market because the margin between the cost of funds and the mortgage rate was lower there than in the rest of the community — is weak. Indeed the analysis of the risk characteristics of various types of loan contract in Section 8.4 makes it more likely that contracts to finance house purchase within the UK may come to look more like those used on the Continent rather than the other way around. The serious front-end loading problems with standard variable-rate loans makes fixed-rate loans for a lower proportion of the purchase price of a home — supplemented by some form of equity or else indexed funding — an efficient risk-sharing contract. Already fixed-rate lending in the UK is on the increase, as Table 8.8 shows. By the third quarter of 1993 50% of new loans had interest rates fixed for more than one year.

Quite how far the type of mortgage contracts used to finance house purchase in the UK will come to resemble those which have been common on the Continent will depend upon conditions in the rental market, on the tax treatment of housing and on the regulation of financial institutions. We turn to these issues in the final chapter.

REFERENCES

Baltensperger, E. and Dermine, J. (1987) Banking deregulation in Europe, *Economic Policy*, April, no. 4, 63–110.

Bank of England (1982) The supplementary special deposits scheme, *Bank of England Quarterly Bulletin*, **22**, 74–85.

Bank of England (1985a) Change in the Stock Exchange and regulation in the City, *Bank of England Quarterly Bulletin*, no. 4, 544–50.

Bank of England (1985b) The housing finance market: recent growth in perspective, *Bank of England Quarterly Bulletin*, no. 1, 80–91.

Bank of England (1987) Change in the Stock Exchange and regulation in the City *Bank of England Quarterly Bulletin*, no. 1, 54–65.

Bank of England (1991) Housing finance — an international perspective, *Bank of England Quarterly Bulletin*, no. 1, 56–66.

Bank of England (1992) House prices, arrears and repossessions, *Bank of England Quarterly Bulletin*, no. 2, 173–9.

Bank for International Settlements (1986) Recent Innovations in International Banking. Report of the Study Group chaired by S. Cross. BIS (April).

Boleat, M. (1985) *National Housing Finance Systems*, Croom Helm, Beckenham.

Boleat, M. (1989) *Housing in Britain*, The Building Societies Association, London.

Cecchini Report (1988) The European Challenge 1992, EEC.

Easton, W. (1985) The importance of interest rates in five macroeconomic models, Bank of England Discussion Paper no. 24, (October).

Easton, W. (1990) The interest rate transmission mechanism in the UK and overseas, *Bank of England Quarterly Bulletin*, no. 2, 198–214.

Elton, E. and Gruber, M. (1992) *Modern Portfolio Theory and Investment Analysis*, 4th edition, Wiley, New York.

Englund, P. (1990) Financial deregulation in Sweden, *European Economic Review*, **34**, 385–93.

Goodhart, C. (1987) Financial innovation and monetary control, *Oxford Review of Economic Policy*, **2**, 79–99.

Goodhart, C. (1989a) *Money, Information and Uncertainty*, 2nd edition, Macmillan, Basingstoke.

Goodhart, C. (1989b) The conduct of monetary policy, *Economic Journal*, **99**, 293–346.

Grilli, V. (1989a) Financial markets and 1992, *Brookings Papers on Economic Activity*, no. 2, 301–24.

Grilli, V. (1989b) Europe 1992 issues and prospects for the financial markets, *Economic Policy*, no. 9, 387–422.

Holmans, A. (1990) *House Price Changes Through Time at the National and Sub-National Level*, Government Economic Service Working Paper No. 110.

Leigh Pemberton, R. (1986) Financial change and broad money, *Bank of England Quarterly Bulletin*, **26**, 499–507.

Leigh Pemberton, R. (1987) The instruments of monetary policy, *Bank of England Quarterly Bulletin*, **27**, 365–70.

Manas, L. (1989) The Impact of 1992 Financial Liberalisation on the Spanish Financial Industry. Mimeo.

Melitz, J. (1990) Financial deregulation in France, *European Economic Review*, **34**, 394–402.

Melitz, J. and Bordes, C. (1989) The Macroeconomic Implications of Financial Deregulation. Centre For Economic Policy Research Discussion Paper no. 309 (June).

Miles, D (1994) Fixed and floating-rate finance in the United Kingdom and abroad, *Bank of England Quarterly Bulletin*, no. 1, 34–45.

Miller, M (1986) Financial innovations: the last twenty years and the next, *Journal of Financial and Quantitative Analysis*, **21**, 459–71.

Price-Waterhouse (1988) The cost of non-Europe in financial services. In *Research of the Cost of Non-Europe*, Commission of the European Communities, Vol. 9.

Tobin, J. (1984) On the efficiency of the financial system, *Lloyds Bank Review*, July, 1–15.

Vives, X. (1990) Deregulation and competition in Spanish banking, *European Economic Review*, **34**, 403–11.

NOTE

This section draws heavily on the author's entry 'Financial Liberalisation Within Europe', in the *New Palgrave Dictionary of Money and Finance* (1992).

CHAPTER 9

Policy issues

9.1 INTRODUCTION

In this chapter we consider the implications of our analysis of housing markets for government policy. There are three main ways in which government policy directly affects the housing market. First, in its tax treatment of owner-occupied and rental housing the government can affect the tenure choices of individuals and the price and quantity of housing. Second, in its regulation of financial institutions the government, or its agencies, can affect the price and quantity of housing finance available to potential home-owners. Third, through legislation on rental and lease-hold agreements governments influence the demand and supply for different types of housing. As well as these ways in which government microeconomic policy affects conditions in housing markets, the conduct of macroeconomic policy may itself be affected by changes in housing markets and in the market for housing finance.

In this final chapter we aim to use the results from earlier chapters to address policy issues in all these areas. In Section 9.2 we look at the tax treatment of housing and of mortgage debt. In Section 9.3 we analyse the way in which current regulation of financial institutions making mortgage loans within the major economies affects the cost and type of credit available to finance house purchase. In Section 9.4 we consider some specific proposals to equalize the treatment of rented property and owner-occupied housing. And in the final section we turn to macroeconomic issues and consider the implications of changes in housing-market conditions for the conduct of policy.

9.2 TAX ISSUES

There are many arguments as to why housing should be subsidized. (Hills (1991) provides a fairly comprehensive list). There are also good reasons why different commodities should, even when there is no case for subsidies to encourage (or penalties to discourage) their uses, *not* be taxed in the same way; distortions in resource allocation may be minimized by taxing at relatively high rates goods with the most price-inelastic demands, while distributional considerations might pull in other directions (see Atkinson and Stiglitz (1980) for an excellent discussion of the issues). For all these reasons there is no presumption that the value of the services of housing, or any capital gains on them, should be taxed in the same way as are other types of income. But while there is no good reason to aim for equality of tax treatment of housing relative to other goods, there is a strong case for the tax system not to discriminate in favour of one type of housing tenure.

In most countries the interest payments on mortgage debt are tax deductible (Table 9.1); in some countries, most notably the UK and (since 1986) the US, the tax treatment of mortgage interest is more favourable than for other types of household debt. In the UK neither the imputed income from home ownership nor capital gains on owner-occupied housing are taxed. In contrast, while the interest on loans used to finance the purchase by landlords of property to rent is tax deductible, both the rental income and any real capital gains from the property are taxed. It is this sort of discrimination against one form of tenure — rather than the way in which owner-occupation is treated for tax purposes — that is the clearest problem. The implications of this differential treatment are clear enough. In Chapter 2 we saw that if the supply of residential property is inelastic favourable tax treatment of owner-occupation will bid up the price of houses; the capitalization of the tax benefits of owner-occupation into house prices increases the cost of renting but without the compensating tax relief. Owner-occupation rates will be higher than if the tax system were neutral with respect to tenure.

All this is quite clear and has long been recognized (see, for example, Atkinson and King (1980)). The interesting issue is how the tax treatment of different tenure types can be made equal. In the UK there are (at least) two options. *First*, tax

Table 9.1   Tax treatment of home owners

UK	US	Japan	Germany	Spain	France
Interest on first £30 000 debt deducted against tax; imputed income untaxed.	Interest on up to $1 mill. on 1st or 2nd home deductible; imputed income untaxed	Interest on debt of 200 000 yen per household deductible; imputed income untaxed	Very limited deduction of interest; imputed income is now taxed	Tax on interest deductible; imputed income untaxed	Interest deductible for 5 years up to a limit; imputed income untaxed

Italy	Sweden	Australia	Canada	Denmark	Finland
Mortgage interest is tax deductible; imputed income is untaxed	Mortgage interest is tax deductible; imputed income is taxed	Neither interest nor imputed income is taxed	Neither interest nor imputed is taxed	Mortgage interest is tax deductible; imputed income is taxed	Mortgage interest is tax deductible; imputed income is taxed

relief on home loans could remain, but the imputed income from home ownership (net of depreciation and maintenance costs) could be taxed and capital gains tax levied on real increases in the value of owner-occupied homes; rental income to landlords (net of maintenance charges, administrative costs and also net of depreciation) would be taxed. This would even up the tax treatment of the income from ownership of property which accrues to landlords and to owner-occupiers. The *second* option is that mortgage interest tax relief to owner-occupiers be removed so that the cost of financing house purchase comes out of post-tax income while the (imputed) income from ownership of housing adds directly to post-tax income. This option would create symmetry in the treatment of the costs and benefits of home ownership; neutrality with respect to tenure is less clearly achieved and would seem to require that so long as landlords pay tax on capital gains then so should owner-occupiers.

The analysis in earlier chapters does not reveal which of these two options is the better; Hills (1991) suggests that the (re-)imposition of tax on the imputed income from home ownership is likely to be so unpopular that the realistic option for more equal tax treatment of housing is that mortgage interest tax relief be abolished, or at least be allowed to become insignificant. (This would seem to be the policy that is being followed by the UK government; in the budget of November 1993 it was announced that the tax rate at which interest on the first £30 000 of mortgage is deductible would fall below the standard rate (25%) in April of 1994. By April of 1995 the rate at which interest is deductible will fall to 15%.) But we are left with the question as to how capital gains on housing should be taxed. The analysis of earlier chapters is helpful here.

In Chapter 4 we saw that real house price increases are quite unlike real increases in equity prices or in the value of gold; because the real cost of housing is a function of the relative price of houses to other goods home owners experience both an increase in the value of their assets and an increase in the present discounted value of their future housing costs when there is a permanent shock to house prices. *Some* home owners gain when prices rise — namely those for whom substitutability between housing and other goods is high and those who had planned to trade down before prices rise; those who have an inelastic demand for housing or who had planned to trade up before an unanticipated price increase lose out. The fact that unanticipated price rises increase the welfare of some home owners and reduce it for others whose economic position (in terms of earned income, house value, stock of wealth) might look identical, makes it hard to establish an equitable rate of tax on real house price increases. The superficially appealing answer might be that capital gains on owner-occupied housing should not be taxed. This has the advantage of getting the tax treatment correct *on average* in the sense that trading up is matched by trading down, so that in aggregate gainers from increases in the real price of houses match losers; house-price rises do not, *in aggregate*, increase real wealth and therefore the average tax rate on capital gains across households ought to be close to zero. Given the difficulty in identifying the gainers and losers from house-price rises it may be that getting the tax rate correct on average is the best that can be done.

This still leaves the issue of the tax treatment of capital gains on rented property. Most people living in the rented sector do not own residential property but a substantial proportion will do so in the future. Those who plan to become owner-occupiers are, other things (in particular inheritances) equal, made worse off by unanticipated increases in house prices. Those who *own* rented property are, however, beneficiaries of increases in their relative price. Horizontal equity between owner-occupiers, landlords and renters would seem to imply that if the tax paid by the first group is unaffected by increases in house prices the tax paid by the second group should rise and that the tax paid by the last group should fall. If landlords were to pass on the benefits of house price increases in lower rents — as one would expect to happen if the price increases were anticipated and the return on rented property were, in equilibrium, tied to the returns on alternative investments — a zero tax would be equitable. But unanticipated price rises can be expected to redistribute wealth from renters to landlords.

This difference in the impact of anticipated and unanticipated price rises provides a useful means of determining the appropriate tax treatment of capital gains on rental property. *If* expectations of price increases are, on average, correct and arbitrage does drive the expected return on investments in rental property to equal the expected return on alternative assets then — on average — higher price rises will be passed on to renters in lower rents. This being so horizontal equity between the three groups (home-owners, landlords and renters) implies zero tax on capital gains to all forms of residential property; this rule implies that the tax rate applied to the capital gains of owners of residential property is equal to the average — across time and owners — benefit stemming from price changes, which is zero.

9.3 THE REGULATION OF MORTGAGE LENDING

9.3.1 THE CURRENT RULES

Deposit-taking financial intermediaries which make mortgage loans within the major, developed economies are subject to several types of regulations. These regulations are specific to financial intermediaries. And because they can affect the balance-sheet structure of lenders, and in particular their funding policy, they can influence the quantity and price of credit available to finance house purchases. In this section we briefly describe the current system of regulation and consider the impact of the rules upon housing markets.

There is now a substantial literature on the economics of financial regulation. Theoretical issues concerning the rationale for, and the optimal structure of, regulation of deposit-taking financial intermediaries have been addressed in several papers (see, for example, the seminal papers by Diamond and Dybvig (1983), and Merton (1978); for excellent reviews of the issues see Goodhart (1987, 1988) and

Chant (1987)). A key issue in the literature has been the nature and extent of information problems in financial markets. The presence of asymmetries of information is central to the role played by financial intermediaries (Diamond, 1984) but their existence is likely to make free market outcomes suboptimal (Akerlof, 1970; Diamond and Dybvig, 1983) and is probably the strongest justification for the existence of regulations which are specific to deposit-takers.

Under a series of agreements reached in the late 1980s and in the early 1990s there will be a common set of rules across the G10 countries for the regulation of deposit-takers involved in housing finance. There is also to be harmonization of regulation within the European Community. Convergence of regulatory standards has gone furthest in the control of insolvency risk. Under the Bank for International Settlements (BIS) agreement of 1988 a set of rules were agreed by regulators in the major economies which would establish common minimum levels of equity (or quasi-equity) for banks. These capital adequacy rules were phased in during the early 1990s. They imply that banks expanding their mortgage lending will have to provide extra capital (equal to 4% of the extra lending if the mortgages are first loans secured against owner-occupied homes). Below we will focus on the design of these capital adequacy rules and analyse their effects upon lending and the cost of mortgages.

As well as capital adequacy rules mortgage lenders face other restrictions, and these can vary depending on the type of institution. Within the UK, for example, banks and building societies face a range of different restrictions. The supervisory regimes, while having much in common, differ in style; restrictions on building societies are more prescriptive, with an emphasis on allowable activities (vires). Both regimes are based around a legislative framework with statutory powers delegated to supervisory bodies. For banks the regulator is the Bank of England to whom authority is granted under the 1987 Banking Act; for building societies it is the Building Societies Commission, which was established following the passage of the Building Societies Act of 1986. Regular meetings between institutions and their respective supervisors occur; at such meetings the extent to which institutions activities comply with both the relevant legislation and with guidance notes issued by the supervisors is assessed.

Both banks and building societies must comply with capital adequacy requirements which establish minimum levels of capital that depend upon the composition of assets. The way in which minimum capital is calculated is similar; but the risk weights (or capital ratios) applied to building society mortgages range from 2% to 4%, depending on the maturity and size of the loan and the credit-worthiness of the borrower, while the risk weight for all bank mortgages is 4%. Both the Banking Act and the Building Societies Act make the maintenance of adequate liquidity a key criterion for authorization, but as with capital adequacy requirements there are differences in the way in which requirements are specified. Banks are required to complete returns which reveal the extent to which asset and liability maturities are mismatched. Building societies are not required to report these 'maturity mismatch ladders' but, unlike banks, they face a limit on the *maximum* stock of liquid assets which may be no more than one third of total assets.

Depositors with both authorized banks and building societies have their deposits insured up to limits. The ways in which the deposit protection schemes are financed differ. Banks make contributions to a standing fund whilst building societies are required to contribute if required. The degree of cover also differs: 90% of the first £20 000 of building society deposits are insured whilst only 75% of that first tranche of bank deposits are covered.

The major differences in regulations for the two types of deposit-taker stems from the fact that the principal purpose of a building society is explicitly defined in the Building Society Act (Section 5) while the Banking Act contains no such definition. Under Section 5 a building society must be established '... for the purpose of raising, primarily through the subscriptions of members, a stock or fund for making to them advances secured on land for their residential use'. In defining what a building society is the Act specifically restricts activities to a limited range. The most important current restrictions are that:

- the proportion of societies' funds which may be raised from the wholesale markets may not exceed 40%;

- the maximum proportion of assets which are *not* first mortgages backed by the value of owner-occupied housing is 25%;

- the maximum amount of unsecured lending to any one individual is £10 000. Furthermore, there are restrictions on the ability to undertake business overseas, on participation in syndicated loans and on the use of hedging and swap arrangements.

These restrictions are likely to be relaxed in the near future. In the summer of 1994 the UK Government announced proposals to allow building societies to raise more funds from the wholesale markets and to make loans to businesses.

9.3.2   THE IMPACT OF CAPITAL REQUIREMENTS

The purpose of capital requirements is to put a lower limit on the equity fund that a deposit taker has and which acts as a buffer to prevent losses on the asset side of the firm's balance sheet, eroding the claims of depositors. Assuming that the capital rules bind — so that lenders are required to hold more capital (or equity) on their balance sheets than they would wish — what effects may they have upon lending? A view commonly heard in the press and from bankers is that because the required return on equity exceeds the cost of debt, rules which force lenders to increase the ratio of equity to debt (or to deposits) increase the cost of funds and either squeeze profit margins or else increase the interest rate charged on loans. If that argument is correct the capital adequacy weight attached to mortgage loans, both absolutely and relative to the weights attached to other forms of mortgage loan, matters. If the marginal cost of financing loans depends upon the proportion raised from deposits (or other types of debt), the mark-up of the mortgage interest rate over the interest rate offered on deposits becomes a function of the capital requirement. Furthermore, if restrictions bite, the relative cost of mortgage debt to other forms of lending will be a function of the relative capital requirements. This will have implications for the amount of investment which is channelled into housing as opposed to other types of investment.

To get a feel for the magnitudes that might be involved consider a UK financial institution funding a marginal mortgage loan in the Autumn of 1993. At that time short-term nominal rates of interest in the money market were around 6%. The interest paid on highly liquid, retail deposits was even lower, but the administrative costs of taking such deposits are significant so we could assume that 6% is roughly the right figure for the cost to a bank or building society of raising debt. The cost of equity capital is less easy to measure. Assuming that stock prices reflect fundamentals — so that the share price is the present discounted value of the expected future earnings per share — we can infer something about the cost of equity from banks' price–earnings ratios. If, for example, we assume that nominal earnings per share are expected to grow at rate g_e and that the share price is the present value of future earnings discounted at the required return on equity, r_e, we can write the current share price, P_0, as

$$P_0 = \sum_{t=0}^{\infty} E_0[(1 + g_e)/(1 + r_e)]^t \tag{9.1}$$

where E_0 are current earnings per share. (9.1) implies that we can write the price–earnings ratio:

$$P_0/E_0 = (1 + r_e)/(r_e - g_e) \tag{9.2}$$

Price–earnings ratios for UK shares at the end of September 1993 were around 20; bank shares had slightly higher PE ratios, which was probably more a reflection of poor current earnings rather than a low discount rate applied to expectations of future earnings. Using 20 as an estimate of the P/E ratio and assuming that nominal earnings were expected to grow at 5% (consistent, for example, with predictions for steady inflation of 2.5% and average real growth of 2.5%) allows us to solve (9.2) for r_e; the implied required return on equity is around 11%. With a cost of equity of 11% and a cost of debt of 6% the weighted average cost of capital using a 4% requirement for equity funding is 6.2%; some 20 basis points higher than the cost of purely debt (or deposit) financed lending. If the capital requirement is 0.08 the weighted average cost of funds is 6.4%.

So the difference in the cost of funds from using more equity than might be freely chosen appears significant, though clearly not prohibitive. But any argument based upon the weighted average cost of funds may overstate the true cost of compliance with capital adequacy requirements, since such arguments are based upon the assumption that the average cost of equity and of debt is the correct measure of the *marginal* cost of funds. But we know that if the Modigliani–Miller proposition is true then the real cost of funds is independent of the debt equity ratio;

although debt may appear cheaper than equity a decision to finance a marginal loan with 100% debt would increase the risk of the company so the cost of existing debt, and the required return on equity, would rise to offset the apparent advantage of using a cheap source of funds (Modigliani and Miller, 1958). Whether the Modigliani–Miller proposition actually holds is another question; there are several reasons — some to do with the tax treatment of debt and equity (Miller, 1977) others connected with asymmetries of information between shareholders and managers of corporations (Myers and Majluf, 1984) — why equity may be more expensive than debt. Empirical evidence in Miles (1991) suggests that unanticipated announcements by UK banks of equity issues have caused share prices to decline, a result consistent with the idea that banks are hurt by having to use more equity (but also consistent with other stories which are compatible with the Modigliani–Miller theorem).

Because it is hard to know to what extent the Modigliani–Miller assumptions are met in the real world it is very hard to assess the true costs of complying with capital adequacy guidelines; nor is the incidence of any costs well understood. But the effects on the allocation of funds of the scheme put in place after the Basle accord could be dramatic if the cost of equity is significantly different from that of debt (or deposits). So it is important to look at the rationale for the rules applied to mortgage loans.

The current capital rules applied within the European Community, and also in Japan and North America, place a capital weight of 0.04 upon (domestic currency) mortgage loans and 0.08 on most other domestic currency loans (e.g. loans to finance corporate investment or non-mortgage loans to the personal sector). One imagines that the justification for these *relative* weights is that mortgage loans were believed to be less risky than most other types of loan, in large part because most mortgages are secured against the value of the house and house prices typically rise in most countries. This justification for the 0.04 weight is a bit weak. First, the relevant thing for lenders and regulators is the risk of the overall portfolio of loans; while it is entirely plausible that an individual loan to finance investment in a small manufacturing company is more risky than an 85% mortgage to finance house purchase, it does not follow that a diversified portfolio of investment loans is substantially more risky than a portfolio of mortgage loans. The key thing is the covariance between the shocks that can affect different manufacturing companies and the covariances between shocks that affect different home owners' ability to service debt. In the light of the mortgage arrears experience in the UK analysed in Chapter 8 it is clear that the key factors in creating repayment problems have been macroeconomic — specifically the sharp rise in inflation in the late 1980s which triggered an even sharper increase in nominal interest rates.

If it is unclear whether the capital weight upon mortgage loans should be twice that on most other loans it is even less obvious that 4% is the right figure.

But *if* one accepts the need to have capital adequacy requirements — and externalities from the bankruptcy of one financial firm on to others stemming from

asymmetries of information does seem a convincing case — one has to sympa-
thize with the regulators given the difficulty of devising a workable rule governing
acceptable capital. And if an implication of compliance with the rules is that the
cost to financial intermediaries of raising funds to make mortgages advances is
higher than it would otherwise be it certainly does *not* follow that resources will
therefore be misallocated. The *raison d'être* of special regulation of financial firms
is that unregulated outcomes are suboptimal and that risks are excessive when firms
are allowed to make decisions in their own private interests. *If* the cost of mortgage debt is higher, the amount of lending lower, and the scale of investment in
residential property smaller as a result of capital requirements, this may represent
a more efficient outcome.

While it is hard to know whether the requirement that equity backing against
the *overall* stock of mortgages held by a financial intermediary be at least 4% is
too tough or too lax a rule, we can use the results on the risk characteristics of
various types of loan contract to say something about how capital weights should
vary *between* different types of mortgage. Because front-end loading problems
are less with indexed contracts, and the risks of repayment problems lower, they
should have lower capital adequacy weights than standard, variable-rate mortgages;
since front-end loading problems can also be severe with fixed nominal rate loans
these should have a higher weight than indexed loans. Of course if loans are
funded in a way which creates maturity mismatch for lenders between assets and
liabilities this creates interest rate risk which may itself require higher capital; but
the main point is that the default risk on indexed mortgages is likely to be lower
than on variable-rate loans and that, *per se*, makes lower capital weights seem
appropriate.

It is even clearer that the capital weight should be lower the smaller is the loan
relative to the house value; but the cost of giving lenders incentives to reduce their
loan to value ratios is that first-time buyers may be forced out of the market for
a prolonged period. In Chapter 8 we argued that part debt–part equity contracts
between lenders and house buyers get around the problem and are superior, in
terms of the allocation of risk, to pure debt contracts. The capital requirement on
these assets may prove crucial to their attractiveness to lenders and borrowers. The
problem that regulators will need to face is in assessing the risk of a portfolio of
equity stakes in residential property. Empirical work is badly needed in this area and
will certainly need to go much further than that presented in Chapter 3 where we
did little more than present back of the envelope calculations on the relative risks of
housing to equity in the UK. One thing that is likely to emerge from any empirical
exercise is that the risk of holding property varies hugely across countries. This
would pose a problem for regulators looking for a simple rule governing the capital
requirements for financial intermediaries throughout Europe. The more promising
implication of diversity in the risk characteristics of residential property throughout
Europe is that the gains from international diversification across property markets
could be great.

9.4   THE SIZE OF THE RENTED SECTOR

9.4.1   MACROECONOMIC IMPLICATIONS OF OWNERSHIP PATTERNS

The size of the rented sector within a country depends upon the relative benefits to households of owner-occupation, the availability of mortgage finance and the incentives of owners of residential property to let. Within the developed economies we have seen that there is significant variability in the importance of the rental sector. In Germany about 60% of households are in the rented sector; in the UK only around 30% of people rent, the majority of whom continue to express a strong preference to be owner-occupiers. In Germany the tax treatment of rented and owner-occupied properties is more equal than in the UK; tax relief is not available on mortgage loans in Germany. In the UK the tax system has clearly benefited owner-occupiers relative to landlords while rent controls and legislation to give tenants security of tenure have (until recently) further reduced the incentives to let property (Black and Stafford, 1988; Kemp and Maclennan, 1993; Maclennan, 1982). Finally, banks and building societies in the UK have been prepared to lend more to home buyers than specialist lenders and banks in Germany.

So one does not need to invoke inherent differences in the tastes and preferences of Teutonic and Anglo-Saxon peoples to explain the very different tenure patterns in the two countries.

The issue I address here is the macroeconomic implications of the economic factors which have created such different tenure patterns in countries. The first point to note is the obvious one that there is nothing inherently superior in one tenure pattern over another. Kemp and Maclennan (1993) make the point nicely.

> One common response is that Britain needs a larger rental sector because our European competitors have bigger rental sectors. This is true...but is hardly an answer — these countries also have higher rates of rabies.

What, then, are the macroeconomic implications of owner-occupation in a country being high? First, the proportion of wealth held *directly* by the personal sector in residential property will, other things (and in particular real house prices) being equal, be higher than in a country with a large rented sector. Of course someone owns rented property so unless this is held by overseas corporations the personal sector in the country where renting is high ultimately holds the assets in some form or another (either as claims on property companies or as less easily realizable claims upon assets held by the public sector). The same point holds for debt used to finance purchases of residential property; in the high owner-occupation economy this debt is held directly by households, in the low owner-occupation country by property companies or by governments whose assets and liabilities ultimately belong to the personal sector. So in terms of *aggregate* assets and liabilities the implications of different tenure patterns, in themselves, are not very significant. The more important effects are on the *distribution* of claims upon property and of debt liabilities. In the UK there have been two important distributional effects stemming from high and rising home ownership. First, on the assets side the dramatic increases in the real value of houses over the century has contributed to greater equality in the ownership of wealth because housing wealth is more equally distributed than other forms of wealth (see Atkinson, 1983). Second, on the liabilities side the high levels of mortgage debt held by recent home buyers has made the impact of increases in the cost of debt fall disproportionately on those who are least able to deal with an adverse shock to disposable income — first-time buyers have tended to have low levels of financial assets precisely because the attractions of home ownership have encouraged them to put what wealth they have accumulated into housing. It is the adverse effects on recent home owners of increasing interest rates — exacerbated by the front-end loading problems analysed in the previous chapter — that has made the removal of distortions in the treatment of rental property a major policy priority for the UK government. We consider ways in which those distortions can be removed in the next section.

9.4.2   REMOVING DISTORTIONS IN THE UK

There are two ways in which the treatment of rented property may have contributed to the dramatic decline in the supply of private rented accommodation within the UK. First rent controls and legislation on security of tenure may have reduced the incentive to let property. Second, and less controversially, the tax treatment of rented property has been relatively unfavourable. Whatever one's views on the distortions caused in the past by rent and security of tenure legislation (and Maclennan (1982) gives a balanced account) the legislation passed by the Conservative Government in its 1988 Housing Act effectively removed new agreements from any controls. So the more interesting issues come back to the tax treatment of property discussed above. In Section 9.2 we argued that the abolition of tax on capital gains on rented property and a decline in the benefits of mortgage interest tax relief for home owners would make the tax system more neutral. It is also desirable to let landlords offset depreciation against tax; the current rules implicitly assume that houses last forever. Sadly this is not true.

Exempting capital gains made by landlords on property from tax and allowing them to offset economic depreciation against rental income would represent a coherent set of reforms to revive the rented sector. Such changes are preferable to temporary and piecemeal measures to stimulate investment in rental property.

9.5   MACROECONOMIC POLICY

There are several important lessons for the conduct of macroeconomic policy from our analysis of the effects of changes in housing markets and in the market for housing finance. In this section we aim to spell these out and in so doing draw together several strands from earlier chapters.

Our theoretical analysis of the impact of liberalization in the housing finance market (Chapter 5), and the empirical evidence from the UK (Chapters 6 and 7), strongly suggest that in the adjustment period following an easing of credit restrictions we would expect to see much lower household saving, higher house prices, deterioration in the current account and significant equity withdrawal. A key message from Chapter 5 is that the adjustment period may prove to be very long — with forward-looking individuals who may have bequest motives the response to the easing of credit restrictions can be drawn out over decades. And because house prices will converge to a new equilibrium slowly and non-monotonically (see Chapter 2) the evolution of household wealth and the pattern of inheritances will be affected for many years. Policy makers in countries where liberalization in housing finance has been quite recent — e.g. the Scandinavian countries — or has hardly started — e.g. Spain, Italy, Japan and, to a lesser extent, France and Germany — should be aware of the kind of adjustments which can come in the wake of liberalization and the time-frame of the transition to new steady states. A government which aimed to cut government spending and increase interest rates because household saving had fallen sharply and remained depressed for years after financial liberalization would be following a misguided strategy. Our analysis reveals that sustained lower savings are the natural market response to the relaxation of constraints which had generated excessive accumulation of net housing wealth. And since current account deficits (or lower surpluses) are a natural consequence of decumulation of housing wealth, a policy of devaluation, or of export subsidies or import restrictions, would be quite inappropriate.

The second set of lessons for macroeconomic policy come from our analysis of the causes behind, and the impact of, house-price changes (Chapters 2 and 4). The main message here is that house price rises should not be presumed to boost real wealth, certainly not at the aggregate level and in many cases not even for individual home owners. Because of this the response of household consumption to increases in the market value of owner-occupied housing may well be muted. A low response of consumption to house-price rises is more likely the less easy it is for home owners to borrow against housing wealth, *or* the smaller are the number of households who want to borrow more but are constrained by the value of their collateral. So in countries where the scope to borrow against housing wealth is very limited or, at the other extreme, in countries where few households face borrowing restrictions at all, then house-price rises may generate small consumption responses. It is those countries where credit conditions in the housing finance market are liberal, but where many households still face binding credit restrictions because other forms of wealth are not easy to borrow against, that house-price rises are likely to have the most powerful impact upon consumption. The UK in the mid 1980s may have found itself in this position; we saw in Chapters 6 and 7 that there was evidence that house-price rises had a greater impact upon consumption then than in the 1960s and 1970s when borrowing against accumulated housing equity had been more difficult.

Perhaps the most important lessons for policy makers to emerge from our analysis of the impact of house price rises are these: first, that sharp price rises should, in an efficient market, tend to be followed by gradual price declines over a prolonged period. This stems from the fact that supply responses to changes in the relative price of houses are likely to be very small in the short run but will build up over time; the kind of overshooting in prices which results from short-run stickiness in the stock of housing (Chapter 2) is analogous to exchange-rate overshooting in modes where there is stickiness in the labour or goods markets (Dornbusch, 1976). Second, because even sustained price rises may have small effects upon household saving, the wider impact of large price rises which are expected to be partially reversed may be quite limited. For policy makers the implication is that in an efficient market house prices, despite being forward-looking variables, may be quite uninformative about future consumer spending. And because the stock of housing is so slow to move in the short run, and the demand for housing is sensitive to expectations on a large range of variables for many periods ahead, house prices are susceptible to large and sudden jumps. But rather than an indication of inefficiency in the market, variability in house prices which is causally unrelated to future changes in consumption is exactly what an analysis of the economics of housing suggests should happen in a world where prices are driven by fundamentals.

9.6   CONCLUSIONS

In previous chapters we have analysed the conditions under which house-price rises increase household real wealth and welfare. We have considered the empirical evidence on the effects of anticipated and unanticipated house-price rises. We developed expressions for the user cost of housing and analysed how changes in the user cost affect the price and quantity of housing in the short and long run. And in Chapter 8 we considered the risk characteristics of various types of financial contract and speculated on the ways in which housing finance may change within the European single market. In this final chapter we have used these earlier results to consider some specific policy issues in the three areas of tax, financial regulation and rental and leasehold agreements. The analysis suggests that tax relief on mortgage interest payments should be abolished, or at least allowed to become insignificant. Capital gains on houses for both owner-occupiers and landlords should be tax-exempt and the latter should be allowed to deduct depreciation from their liability to tax. Regulations, and in particular capital adequacy requirements, should be sensitive to the relative risks of different types of mortgage contract. Debt–equity contracts — because they have the potential to allow better risk-sharing between owners and providers of funds — should not be discouraged by regulation. Finally we have argued that many propositions which are superficially plausible are likely to be a poor guide to the formulation of macroeconomic policy: house-price rises cannot be assumed to generate higher spending for home owners; sharp house-price rises followed by gradual declines are not necessarily a sign of bubbles or inefficiency which require action to dampen; and sustained reductions in saving rates and worsening of current accounts are natural responses to easing of conditions in mortgage markets rather than phenomena requiring offsetting changes in monetary or fiscal policy.

REFERENCES

Akerlof, G. (1970) The market for lemons: qualitative uncertainty and the market mechanism, *Quarterly Journal of Economics*, **84**, 488–500.

Atkinson, A. (1983) *The Economics of Inequality*, 2nd edition, Clarendon Press, Oxford.

Atkinson, A. and King, M. (1980) Housing policy, taxation and reform, *Midland Bank Review*, Spring, 7–15.

Atkinson, A. and Stiglitz, J. (1980) *Lectures on Public Economics*, McGraw-Hill, London.

Bank of England (1991) Housing finance — an international perspective, *Bank of England Quarterly Bulletin*, no. 1, 56–66.

Black, J. and Stafford, D. (1988) *Housing Policy and Finance*, Routledge, London.

Chant, J. (1987) Regulation of Financial Institutions — A Functional Analysis. Bank of Canada Technical Report No. 45.

Diamond, D. (1984) Financial intermediation and delegated monitoring, *Review of Economic Studies*, **51**(3), 393–413.

Diamond, D. and Dybvig, P. (1983) Bank runs, deposit insurance and liquidity, *Journal of Political Economy*, **91**, 401–18.

Dornbusch, R. (1976) Expectations and exchange rate dynamics, *Journal of Political Economy*, **84**(6).

Goodhart, C. (1987) Why do we need a central bank? *Oxford Economic Papers*, **49**(1), 75–89.

Goodhart, C. (1988) *The Evolution of Central Banks*, MIT Press, Cambridge, Mass.

Hills, J. (1991) *Unravelling Housing Finance*, Clarendon, Oxford.

Kemp, P. and Maclennan, D. (1993) Private rental housing: decision time, in *Housing Finance Review*, Joseph Rowntree Foundation, York.

Maclennan, D. (1982) *Housing Economics*, Longman, London.

Merton, R. (1978) On the cost of deposit insurance when there are surveillance costs, *Journal of Business*, **51**, 439–52.

Miles, D. (1991) What is different about financial firms, *The Manchester School*, **LIX**(1), 64–79.

Miller, M. (1977) Debt and taxes, *Journal of Finance*, **32**, 261–275.

Modigliani, F. and Miller, M. (1958) The cost of capital, corporation finance and the theory of investment, *American Economic Review*, **48**, 261–297.

Myers, S. and Majluf, N. (1984) Corporate financing and investment decisions when firms have information that investors do not have, *Journal of Financial Economics*, **13**(2).

Index

Index compiled by Lynette Lee Davidson